*Cathedrals and
Abbeys of England
and Wales*

Nec enim terram tenere deorsum, sed coelum potius desuper quaero

Cathedrals and Abbeys of England and Wales

The Building Church, 600–1540

RICHARD MORRIS

W. W. Norton & Company Inc
New York

726
Mor

AUTHOR'S AND PUBLISHER'S ACKNOWLEDGMENTS
The author and publisher are indebted for permission to
reproduce passages from published works: to Dr H. M.
Taylor, Professor Martin Biddle and Phillimore Ltd for
extracts from *Tenth Century Studies*; to Dr H. M. Taylor,
Professor Peter Sawyer and the Council for British
Archaeology for extracts from CBA Research Reports 13
and 27; to Dr John H. Harvey and Wayland Publishers
Ltd for extracts and translations from *The Mediaeval
Architect*; to B. T. Batsford Ltd for extracts from Francis
Bond's *Gothic Architecture in England*; to Faber and Faber
Ltd for the extract from *The Spire* by Mr William Golding; to Dr A. R. Bridbury and the Harvester Press for
extracts from *Economic Growth*; to the Harvard Univer-
sity Press for the extract from *The Renaissance of the
Twelfth Century* by Charles H. Haskins; to World Pub-
lishing Co. for extracts from *Gothic Architecture and Scholasticism* by Erwin Panofsky; to Nelson Ltd for the extract
from *Theophilus: De Diversis Artibus* in the translation by
C. R. Dodwell; to Wilfred Mellers and Gollancz Ltd for
extracts from *Caliban Reborn*. Extracts from Dr L. F.
Salzman's *Building in England down to 1540*, Alfred
Clapham's *English Romanesque Architecture After the Conquest*, A. C. Crombie's *Robert Grosseteste and the Origins of
Experimental Science*, and *The Architect: Chapters in the History of the Profession*, edited by Spiros Kostof, are quoted
by permission of the Oxford University Press. Extended
quotations from papers in journals are used by kind
permission of the following scholars: Dr Richard Gem,
Mr Jim Gould, Dr John H. Harvey, Professor Jacques
Heyman, Mr John James, Dr J. R. Maddicott, Dr D. M.
Metcalfe, Professor E. Miller, Dr Warwick Rodwell and
Dr Lon Shelby. Figures 3, 5, 6 and 9 have been redrawn,
in each case with permission, from originals published
or generously made available by Professor Martin Biddle and Mrs Birthe Kjølbye-Biddle, Dr H. M. Taylor,
Dr Richard Bailey and Mr Derek Phillips. Special
thanks are due to Mr Graham Challifour, Mr Simon
Pentelow and Mr Derek Phillips for the provision of
certain black-and-white photographs. In connection
with colour photography the author and publishers wish
to express gratitude to Dr John Baily (Plates 1, 3, 4 and
8), the British Tourist Authority (Plates 6, 7, 12, 13, 14
and 15) and Professor Rosemary Cramp (Plate 11). The
remaining colour photographs were taken by the author.

Contents

List of Plates

List of Line Drawings

List of Colour Plates

Introduction

HERE ARE ABOUT 19,000 churches in England and Wales.* More than 9000 of them were built or founded during the Middle Ages. The great majority were established as parochial churches or chapels: that is to say, they were buildings erected for the use of lay populations in particular districts.

Alongside these neighbourhood buildings there existed another type of ecclesiastical structure which for convenience we may call the greater church. Cathedrals, monastic churches and the churches of some collegiate establishments fall into this category. A few of them were exceptionally large. Old St Paul's fell just short of one-eighth of a mile in overall length. Winchester and St Albans stretched to 554 feet and 550 feet, respectively. Not all the greater churches were laid out on such a lavish scale, however, and size alone did not distinguish the majority from the parish churches, some of which approached or even exceeded their dimensions. The leading features of a great church were its layout, which generally took the form of some variation on the cruciform theme, and its internal arrangements, which ensured liturgical privacy for the resident community of monks, nuns or canons. The purpose of the community was twofold: to praise God by maintaining the *opus Dei*, and to pray for the benefit of the souls of the dead. Great churches served a variety of public functions in the Middle Ages but they were not, in the modern sense, public buildings.

It is logical to consider the greater church buildings as a group, because the men who were responsible for their construction worked within a homogeneous tradition of design. 'Cathedral' is a word which has no special architectural significance. It denotes a church that contains a bishop's chair (*cathedra*). Some of the churches we now know as cathedrals, such as Gloucester and Southwell, were not originally intended to function as such, but started out as monastic or collegiate buildings. Hence although the churches visited in this book are of two basic kinds – churches of bishops, and churches built for the use of groups of men and women living a life in common according to a code of discipline – the distinction is institutional rather than architectural. Both types were shaped to accommodate the same sort of liturgical needs.

I

* This figure excludes churches, chapels and meeting-houses of Nonconformist denominations

Cathedrals in England and Wales fall into four main groups. There are twenty-eight sees of pre-Elizabethan origin (twenty-four in England, four in Wales) and five sees of more recent creation where buildings of considerable size and antiquity have been promoted to cathedral status (four in England, one in Wales). To these may be added the cathedrals which use or have used former parish churches (eleven in England, one in Wales) and those which occupy churches of post-medieval or modern construction (four in England). Of the four groups it is the first two which concern us; the parish church and modern cathedrals are not considered further here.

Turning to the non-cathedral greater churches, over 250 monastic and collegiate buildings survive, either in full or partial use, or as substantial ruins. Apart from one or two, like Westminster, which occupy a special judicial position, virtually all those that remain in use are now operated as parish churches, and owe their survival to parochial or civic intervention during or after the Dissolution. About sixty major churches fall into this category. In some cases, as at Beverley, virtually the entire building remains functional. More often only a fragment of the original has been preserved intact, such as the presbytery and transept at Abbey Dore, the nave at Bolton, or even a single aisle, as at Crowland. Not surprisingly, Orders which preferred remote settings for their churches, such as the Cistercians, are poorly represented in this list, whereas buildings which belonged to the more extrovert and urbanized Orders, notably the Benedictines and Augustinians, have survived in greater numbers. The policy of including here only those churches which happen to have been retained for parish worship may seem harsh, since it leads to the exclusion of many of our most famous ruined structures, such as Fountains, Rievaulx and St Augustine's, Canterbury. On the other hand, the qualification does ensure that at least a part of each church considered survives complete, and it is a useful if somewhat arbitrary means of reducing the group to a manageable size. Nevertheless, because of the need for limitation it has not been possible to include all the non-cathedral greater churches which remain in use, and forty-two out of the sixty have been selected for discussion. When these are added to the thirty-three cathedrals a total of seventy-five buildings is reached. It is this group which forms the subject of the book.

The book covers greater churches in England and Wales, although it may seem that the Welsh churches have received rather less than their fair share of attention. The imbalance is the outcome of history. Wales never did possess many great churches, and few of those which did exist are in use today. Many of the best, such as Neath, Strata Marcella and Tintern, were abandoned in the sixteenth century. Tallie remained in use until *c*. 1770 but is now a ruin, and the Blackfriars' church at Rhuddlan has likewise been deserted. The Cistercian church at Margam survives. Of the four ancient cathedrals only St David's measures up to English counterparts in terms of scale or architectural interest, while all of them derive from the English medieval building tradition.

2

Books about churches are numberless. It might be imagined that little remains to be said about them that has not been said already. But with few exceptions all the recent works on great churches have been devoted to the cathedrals, thus leading to the unnatural exclusion of such buildings as Selby, Tewkesbury and Sherborne. Moreover, it is the surfaces rather than the spaces and skeletons of churches which in the past have tended to engage the attention of writers. Historical and aesthetic, rather than functional or structural (in the engineering sense) interests have tended to prevail. Where these topics have been treated it has usually been on a specialized basis. The rapport which existed between architects, historians and archaeologists in the nineteenth century has largely been lost, with the result that works on the construction, appreciation and investigation of churches are now addressed to separate audiences. This book differs from some of its predecessors in that it seeks to examine the greater churches as a unity. It considers their origins, explores the methods and motives of the men who built and paid for them, and attempts to throw light on how they were used at different stages in their history. The demands of form have required the refraction of the central idea of the greater church into a series of thematic chapters, but the underlying aim has been to treat the greater church as an entity.

Throughout the book my main preoccupation has been with Man rather than God. Great churches were built with sweat, skill and cash, not by miracles. A good deal of sentimental nonsense has been written about our cathedrals and abbeys. Much of it derives from the emphasis which monastic historians placed upon the pious aspirations of medieval patrons. Uncritical acceptance of this propaganda, encouraged by the fact that some of it is true, has sometimes caused us to forget that the motives of patrons were often mixed, and that it was not the patrons who cut the stone, dragged the sledges or forged the tools. The men who usually performed these tasks did so because they were paid to. That is not to deny that a living faith was a powerful stimulus to churchbuilding; rather it is to recognize the circumstances in which that faith operated. For every bishop, abbot or lord who hoped to immortalize his name or provide for the security of his soul through some great enterprise of ecclesiastical building there were several hundred craftsmen and unskilled people who sold their labour, and often their lives and health, to do the work. There were, too, thousands of ordinary folk who gave resources in cash and kind to pay for it.

They still do. More people now file through the nave of Canterbury Cathedral in a year than were alive in all the land when the nave was built late in the fourteenth century. A few of them chip pieces off mouldings and monuments as souvenirs. Many are surprised to discover that cathedrals are still in constant use for worship. Yet in a way the circumstances are not so very different from those which obtained in the Middle Ages, when pilgrims flocked to visit the shrines of saints, chattered during the offices and pressed forward to glimpse or touch holy relics. Then, as today, the church authorities were usually short of money for new building or repairs. Funds were raised by the sale of spiritual privileges and petty relics; now they sell postcards, books and 'Minutes of History'. A great church is and always has been an economic phenomenon. Being so, it is a supreme paradox: at once a denial and an affirmation of the Christian faith. But however we view the great church we may agree that it helps to pierce the worst darkness which threatens to envelop us: the darkness of indifference.

Author's Acknowledgments

Many people have helped me to write this book. My thanks are addressed particularly to Dr Christopher Arnold, Mrs Georgina Berridge, Mr Leo Biek, Mr Henry Cleere, Miss Christina Colyer, Dr Eric Gee, Mr Brian Hartley, Dr John Hunter, Mr Marcus Huxley, Dr Derek Keene, Mr Andrew Parrott, Dr Warwick Rodwell, Dr H. M. Taylor and Mr Christopher Wilson, all of whom answered questions on particular matters or gave advice at various times. Ideas which emerged during several long and stimulating discussions with Mr Derek Phillips and Mr David Tasker are incorporated here, and I am particularly grateful to Professor Peter Sawyer for permission to read chapters of his book *From Roman Britain to Norman England* in advance of publication. I am also indebted to Mr Emil Godfrey for his company and practical wisdom on a number of tours of Beverley Minster, and to Mr Tim Tatton-Brown and Mr Hendrik Strik for an instructive expedition into the roofs of Canterbury Cathedral. My special thanks go to Mr Stephen Coll, who assisted with the preparation of the Gazetteer, Mr Dick Raines and Miss Judith Sheard, who drew figures for the text and the comparative plans, Mrs Alison Turner for her help with the typescript and the staff of the National Monuments Record for their friendly help. Dr John Baily, Dr Lawrence Butler and Professor Peter Sawyer read portions of the text while it was still in draft. They suggested many improvements, most of which have been incorporated and for which I am deeply grateful. Lastly, my thanks go to my wife for her immense tolerance and practical assistance while the book was being written.

Ingmanthorpe
June 1978

Note on References

References for important facts, arguments or quotations are given by the 'Harvard' or author-year system. In this system references are embedded in the body of the text and consist of the author's name, the year of publication or the edition cited, and (if relevant) page number(s). Named references are gathered into a single alphabetical sequence in the Bibliography at the end of the book.

1
First Things

I T IS OFTEN forgotten that the history of the English Church went back almost as far before the Norman Conquest as the Reformation came after, while in the west of the country, and in Wales, an unbroken thread of Christian tradition and action reaches back to the Christianity of Roman Britain. It is worth pausing to examine this Roman background. For one thing there are signs that the Anglo-Saxons took an interest in Imperial affairs, and for another it is fairly certain that important, though not necessarily very large churches were constructed in Britain during the fourth century. More important still is the extent to which Roman building methods and architectural forms came to influence the techniques and designs of medieval builders.

Archaeology has so far done relatively little to illuminate the history and organization of Christianity in Roman Britain. To a great extent commentators have had to make do with *disjecta membra* for their discussions: objects of possible Christian significance, graffiti and ambiguous inscriptions. In the major towns the presence and importance of the Church have been measured more from the short life-span of pagan temples than from tangible indications of Christian activity. In England the catalogue of key sites is still brief, although to the church at Silchester, now re-excavated (Frere 1976), we may add the Christian building at Icklingham, Suffolk (West 1976), and perhaps the putative church at Richborough (Brown 1972). Here and there rural sites have produced indications of Christianity, notably at the wealthy villa at Lullingstone where excavation revealed a suite of rooms set aside for worship, and in the eclectic art of fourth-century mosaics at Hinton St Mary and Frampton. The fourth-century Christian silver treasure found at Water Newton is of remarkable interest; if this was originally in congregational rather than private ownership it makes a striking contrast with the image of Romano-British ecclesiastical poverty which has sometimes been portrayed. Romano-British Christian cemeteries are now known at several sites, including the major example at Poundbury in Dorset.

Excavated objects suggest that there were Christians in Britain as early as the second century AD, but the formal history of Christianity in the island begins in 312, when the faith was officially adopted throughout the Empire. Two years later we catch a glimpse of a trio of British bishops attending the Council of Arles. We know their names: Restitutus, Eborius and Adelphius. It has been suggested that those who attended at Arles (from York, London and perhaps Colchester or Lincoln) were the metropolitans from three of the four provincial capitals, and that each of the cantonal capitals is likely to have had a bishop. British clergy are again mentioned as having been present at the Council of Rimini in 359. So far only Silchester has provided a church, and even there confirmation of the Christian identity of the building is not absolute. The dioceses at this time may have corresponded with the various tribal districts or *civitates*, and it is usually assumed that they were served by bishops working on a peripatetic basis. However, it is intriguing to notice that the church recently excavated at Icklingham possessed a font (West 1976); this implies a degree of localization in Christian organization (perhaps a resident priest) which may be at odds with the received picture of an evangelical ministry depending

KEY: Map locating churches discussed or mentioned in the text.

1 Abbey Dore	34 Fountains	67 Rievaulx
2 Arundel	35 Glastonbury	68 Ripon
3 Bangor	36 Gloucester	69 Rochester
4 Bardney	37 Great Malvern	70 Romsey
5 Bath	38 Hereford	71 St Albans
6 Beverley	39 Hexham	72 St Asaph
7 Binham	40 Howden	73 St Bartholomew, Smithfield
8 Blyth	41 Jarrow	74 St Bees
9 Bolton	42 Lanercost	75 St David's
10 Boxgrove	43 Lastingham	76 St German's
11 Brecon	44 Leominster	77 Salisbury
12 Bridlington	45 Lichfield	78 Selby
13 Brinkburn	46 Lincoln	79 Selsey
14 Bristol	47 Lindisfarne	80 Sherborne
15 Bury	48 Little Malvern	81 Shrewsbury
16 Canterbury	49 Llandaff	82 Southwark
17 Carlisle	50 London St Paul's	83 Southwell
18 Cartmel	51 Malmesbury	84 Tewkesbury
19 Chester St John	52 Margam	85 Thetford
20 Chester St Werburgh	53 Melbourne	86 Waltham
21 Chichester	54 Milton Abbas	87 Wells
22 Christchurch	55 New Shoreham	88 Westminster
23 Coventry	56 Northampton	89 Whitby
24 Crowland	57 North Elmham	90 Wimborne
25 Cullompton	58 Norwich	91 Winchcombe
26 Deerhurst	59 Nun Monkton	92 Winchester
27 Derby	60 Old Malton	93 Winchester St Cross
28 Dorchester	61 Old Sarum	94 Worcester
29 Dunstable	62 Oxford	95 Worksop
30 Durham	63 Pershore	96 Wymondham
31 Ely	64 Peterborough	97 York
32 Evesham	65 Ramsbury	98 York, Holy Trinity
33 Exeter	66 Ramsey	

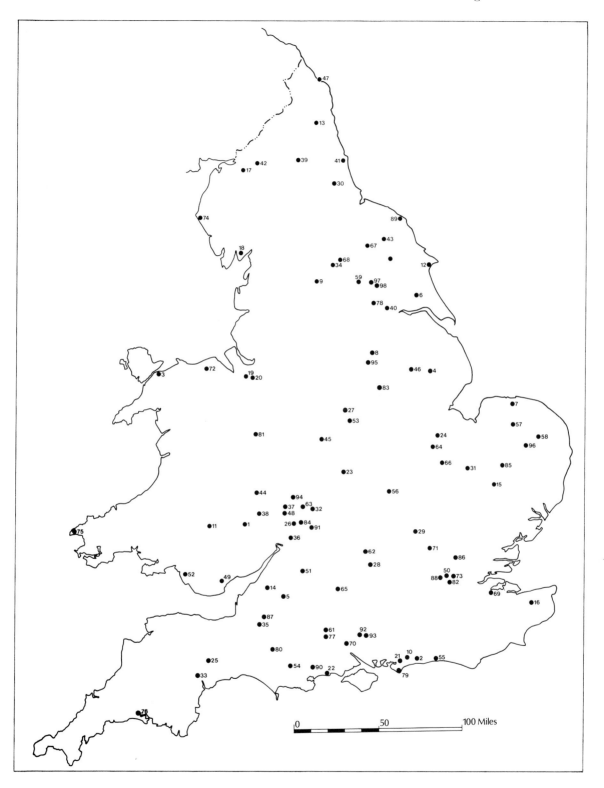

Fig. 1 Churches discussed or mentioned in the text

entirely upon major episcopal centres. At all events, while there is insufficient evidence available to refute the suggestion that Christianity in fourth-century low-land England was anything other than a minority religion, there is at least a growing body of evidence to show that it was less extraneous than has so far been claimed.

Hitherto archaeology has failed to produce (or at least to identify) any major Romano-British church or episcopal complex. The problem here is one of recognition. Each bishop would have been assisted by a small body of priests and deacons, or *familia*. If conditions in Britain were analogous to those in Gaul and elsewhere in the Empire then it is likely that the buildings occupied by the *familia* would have been domestic in character, with facilities for administration, accommodation and worship combined within one complex. Such complexes have been investigated abroad, as for example at Merida in southern Spain, Aquileia, and at Salona (Radford 1968, 19–36). In each case the episcopal church formed only a part of a larger suite of rooms and structures. Without the evidence of internal decoration or ritual arrangements it could thus be difficult to discriminate between a Romano-British cathedral complex and some other types of urban building. The concept of the church as a distinctive architectural form was emerging in the fourth century, but it may have arrived too late to have had much impact in Roman Britain.

In the fifth century the picture begins to blur. Christianity undoubtedly persisted for some time, but during the 440s our sources fail us and we lose sight of all but the very barest outline of events. It has been argued that Romano-British Christianity was essentially an institutional religion, in which case the gradual deterioration of security and the breakdown of central government would have caused it to wither. Elsewhere, however, in the western and northern regions of England, in southern Scotland and in Wales, Christianity survived, and that it could do so might be taken as a measure of the strength of the faith in late Roman Britain as a whole.

The stages by which Roman *Britannia* was transformed into Anglo-Saxon England continue to perplex and fascinate scholars. The idea that Romano-British society disintegrated utterly in the fifth century and had no discernible influence on the Germanic culture which succeeded it is now regarded by many historians as at best an over-simplification and quite possibly as fundamentally wrong. English mercenaries (*foederati*) were present in Britain *before* the Imperial government shed its administrative responsibilities for the island in 410. At first they were used to ward off Pictish aggression, but after a time it seems that they became something of a liability to their employers, who were forced to hire further contingents of *foederati* in order to maintain control. An approximate timetable for subsequent events was put forward by the late Dr John Morris, working from fifth- and sixth-century British and Continental sources, who envisaged four main stages, the first being a continuation of Roman Britain under its own rulers until *c.* 440, followed by a revolt by the Saxons (*c.* 440–57) and then a period of recovery by the British (*c.* 460–95). British domination may have continued for as long as seventy-five years, until a second, successful Saxon revolt towards the end of the sixth century (Morris 1968, 59). This

8

framework of dates is necessarily tentative, but it does give some idea of the probable complexity of fifth- and sixth-century circumstances, and challenges the old notion of outright conquest.

Connection or conversion?

The Saxons were of course pagans, and their revolt would have stifled any organized clerical activity in areas under their control. Bede (HE I.22) noted censoriously that for their part the British refused to have any missionary dealings with the English, an attitude which he maintained had persisted down to his own time (HE II.20). Thus by the end of the sixth century we are unable to recognize any trace of an organized Church in areas under Anglo-Saxon control. But by no means everything Roman was either destroyed or forgotten. Reminders of the Imperial past were everywhere, including large buildings, fortifications, villas, boundaries and road systems. It is fairly clear that a very large section of the indigenous population stayed where it was, subject only to redistributions of land and alterations of tenure and control. Thus while the Church was extinguished it is not impossible that some individual *churches* survived, if not in the sense of living Christian communities then at least as recognizable Christian structures, to be commemorated in parts of eastern as well as western England by the place-name Eccles (from Latin *ecclesia*, a church: Cameron 1968; Gelling 1977; 1978, 82).

Roman law forbade burial inside the walls of a town. This custom was respected by the English at certain places, while it is interesting to notice that pagan burial grounds around some Roman cities in parts of Gaul and Upper and Lower Germany remained in use into the Christian period and with the establishment of a church have continued down to the present (Biddle 1976, 66). At the Rhineland towns of Xanten and Bonn, for example, the focus of medieval settlement shifted from the Roman *coloniae* to churches which developed on the sites of Christian martyr-graves in extra-mural cemeteries. Could this have happened in England? There is one site where it seems possible: St Albans. St Albans Abbey lies outside the Roman town of Verulamium, beside a Roman road and in the Roman cemetery area. It is the reputed site of the martyrdom of St Alban. Bede, writing in about 730, stated that the cult was flourishing in his day and that it was housed in a building of Roman construction (HE I.7). A *prima facie* case for continuity could thus be made out for St Albans (Levison 1941), and while St Albans provides the only obvious English candidate for the sequence of cemetery-shrine, *locus sanctus* and medieval church which is found on the continent (Radford 1971, 6), there are a number of parish churches which by their siting in relation to former Roman settlements and cemeteries suggest early histories of this nature. Even so, while it may not be totally fanciful to suspect individual instances of continuity it is all but certain that such cases would have been exceptional in areas directly under pagan English control. For the origins of our dioceses, and the sites of our cathedrals and great churches we must look to events in later centuries.

Missionaries

St Augustine arrived in Kent in 597. He came with forty companions and was received with tolerance by Ethelbert, the King of the region. Augustine was not the first Christian to cross into Kent; he had been preceded by Liudhard, a Frankish bishop, who had accompanied Bertha, Ethelbert's Frankish Christian bride, about ten years before. A gold medallion which belonged to Liudhard has been recovered from the churchyard of St Martin's, Canterbury (Grierson 1952–4), and there are hints in Pope Gregory's correspondence of Frankish interest in English affairs. Within four years of Augustine's arrival Ethelbert accepted baptism, and we are informed by Bede that Augustine reconditioned an existing Romano-British church in the town of Canterbury for use as his cathedral. During the next fifty years (or more) it is possible that the shells of other surviving Christian buildings were reused in this way, but Canterbury is the only place where we are specifically told that this was done.

Bede also records that Pope Gregory instructed Augustine to establish primary ecclesiastical centres at London and York, and that thereafter each metropolitan was to consecrate twelve bishops at certain, unspecified 'other places' (HE I.29). This intended total of twenty-six sees tallies quite closely with what we know of the administration of late Roman Britain, in particular the existence of twenty-seven or twenty-eight *civitates*, and it is tempting to guess that there were documents in the papal files which portrayed *Britannia* as it had been two centuries earlier. If so, then it may have been Gregory's intention to revive a lapsed ecclesiastical system rather than to start completely afresh. However this may be, events were to show the extent to which Gregory was out of touch with contemporary political realities. London, for example, was inaccessible to Augustine in the first instance, and for this reason Canterbury became the primatial see. York was not raised to metropolitical status until 735.

Augustine worked in England for about seven years. It is said that he attended two meetings with British bishops but that on each occasion, probably for the reasons already given, he found them unsympathetic to suggestions that they should co-operate in converting the English. Only three dioceses were established during the period: Canterbury, Rochester and London. Outward expansion from this bridgehead was slow; indeed, after Ethelbert's death in 616 the entire mission came very close to collapse. There was a relapse into paganism, Mellitus and Justus (the bishops of London and Rochester) withdrew to Gaul, and although Eadbald, Ethelbert's son, was converted and the bishops were recalled another ten years were to pass before the mission gained any momentum outside the south-east. Ethelbert's daughter was married to Edwin, King of Northumbria, and Paulinus, who had joined the mission in 601, was permitted to accompany her as her chaplain. The circumstances were reminiscent of those which had surrounded the arrival of Bertha and Liudhard in Kent nearly forty years before.

Edwin and his advisers were impressed by Paulinus' teaching, and in 627 they were baptized in a small wooden oratory which was erected for the occasion and which probably stood somewhere in the vicinity of the headquarters building of the former legionary fortress at York. Churches were built in Lincoln and in the district of Leeds at about this time (HE II, 14, 16), but progress was brought to an abrupt halt in 632 when Edwin was defeated and killed in battle by Penda, the pagan King of Mercia, and his ally Cadwallon, the Christian King of Gwynedd. Deprived of royal support, Paulinus left the region and ended his days at Rochester. His deacon, James, retreated to Catterick, and a stone church which was under construction at York to replace the wooden oratory was left unfinished. One consequence of the demise of the Roman mission in the north followed almost immediately: Oswald, Edwin's effective successor as King of Northumbria (633–41), invited the Irish monks at Iona to send a mission to his kingdom.

Iona was a monastic centre. Monasticism seems to have arrived in Britain, in south-west England and in Wales, late in the fifth century. Individual religious, living a solitary, eremitical life, may have been present before this time, but the concept of organized monasticism – that is to say, groups of men or women living a common life under the direction of an abbot or abbess, according to a code of discipline – cannot be discerned in Britain much before *c*. 500. The idea seems to have been acquired directly from the Mediterranean, ultimately from Egypt (Thomas 1971, 20ff). During the sixth century a number of monasteries were established in Wales (one may mention Bangor, Llancarfan, Llantwit Major and St David's) and we are informed of the presence of monastic bishops. Monasticism spread to Ireland in the sixth century, from there to Iona, just off the Isle of Mull, in the 560s, and thence to Lindisfarne, at the invitation of Oswald, in 634–5. During the next thirty years Aidan and his successors worked with royal support to extend the influence of their mission.

Meanwhile Fursa, another Irishman, was given the old Saxon Shore fort of Cnobheresburh (Burgh Castle, in Suffolk) by Sigeberht, King of East Anglia, for the

1 Burgh Castle

emplacement of a monastic community (Rigold 1977, 72). A see was established at Dorchester (a joint effort by Oswald of Northumbria and Cynegils of Wessex), and at about the same time Bishop Felix was given a see at *Dommoc* – wherever it was (Whitelock 1972, 4) – to serve East Anglia. Felix came from Burgundy, perhaps even from one of the monasteries which had been started there by the Irish missionary Columbanus towards the end of the previous century (Campbell 1971). New churches were founded at Lastingham, Whitby and elsewhere, and in the 650s a see was established at Lichfield.

The presence of such men as Felix of Burgundy and Agilbert (a Gaul with an Irish background who became Bishop of Dorchester) reminds us that there were several sources of evangelical energy in seventh-century England. There was no doctrinal clash between Canterbury and Lindisfarne, but circumstances did place a certain strain upon relations between the two centres. Nothing which resembled Gregory's preconceived blueprint for the structure of the English Church had been achieved. The dioceses were exceptionally large by Roman standards. Diocesan boundaries – if they even existed in any practical sense – tended to coincide with tribal or political frontiers and were often ignored by monks who conducted a mobile ministry and moved about on their own initiative. In Northumbria controversy on such matters as the correct method of calculating Easter and the proper form of tonsure was settled, in favour of Rome, at the Synod of Whitby in 664, but more fundamental developments were instigated by Theodore, a monk from Asia Minor, who was appointed to the see of Canterbury in 668 and arrived in England in the following year.

Consolidation

Theodore, Bede noted, was the first archbishop to enjoy the obedience of the entire English Church (HE IV.2). On his arrival he found that, with the exception of the Diocese of Winchester, which had been created by splitting Dorchester in 662 (apparently because Cenwalh, King of the West Saxons, had become exasperated with Agilbert's inability to speak the Saxon language), there had been no recent progress in the formation of dioceses. Moreover, a number of the sees which had been brought into being earlier in the century were vacant at the start of Theodore's pontificate. In 672 a conference of bishops was organized at Hertford, at which proposals for the observance of canonical decrees and for an increase in the number of dioceses were on the agenda. A decision on the question of dioceses was deferred (HE IV.5), but before long new sees were added: Elmham, Hereford, Lindsey and Hexham (in the 670s), followed by Worcester, Leicester and Selsey (in the 680s). With the addition of Sherborne (705) the primary diocesan map was complete, although in several cases (such as Selsey and Leicester) the early existence of the see was intermittent; it was not until the second quarter of the eighth century that the pattern was rendered stable, surviving without much alteration until the disruption caused by the Danish attacks in the ninth century. Theodore was an able administrator.

He travelled widely in England and laid the foundations for a unified Church in a period when political differences divided the country into a jig-saw of tribal kingdoms.

Two other men stand out as important figures at this time: Wilfrid, who was reared in the Hibernian tradition at Lindisfarne, and Benedict Biscop, also a northerner. Both spent time abroad, in Italy and in Gaul, and both returned firmly persuaded of the virtues of certain strains of continental monastic practice. In 661 Wilfrid introduced a continental observance at his monastery at Ripon. He went on to recondition the church at York and to oversee the construction of a church at Hexham. Benedict Biscop founded important monastic colonies and churches at Monkwearmouth (674) and Jarrow (681). These establishments are often described as 'Benedictine', but strictly speaking the term does not apply. The Rule of St Benedict was only one among a number of observances which were consulted, borrowed or developed in order to regulate the organization, routine and objectives of individual monastic communities during the sixth, seventh and eighth centuries. The concept of a monastic Order did not yet exist; the Benedictine Rule was not accepted as a general basis for monastic obedience until the Council of Aix-la-Chapelle in 817, and even Charlemagne had had difficulty in obtaining a complete copy. Cluny, the first house to be organized closely on the 817 model, was not established until 910. However, the new projects inspired by Wilfrid and Benedict Biscop undoubtedly reflected continental taste and technology, and in the years that followed these northern churches became the foci of a rich and vigorous culture. Literary activity, the arts and architecture flourished. At York a school was founded which acquired an international reputation. Missionary activity was carried into Germany. By the middle years of the eighth century Northumbrian monasticism was no longer derivative: it was influential.

If we examine the English Church as a whole at this period it is interesting to notice that ten out of the seventeen dioceses were based on former Roman towns. This would suggest that these places had retained, or reacquired, an importance as administrative or political centres, even if the majority cannot be regarded as urban in any commercial or institutional sense. Of the character and whereabouts of the churches concerned we are for the most part ignorant. Augustine's refurbished Roman church probably underlies the later cathedral at Canterbury and awaits an opportunity for investigation. The precise sites of the cathedrals at York, Lichfield, Hereford, Dorchester and Worcester have yet to be located, although in most cases the presumption is that they lie either beneath or very close to their medieval successors. *Dommoc* and Selsey have been claimed by the sea. The church of St Nicholas, Leicester, may occupy the site of the seventh-century church, which in turn was built amid the ruins of a Roman bath-house. Wilfrid's church at Hexham was inefficiently excavated in the 1890s during a rebuilding of the abbey, while at the other end of the country part of the outline of what could have been the church of 604 at Rochester was recovered by excavation in 1889. Of the first cathedrals, only Winchester has been thoroughly examined by modern archaeological methods.

13

Until recently the location of the see of Lindsey has posed a problem. Commentators have placed it variously at Stow, Caistor, Louth and Horncastle, but a fragment of Bede, apparently unknown in the Middle Ages, connects the see with a place with the status of *urbs* (. . .*hac et in urbe sibi seseque sequentibus almam fecit presulibus sedem, qua* . . .) (Lapidge 1975, 805–6). Bede tended to reserve the term *urbs* for fortified places (such as Bamburgh and Aylesbury), plus important towns such as Canterbury, London and Rome. It seems unlikely that any of the other candidates for the see of Lindsey would fall into an *urbs* category, whereas Lincoln would. More conclusive, however, is the reference to the bishop of Lindsey at the Council of Clofesho in 803, in which he was styled *Eadwulf Syddensis civitatis episcopus*. In this context *Syddensis* means 'south'. In the past this has led historians to look for the see elsewhere, but the use of the word in combination with the term *civitas*, which in this list was reserved for genuine *civitates* plus former Roman towns such as Worcester and Rochester, suggests that it was the south city of Lincoln (as against the upper *colonia* to the north) which was meant.

In the course of the eighth century the balance of power shifted from Northumbria to Mercia. Under the leadership of King Offa (757–96), a ruler of European stature, Mercia grew to become a dominant kingdom. The area within Offa's dominion extended from the Thames to the Humber, and in 788 the Mercian see of Lichfield was promoted to metropolitan status. The first Archbishop of Lichfield was the last, however, and shortly after Offa's death in 796 the status quo was restored, although not before Cenwulf, Offa's effective successor, had toyed with a plan for transferring the seat of the southern metropolitan to London (Stenton 1971, 225–7).

Danish attacks on England opened with a raid on Lindisfarne on 8 June 793. During the ninth century the Danish attacks grew more prolonged and systematic. Cathedrals and monasteries were natural targets for the raiders. They contained articles of value, they were not well defended and the inmates could be taken as slaves. By the 860s monasticism in Northumbria had been severely weakened, although houses of various kinds persisted, as for example at Crayke, near York (perhaps a double monastery?), Heversham, Norham and Ripon. The community of St Cuthbert abandoned its home at Lindisfarne and made its way, via Norham and Carlisle, to Chester-le-Street (Sawyer 1978a). Elsewhere the Danes caused further disruption. Not all religious communities fell victim to attack. Some disappeared because the Danes deprived them of their estates. Others collapsed following the displacement of local leaders who had previously taken an interest in their fortunes (Sawyer 1978).

Dioceses, too, were casualties of the troubles. Hexham fades from view *c.* 822. The sees of *Dommoc* and Leicester were permanently eliminated. The see of Lindisfarne was transferred to Chester-le-Street, while those of Elmham and Lindsey disappear into temporary obscurity. In a letter prefixed to his version of Gregory's *Pastoral Care*, Alfred (871–99) deplored the low standards of Latinity on both sides of the Humber. Only a century had passed since the days of Alcuin, when York had maintained one of the leading libraries of northern Europe.

By *c*. 900 the number of functioning dioceses seems to have dropped from the eighth-century total of seventeen to twelve: Canterbury, Chester-le-Street, Dorchester, Hereford, Lichfield, London, Rochester, Selsey, Sherborne, Winchester, Worcester and York. The tenth century saw improvements and changes. The growing importance of Wessex led to the creation of three new dioceses in that area: Crediton, Ramsbury and Wells, all in 909. A further subdivision in 930 led to the formation of a Cornish diocese based on St Germans. Elmham was revived at about this time and continued until the Conquest. Lindsey seems to have been re-established *c*. 954, although its subsequent institutional continuity is doubtful. According to tradition pre-Conquest Lindsey was subject to the authority of Dorchester (an immense diocese which had inherited the territory of Leicester), but it may be that for practical purposes Lindsey was regarded as falling more within the sphere of York's influence.

In the middle years of the tenth century a reformist movement gained momentum. Its prime movers were King Edgar (957–75) and a trio of bishops: Dunstan, Oswald and Aethelwold, appointed to the key sees of Canterbury (960), Worcester (961) and Winchester (963), respectively. The revival drew inspiration from contemporary monastic reforms on the Continent. Among other things it sought to substitute a standardized Rule for the more fluid observances to which religious houses had previously, and often casually, subscribed. This Rule, the *Regularis Concordia*, was worked out at a conference held in Winchester in 970 which was attended by ecclesiastical dignitaries from all over the country and from certain continental houses. A number of communities were reformed or refounded on the Benedictine model, including Crowland and Ely and the cathedral establishments at Winchester and Sherborne. The monastic cathedral was nothing new – the concept went back to the British Church of the sixth century – but it remained almost exclusively a feature of English ecclesiastical organization. The impact of the reforms was greatest in the midlands, in the fenland and in Wessex: areas which broadly corresponded with the houses of Abingdon, Ramsey and Glastonbury with which the three chief reformers had been closely connected. However, the initial fervour soon died down. Even at Worcester the reform does not appear to have been rigorously implemented (Sawyer 1975) and further north the revival was less influential. Indeed, beyond the Humber, despite a succession of monastic bishops at York, it was hardly felt at all. The collapse of Northumbrian monasticism in the ninth century may not have been complete, but almost without exception the major churches were now served by small bodies of secular canons.

The distinction between monks and canons has not yet been drawn. Monks, although withdrawn from the world and living according to a closely regulated regime, were not usually members of the priesthood. Canons, on the other hand, were ordained members of the clergy and earned the title 'secular' from the fact that they served, and often lived, in the everyday world. This exposure to outside influences was something of a danger, and in the absence of formal controls could lead to a decline into laxity and incontinent behaviour. From the ninth century onwards, therefore, we find a growing tendency for bishops to organize their canonical families along monastic lines, according to a Rule. One Rule in particular, the Rule of St Chrodegang (Bishop of Metz, d. 766), was widely observed on the Continent and was especially influential in Lorraine. During the eleventh century a number of foreigners were recruited into the English episcopate, including several who had been either born or educated in Lorraine. These included Leofric (Exeter), Giso (Wells), Walter (Hereford) and Hermann (Sherborne). At Exeter there was a copy of the Rule of St Chrodegang in the library, and at Wells we hear that Giso built facilities which enabled him to bind his canons into a family living a life in common. Harold's church at Waltham, founded in 1061, was consciously modelled on Lotharingian practice.

The northern province seems to have evolved its own brand of canonical rule in this period. The last three Anglo-Saxon Archbishops of York saw to the construction of refectories and dormitories – prerequisites for a life in common – at Southwell, Beverley and York. At Southwell prebends were established on the eve of the Conquest. In essence a prebendal system involved a shift of emphasis away from monastic collectivism towards an arrangement whereby a proportion of the communal resources was divided and shared out among the canons. Each canon received for his support a regular income deriving from a portion of the church's endowment.

Apart from the removal of the see of Chester-le-Street to Durham in 995 there were no further adjustments to the diocesan map until the reign of Edward the Confessor (1042–65). The Cornish see of St Germans was merged with Crediton in 1046, and in 1050 the see was transferred to Exeter. Eight years later Ramsbury was reunited with Sherborne; eight years after that Duke William of Normandy invaded England.

The Norman Conquest

The Norman Conquest led to a reorganization of the English Church. The diocesan pattern was rationalized, and reforms implemented by Norman abbots and bishops drew many of the English houses into intimate relation with continental foundations. In the process English monasticism acquired a coherence and vitality which gave the Church an entirely new dynamic.

Far-reaching as they were, Norman diocesan alterations involved the creation of only two new sees. The main changes were accomplished by adjusting the inherited pattern, and in particular by shifting episcopal chairs from the countryside to towns. The first changes were made nine years after the Conquest. They involved the removal of the sees of Dorchester to Lincoln, Elmham to Thetford, Lichfield to Chester St John, Selsey to Chichester and Sherborne to Sarum. In some cases the new arrangements did not last. In 1094 the East Anglian see was moved again, from Thetford to Norwich, and in the following year the midland see was transferred from Chester to the priory church at Coventry. Meanwhile, the see of Wells had been removed to Bath (1088).

Fig. 2 English dioceses on the eve of the Norman Conquest

An interesting document known as *The Shires and Hundreds of England* (Morris 1872, 145–6), compiled some time between 1094 and 1109, provides a survey of dioceses which were then in existence. The list is intriguing because it mentions former suffragan cathedrals. York, for instance, is credited with five 'bishoprics', including Ripon, Beverley and Whitby. Lincoln formerly comprised three (unspecified, but presumably Lincoln, Leicester and Dorchester), while in the south-west there had originally been a bishop's chair at Bridport as well as at St Germans. The possibility that there were subsidiary *cathedrae* in churches other than those normally accepted as cathedrals in the late Saxon period (e.g. at Hoxne, Suffolk) accords with a remark in the *Anonymous Life of St Oswald*, probably written at Ramsey late in the tenth century. In the middle of a discussion of the church at Ripon the author observed that it contained a pontifical chair.

The Diocese of Ely was formed in 1109 by detaching Cambridgeshire from the sprawling east midland diocese of Lincoln. The finishing touch to Norman reorganization was made in 1133 with the creation of the Diocese of Carlisle, apparently extracted from the southern sector of Glasgow. This was a disputed area, however, and for much of the twelfth century the bishops divided their time between Carlisle and an estate based on Melbourne in Derbyshire. At the end of the reign of Henry I the total of English dioceses again stood at seventeen, of which the churches in eight had kept to the same site or precinct since the seventh century. Apart from the removal of the see of Sarum from its inconvenient hilltop environment to a new site beside the Avon in 1219, this network remained unchanged until the Reformation.

The twelfth century was also a period of reorganization in Wales, where at least four dioceses had been in existence since the sixth century. Apart from St David's these dioceses seem to have been run on a peripatetic basis and correspond with the kingdoms of Glamorgan, Gwynedd and Powys. A diocese coinciding with the kingdom of Gwent might be expected but cannot be discerned. Norman changes involved the establishment of sees at Llandaff (Glamorgan, possibly incorporating the territory of a vanished diocese of south-east Wales; 1107), Bangor (Gwynedd; before 1092) and St Asaph (Powys; 1147) and the creation of constituted bodies of secular canons.

The Norman reformers had a decisive influence upon the institutional character of cathedral bodies in England and Wales. We have seen that in late Saxon England there was considerable diversity in the standing and administrative structure of the cathedrals. In the north and parts of the west a canonical system prevailed, while in parts of the midlands, the south and the fenland a monastic organization was favoured. Over much of the country the two systems existed side by side. Both types of organization tended towards the communal and monastic, but so far as the secular churches were concerned the numbers of canons were generally too low to permit any kind of elaborate interior organization. Five canons formed the staff at Rochester, for example, there were five at Lichfield and even metropolitan York was served by only seven. There was thus no scope for a hierarchy of officials, and episcopal functions were rarely delegated.

The Normans, by contrast, in common with their neighbours in Maine, Brittany and elsewhere, had from the end of the first quarter of the eleventh century moved towards a system which involved a chapter of canons led by a dean and a small group of capitular dignitaries. A dean is mentioned at Rouen as early as 1024, and at Lisieux it appears that a chapter with a full complement of dignitaries was in existence soon after 1050. In addition to the dean the key figures were the precentor (in charge of music and musical training), the treasurer (responsible for finance, possessions and fittings) and the *magister scholarum* (who supervised the school). In the twelfth century the office of *magister scholarum* expanded into that of chancellor, with additional secretarial and doctrinal functions. These offices were usual but they sometimes varied, particularly at this formative stage. The chapter at Coutances, for example, was headed by a *cantor*, and other offices such as *succentor* and sacristan are encountered. An important feature of the chapter system lay in the way in which a proportion of the cathedral endowment was split up into prebends which were individually assigned to canons who had stalls in the church.

England had already had a taste of this kind of arrangement at London, where reforms along continental-Norman lines had been implemented during the reign of Edward the Confessor. After the Conquest the Normans extended the idea to eight other cathedrals – first at Lincoln, Sarum and York, then at Chichester, Exeter, Hereford, Lichfield and Wells – and at all four cathedrals in Wales. It used to be thought that the chapter at Bayeux was the prototype upon which the English chapters were modelled, but it is now clear that the capitular system in Normandy itself was still in a process of evolution at the time of the Conquest. Hence the arrangements devised in England are probably to be regarded as a conflation of ideas from Normandy (and beyond), rather than as a direct importation from any single continental cathedral. There are signs of co-operation between the bishops responsible for establishing the first three post-Conquest chapters. Thomas of York, Osmund of Sarum and Remigius of Lincoln witnessed each other's foundation charters; all three were reorganized by 1092–3; and, in two cases at least, they contrived to consecrate their new cathedrals in the same year.

Side by side with the secular cathedrals existed the cathedral priories. The monastic cathedral had no parallel on the continent. However, the Normans took to the idea in England and went on to develop it. Lanfranc, the first Norman Archbishop of Canterbury (1070–93), reorganized the cathedral along strict Benedictine lines (Knowles 1951). This provided a balance to York where as we have seen the new constitution was modelled upon arrangements already existing in Norman secular cathedrals. Elsewhere the nature of reform appears to have depended upon the outlook of each individual bishop, or upon the ability of the existing establishment to resist it. Winchester and Worcester, already monastic, were maintained as Benedictine houses. Durham and Rochester, previously secular, were refounded as Benedictine monasteries. At the new cathedrals of Ely and Norwich the Benedictine Rule prevailed. Change was also accomplished through transfer. Giso of Wells, for example, who had been appointed in 1060, was permitted to remain in office until his death in 1088, whereupon his successor, John of Tours, removed the see to the Benedictine priory at Bath. The cathedral founded at Carlisle in 1133 was staffed with Augustinian canons. Before leaving the monastic cathedrals it is worth pointing out that these houses were ruled by priors; the bishops, who very often came from a secular background, were looked upon as titular abbots. Relations between the two were sometimes strained.

We must now consider the circumstances of the non-cathedral greater churches. Monasticism in England and Wales from the Conquest to the Dissolution is an immense subject, involving more than twenty-four different orders of monks, canons

2 *Durham: from the south-west*

and friars and over a thousand houses of varying status and size. Nothing more than the briefest outline is attempted here.

The history of the religious orders from 1066 down to the 1530s can be traced in terms of three main waves (the dates given are those of the principal periods of expansion): Benedictine and Cluniac houses (1067–1130), together with houses of Augustinian canons (1100–1260); houses of the reformed orders, mainly Cistercian, and houses of canons operating a Cistercian-based rule (1125–1220); and last, the friars or preaching orders, whose heyday lasted from *c.* 1225 until the early fourteenth century.

Of these three it is the first two, and in particular the first, which provided the

3 Rochester: Benedictine cathedral priory

majority of the buildings considered in this book. The friars, in theory at least, lived a frugal existence and eschewed the ambitious churches and complicated layouts of economic and conventual buildings which characterize the sites of the other two. Although from the last quarter of the thirteenth century the friars did begin to build

4 Tewkesbury: Benedictine abbey

sizeable churches, these structures were plain in outline, built for capacity, and came too late to have much impact upon the planning of their monastic counterparts.

Three orders formed the spearhead of Norman reorganization: the Benedictines, the Cluniacs and the Augustinian canons. The Benedictine order was used as an instrument of authority by the early Anglo-Norman kings, and this goes some way towards explaining the rapidity with which old houses were reformed and new ones founded. In its heyday the order mustered about 240 houses in England and Wales (excluding many of the alien cells), and over half of the churches examined below either originated or were refounded as Benedictine establishments. Among these were several, such as Crowland and Malmesbury, which achieved some importance as intellectual and artistic centres in the twelfth century.

The Cluniacs had their own observance, and contrasted with the Benedictines on account of their more elaborate liturgy and hierarchical organization. Cluny contributed some seminal ideas in the field of church design, but in England the houses were never particularly numerous, being outnumbered *c.* 5:1 by the Benedictines.

The Augustinian order founded its first house in England at Colchester in the 1090s. As we have seen, communities of priests living some sort of life in common according to a quasi-monastic rule were widespread in England before the Conquest. Many of these, such as Hexham and St Germans, were regularized as Augustinian houses during the twelfth century. Augustinian establishments often

5 Cartmel: Augustinian priory founded late in the twelfth century

resembled continental models in their organization and became particularly numerous during the reigns of Stephen and Henry II. Their churches, however, tended to be smaller than those of Benedictine houses and often differed in design. Unlike the black monks, the Austin canons maintained their appeal for a considerable time; new foundations were made throughout the Angevin era and on into the thirteenth century.

Success can bring its own problems, among them the risk of subverting progress towards the objective for which one set out. It was natural that the growing affluence and intellectual pretensions of the Benedictine and Cluniac orders should provoke a reaction. Reformed orders intent on reviving the primal ideals of monasticism emerged in Burgundy and Maine during the eleventh century. One, centred on the Abbey of Cîteaux, quickly grew influential. Led by a succession of abbots of unusual ability the Cistercians sought to reinstate a sense of fervent austerity which was felt to be lacking in other contemporary orders. In order to guard against any internal relaxation Cistercian houses were organized on a much more cohesive basis than those of black monks or canons. A system of regular visitations and meetings was instituted in order to foster a sense of corporate identity and to maintain discipline. Emphasis was laid upon manual labour, in direct contrast to the Cluniacs, and a second order of laybrothers was recruited to assist in agricultural work.

This return to simplicity extended to aesthetics and architecture. Bernard of Fontaine, the most famous of the Cistercian leaders, condemned the ostentation and irrelevant iconography of the Cluniac buildings: 'The walls of the church are glorious, but its poor are needy. Its stones are decorated with gold and its children are forsaken for lack of clothes. The eyes of the rich are pleased by the offerings of the poor. Aesthetes find things in which to take pleasure but the poor find nothing to sustain them' (Mortet 1911, 366–70). Cistercian houses in England and Wales were deliberately located in remote or secluded areas. Cistercian churches were designed to mirror the ascetic ideals of those who worshipped in them; this requirement undoubtedly helped to channel twelfth-century architectural invention into the abstract symbolism of Gothic. In the wake of the Cistercians came reformed orders of canons: notably the Premonstratensians, the Gilbertines (an order of English origin) and the Victorines. Mention must also be made of the numerically small but influential Carthusians; the Cistercians were agriculturalists and eventually fell victim to their own prosperity; the Carthusians retained their integrity to the end.

By the middle of the thirteenth century the epoch of monastic expansion was over. Leaving aside the preaching orders there were few new foundations, although a number of collegiate churches were established. These were served by groups of secular canons who led a common life according to specific rules. In some cases the clergy performed parochial duties; in others the college was created for the purpose of offering masses for the soul of the founder.

The high point of English monasticism was reached in the years around 1300. The century which followed saw changes in the equilibrium of the national economy which had an increasingly adverse effect on the affairs of many monasteries. These

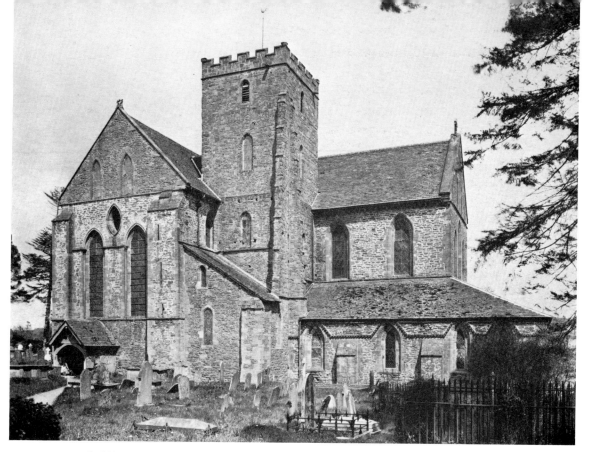

6 Abbey Dore: Cistercian abbey founded 1147

problems were intensified by heavy taxation in support of Edward III's war effort in France, by a series of epidemics and by social unrest. They persisted into the fifteenth century, to be aggravated by civil war and demographic changes which worked to the disadvantage of monastic landlords. Surprisingly few houses were closed during this period, however, and close on nine hundred were still in existence at the accession of Henry VIII in 1509. Houses with a net annual income of £200 or less were suppressed from 1536; the larger establishments were dealt with in 1539–40.

The Dissolution led to the summary destruction of buildings which, if they had survived, would rank today among the masterpieces of European architecture. Some of the most serious casualties were Abingdon, Hyde, Bardney, Reading and Winchcombe, all obliterated above ground. Several royal foundations were destroyed, including Vale Royal and Henry II's church at Waltham. The chapter-house at Westminster was discarded, though not entirely wrecked, and survives today as a partial replica. Quite often an aisle or a nave was saved from destruction because it was already in use for parochial worship. This accounts for the relatively large residue of Benedictine and Augustinian buildings and the high fatality rate of churches which belonged to the reformed orders; these latter generally excluded laymen and hence inspired little local affection. None of the nine major Cluniac priory churches survives as more than a ruin.

In certain instances, as at Selby and Tewkesbury, the parishioners managed to acquire almost all the church, although in some such cases (as at Great Malvern) destruction had already been started before the transaction was confirmed. The usual story is of the immediate removal of roof lead together with all articles of value followed by steady deterioration, often accelerated by those who used the churches as quarries for second-hand building material.

A handful of the great monastic churches survived without parochial intervention. In step with the suppression of the monasteries went a programme of diocesan reorganization. By continental standards the English dioceses were still large. The original proposals for restructuring the pattern were extensive. A memorandum drafted by Henry VIII himself in 1539 or 1540 notes: '. . . it is thowght therfore unto the kynges hyghtnes most expedient and necessary that mo bysshopprycys, colegyall and cathedralle chyrchys, shulbe establyshyd in sted of thes forsayd relygyus housys . . .' (Wright 1843, 263). The 'Byshopprychys to be new made' included Waltham (Essex), Dunstable (Bedfordshire), Bury (Suffolk), Shrewsbury (Stafford-shire and Shropshire), Worksop (Nottinghamshire and Derbyshire) and Fountains (Lancashire plus the Archdeaconry of Richmond). In the event, however, the plan was curtailed and only six churches were accorded cathedral status. The Benedic-tine Order supplied four: Chester St Werburgh, Gloucester, Peterborough and Westminster. The dioceses of Chester and Gloucester were formed by detaching portions of Lichfield and Worcester. Peterborough was cut out of Lincoln. West-minster never seems to have acquired a territory of its own and enjoyed only a fleeting period as a cathedral. Oxford and Bristol, the other two churches promoted at this time, were former Augustinian houses.

It was not until the nineteenth century that there were further significant changes. Redistributions of population and a newly-awakened instinct for reform called for the redrawing of boundaries and the creation of new dioceses . The first change came during the reign of William IV with the creation of the Diocese of Ripon (1836); then followed Manchester (1848), St Albans and Truro (1877), Liverpool (1880), New-castle (1882), Southwell (1884), Wakefield (1888), Birmingham and Southwark (1905), Chelmsford, St Edmundsbury and Ipswich, and Sheffield, all in 1914. The years since the First World War have seen the formation of six more dioceses: Blackburn, Bradford, Coventry, Derby, Guildford and Portsmouth. In Wales dio-ceses based on Brecon, Newport and Swansea have been added to the pattern. In the majority of instances the cathedrals in these new dioceses use former parish churches, although several, such as Guildford, Liverpool and Truro, occupy build-ings expressly designed as cathedrals. In six cases (Brecon, Manchester, Ripon, Southwell, Southwark and St Albans) the bishopric centres on a medieval building which is, or was, of cardinal importance. The church at Derby dates mainly from the eighteenth century but retains a late medieval tower of the first rank.

2
Commentators

*The men of the Renaissance discovered suddenly that the
world for ten centuries had been living in an ungrammatic
manner, and they made it forthwith the end of human
existence to be grammatical. And it mattered thenceforth
nothing what was said, or what was done, so only that it
was said with scholarship and done with system. . . . A
Roman phrase was thought worth any number of Gothic
facts.*

Ruskin

THE ARCHITECTURAL historian acts as an intermediary between the
medieval builders and ourselves. When we point to 'Decorated tracery',
discuss the 'Perpendicular style' or refer to the 'Benedictine plan' we are
using the terminology and taxonomy of recent scholarship rather than the language
of the builders responsible for the features we describe. We depend upon accounts
written by those who have studied and investigated churches for important facts
about the structural character and evolution of the fabrics and sites. This chapter
assesses the extent of our debt to these commentators, and traces aspects of the
growth of the study of great churches as history.

Early commentators

The Anglo-Saxons were proud of their churches but when they wrote about them
they were often vague when it came to providing details about layout and appearance. Eddius' contemporary description of the minster built by Wilfrid at Hexham
in the 670s is typically impressionistic. It mentions columns, *porticus*, stair-turrets,
walls of great length and height, a crypt, galleries and other features, but tells us
nothing of their co-location.

Furnishings and fittings often attracted more attention than the structures which
housed them. In his poem *De Pontificibus Ebor: Carmen* Alcuin recorded the lavish
outlay which was made for a new altar dedicated to St Paul at York in the second half
of the eighth century. The *Liber Eliensis* mentions an extension which was made to the
church at Ely in the 1000s, when a certain Leofwine 'began to extend the walls of the
church and to enlarge them to the south side, and at his expense completed them,
joined to the remaining work. He also built in one porticus an altar in honour of the
most blessed Mother of God, and above it a throne, the height of a man, in which was

to be seen an image of her, with her Son on her lap, remarkably worked with gold and silver and jewels with a magnitude of inestimable price' (Blake 1962, 132; transl. Gem 1975, 29). At Beverley we hear that a new presbytery was added to the minster in the 1060s by Archbishop Ealdred (1060–9). Little is said of the building, but we are told that above the entrance to the choir the archbishop commissioned 'a *pulpitum* of incomparable work of bronze and gold and silver, and on either side of the loft he set up arches, and in the middle, above the loft, a higher arch, carrying on its top a cross likewise of bronze and gold and silver, skilfully fashioned of Teutonic work' (Raine 1879, 354; transl. St John Hope 1917, 51).

After the Conquest observers of building activity often reported upon technical developments and stylistic innovations. In 1174 the eastern arm of Christ Church, Canterbury was severely damaged by fire. Gervase, a monk at the cathedral priory, wrote an exceptionally detailed account of the rebuilding that followed. It takes the form of a diary of events. Here he tells of the method which was adopted for vaulting the aisles:

> The master (i.e. the master-mason, William of Sens) began, as I stated long ago, to prepare all things necessary for the new work, and to destroy the old. In this way was the first year taken up. In the following year, that is, after the feast of St Bertin (5 September 1175) before the winter, he erected four pillars, that is, two on each side, and after the winter two more were placed, so that on each side were three in order, upon which and upon the exterior wall of the aisles he framed seemly arches and a vault, that is, three *claves* on each side. I put *clavis* (the boss of a ribbed vault) for the whole *ciborium* (the compartment of a vault) because the *clavis* placed in the middle locks up and binds together the parts which converge to it from every side.
>
> (Transl. Willis 1845, 48–9)

The awkward explanatory asides in Gervase's narrative are particularly interesting because they are suggestive of the difficulties which faced medieval commentators who were either not versed in the technical language of stonemasons or who chose to paraphrase it for the benefit of the uninitiated reader.

At Ely the central tower collapsed in 1321. Seven years later

> . . . the ingenious wooden structure of the new tower, designed with great and astonishing subtlety, to be erected on the said stonework, was begun. And at very great and heavy cost – especially for the huge beams required for that structure, which had to be sought far and wide, found with much difficulty, bought at great price, and carried to Ely by land and water, and then cut and wrought and cunningly framed for the work by subtle craftsmen . . .
>
> (Monk of Ely, *Anglia Sacra* i, 643; transl. Salzman 1967, 390)

Medieval descriptions of new buildings were frequently larded with such adjectives as 'astonishing', 'cunning' and 'subtle', but in this instance the epithets were justified. The 'ingenious wooden structure' of the Ely tower was of an advanced and daring kind (Quentin Hughes 1955).

Sir Gawain and the Green Knight, a narrative poem written during the reign of Richard II, contains a description of a castle which bristled with up-to-the-minute features:

> The knight remained on horseback and tarried on the bank
> Of the deep double ditch that enclosed the place;
> The wall waded deep in the water,
> And rose aloft to an immense height,
> Of hard hewed stone up to the cornice,
> Fortified under the battlement in the best manner;
> And in addition interval towers full gay were arranged between,
> With many fine loop-holes neatly pierced;
> A better barbican that man had never looked upon;
> And beyond he beheld a hall standing high,
> Towers set between, thick with spirelets,
> Fair turrets sited with subtlety, wondrously slender,
> With carved summits, fashioned with great skill;
> Chalk-white chimneys he perceived in plenty,
> Upon tower roofs that glinted full bright;
> So many pinnacles were scattered everywhere
> Among the castle embrasures, densely clustered,
> That it seemed they must have been cut out of paper.

(lines 785–802)

Medieval commentators paid less attention to the architectural achievements of previous generations. This was partly because patrons and the builders they employed were often intent upon surpassing them. Gothic builders worked in a progressive tradition. Each fresh enterprise was recorded as 'the new work', as at Durham in the 1150s when Geoffrey of Coldingham recorded that Bishop Hugh de Puiset initiated 'a new work at the east end of the church', or at London, St Paul's in 1339 when 'the quire was transferred from the nave of the church . . . where it had stood for seven years because of the danger of the bell tower, into the new work . . .' (*Ann. Paulini*, 338; transl. Salzman 1967, 391). There were occasions when a client or his master-mason sought to protect some admired feature, such as the richly-carved Norman doorway at Malmesbury, or to rebuild in a manner which was in keeping with an earlier style. At Beverley, for example, the fourteenth-century nave was intended to recollect the idiom of the Early English eastern arm and transept. John Leland remarked perceptively that the minster was of a 'faire uniforme makeing'. A similar policy was adopted at Westminster, where work on the nave of the church begun by Henry III continued on and off for more than two centuries. And was it affection which ensured the preservation of so many Norman doorways in the walls of parish churches rebuilt at a later date? Nevertheless, although patrons may have been less ruthless towards earlier work than has sometimes been claimed, on the whole it was the impulse to modernize which prevailed.

Modernization, as Gervase pointed out, might require the removal of what was already there. Nowadays no dean and chapter or local philanthropist would be likely to order the demolition of, say, the eastern arm at Wells or the central tower at Pershore in order to make way for something more convenient and up to date. Yet medieval churchmen and their builders were possessed of an almost unassailable confidence in the artistic validity of new work which enabled them to undertake such operations almost as a matter of routine. From the era of the Plantagenets through to that of the Tudors it could be said of many a great church that it was never finished, only temporarily abandoned. A church could stand complete – many Cistercian abbeys did, and enjoyed several centuries of quietude – but often it was not long before the next campaign of enlargement or adaptation to changing ritual needs returned the church to an unfinished state. Between *c.* 1200 and 1540 the eastern limbs of about two-thirds of Anglo-Norman cathedral and abbey churches were rebuilt or substantially modified. It is noticeable that many of the exceptions, such as Chichester, Durham and Hereford, were provided with large eastern extensions. At Canterbury building was in progress on an average of one year in three. At Chester it approached one year in two. Campaigns were normally organized in bursts, punctuated by years of inactivity which allowed the monastic economy to recuperate and when the offices could proceed undisturbed by clamour and dust. But some churches, such as York, were the scene of almost incessant building. There might be technical fumbling, as there was at Beverley around 1200 when the men engaged to remodel the central tower carried on doggedly despite signs that their alterations would provoke a collapse; and there could be aesthetic miscalculations as, arguably, in the internal elevation of the north transept at Hereford, designed *c.* 1250. But there seems to have been little heart-searching over the propriety of knocking down something old in order to do better. When the east end of St Hugh's Choir at Lincoln was dismantled in the 1250s to make way for the Angel Choir there were citizens alive who could remember the consecration of St Hugh's chevet half a century before.

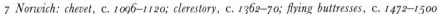

7 Norwich: chevet, c. 1096–1120; clerestory, c. 1362–70; flying buttresses, c. 1472–1500

The main obstacle to new work was lack of money. After the great construction boom of *c.* 1080–1170, when almost all great churches of pre-Conquest vintage were methodically replaced by large, cruciform, aisled churches with central towers and capacious naves, few religious houses could afford to rebuild again in a single operation on a comparable scale. Instead renewal was undertaken in stages, taking a choir, a nave, a transept or a tower at a time. It was this process of piecemeal alteration which gradually transformed the unitary Anglo-Norman churches into the heterogeneous structures we know today. A glance at the Gazetteer reveals how often the greater English church is an anthology of styles, comprising contributions from a succession of craftsmen made over several centuries.

But medieval patrons and builders were makers, not writers of architectural history. By the sixteenth century the origins of the earlier styles and the periods at which they were used had been forgotten. When Leland visited Leominster late in the 1530s he found the church as being 'large, somewhat darke, and of auncient buildynge' and thought that 'insomoche that there is a great lykelyhod that it is the churche that was somewhat afore the Conquest'. About 160 years later Nicholas Hawksmoor was even further from the mark when he suggested that the Norman portions of St Albans dated from the reign of Offa, King of Mercia (757–96). Not until the early years of the nineteenth century was the study of the structural and liturgical development of great churches placed upon a logical basis.

The death and resurrection of Gothic: 1540–1800

The Renaissance killed the medieval building style, and the Age of Reason very nearly buried it. Today it may seem remarkable that even the basic particulars of an idiom which dominated northern Europe for four centuries should have passed beyond recall so quickly. But forgotten they were, at least in England, and during the eighteenth and nineteenth centuries the history and method of medieval architecture had to be learned anew.

This state of architectural amnesia arose for three main reasons. In the first place the Reformation cleared away a large number of major ecclesiastical buildings from the scene and expropriated the resources of many of the survivors. This reduced opportunities for further work in the vernacular tradition. It also led to the disbandment or shrinkage of works organizations which hitherto had functioned as nurseries of Gothic design.

As a style, however, Gothic was still viable (Bath), even virile (Ripon nave), and the decisive blow to its future was dealt not by the suppression of monasticism but by what amounted to a political decision. The abandonment of Gothic was swiftest at the political centre, and hence in projects commissioned by patrons who wished to show their loyalty to the state. It was still possible to build in Gothic up to *c.* 1600 in Bath or Mold, or beyond (Staunton Harold, Chadderton), but not in London. Similarly, Burghley, Thynne (until *c.* 1550) and Sharington were in Court and

8 Bath Abbey: c. *1500–39, on the site of an older church*

subscribed to Classicism in their new country houses, whereas Savage, Percy and Walter were out of Court and still Gothic. Even so, sixteenth-century secular building, from Thornbury to Nonsuch and Burghley, was still Gothic in proportion though becoming Classical in dress. Only after *c.* 1600 was Classicism understood as a thought-out system rather than a conceit. (The same process may be seen in reverse during the period *c.* 1770–1830 when Gothic was readopted, as for example in the mongrel east window of St Mary's, Battersea (1777).) In Oxford there was an adherence to the principles of Gothic design until as late as the middle years of the seventeenth century (Harvey 1947, 145–6), while at Leeds the church of St John the Evangelist (1631–4) is a remarkable example of 'Gothic survival'.

Connected with the altered politico-religious climate was a change in the manner whereby large-scale building operations were directed. Previously it had been usual for supervision of both technical and artistic matters to rest in the hands of the master-mason. Gothic was the product of a craft tradition wherein new ideas were generated and developed empirically. Renaissance architecture, in contrast, was intellectual in its basis, and hence depended upon design sources and principles which were extrinsic to the accumulated experience of English medieval masoncraft. Access to these sources presupposed facilities for travel abroad to study paradigms and the booklearning of a liberal education: opportunities which were not normally open to the artisan in combination. The appearance of pattern-books, expositions of the Classical orders, and treatises on building methods and surveying furnished the patrons with a vocabulary with which to dictate their taste. Some of these volumes, such as John Shute's influential *First and Chief Groundes of Architecture* (1563) were published in English on the heels of the Dissolution, but most of them were imported from the continent. Alberti, Blume, Palladio, Serlo and de Vries were among the authors most often consulted.

The availability of these textbooks meant that buildings could be designed and erected under the superintendence of men who had little or no direct experience of the techniques and site skills involved. Control of the detail, as well as the outline, of new projects now passed to the patron, although in practice much was delegated. The functions of the medieval master-mason devolved upon several personalities: design and overall control to the patron or his assistant, day-to-day co-ordination of works to his steward, and the handling and assembly of materials to the artisan. So opened the rift between designing and making which has continued to widen down to our own day. The espousal of Classicism, sealed in the seventeenth century, substituted a derivative ethos for the experimental impulse which had animated the best of medieval achievement. The Elizabethan arts might be seen as a uniquely successful conflation of the two, but for the builder the eventual effect was to be as if a nerve between brain and hand had been severed.

For a time medieval architecture was despised for its crudity, asymmetry and disregard for the 'true' principles of Classical geometry and proportion. The very term 'Gothic' was coined in a spirit of contempt. Sir Henry Wotton, writing in 1624, referred to the 'natural imbecility' of the pointed arch. John Evelyn thought of medieval cathedrals as the outcome of a 'fantastical and licentious manner of building: congestions of heavy, dark, melancholy monkish piles, without any just proportion, use or beauty'. Wren's son deplored the 'misshapen pillars' and 'unreasonable thickness of the walls, clumsy buttresses, towers, sharp-pointed arches, doors and other apertures without proportion; nonsensical insertions of various marbles impertinently placed' and concluded that Gothic was 'not worthy the name of architecture' (*Parentalia*, 306). More appreciation was shown for some of the buildings of the Tudor age. Bacon, normally no great connoisseur of Gothic art, wrote in his assessment of Henry VII that 'He was born in Pembroke Castle and lieth buried at Westminster, in one of the statliest and daintiest monuments of Europe both for the chapel and for the sepulchre. So that he dwelleth more richly dead, in the monument of his sepulchre, than he did alive in Richmond or any of his palaces.' Wren thought that it was 'a nice embroidered work'. Meanwhile architects turned to early Christian Rome and Ravenna for ideas. They used new forms (the dome), new spatial areas (the oval), new decoration (Corinthian naturalism) and took a new delight in the theatrical, from the Somerset House porch to Blenheim, and the Italian Temple church at Llandaff, begun in 1734 and picturesquely set amid the decomposing remains of the medieval cathedral.

But the period when Classical was permissible in the greater churches was short lived. It lasted from about 1600 to 1750. And even then old forms lingered. Wren employed flying buttresses – of the kind denounced by his son – at St Paul's (though discreetly masked by brick screens) and the ordinance of his cathedral owed a good deal to medieval example, especially to Ely. The English tradition of tower building, which went back at least to the ninth century, scarcely faltered. At Westminster, for instance, Wren produced designs for a pair of towers to complete the late medieval west front; the designs were adapted by Hawksmoor and finally seen through to completion by James in 1745.

The modern church at Llandaff was unusual in that ecclesiastical expenditure upon new enterprises at this time was, in general, low. In many cases resources were barely sufficient to cover routine maintenance. The more affluent cathedrals managed to run small works departments which continued, in attenuated form, the tradition of a permanent lodge that went back to before the Reformation. But parishioners who worshipped in ex-monastic churches too large for their needs lacked the income from rents, endowments and fines which accrued to the cathedrals. It was not always possible to keep these buildings sound. At Selby, where the abbey church was taken over by the town as its parish church in 1618, the central tower fell in 1690 and had to be rebuilt. The south transept was abandoned. The north transept at Pershore collapsed in about 1686; the gap was filled with a wall which embodied some seventeenth-century Gothic detail. The parishioners of Crowland inherited the western portion of the Benedictine abbey. They occupied the nave until 1688, when the doubtful condition of the roof prompted them to retreat into the north aisle. This precaution proved wise: about thirty years later the roof fell in. Great Malvern deteriorated to a ruinous condition in the eighteenth century. An appeal for its restoration was launched in 1815. Brinkburn was derelict until Thomas Austin repaired it and returned it to use in 1858. When Hawksmoor surveyed Beverley Minster in 1715 he found the gable of the north transept leaning four feet out of plumb. However, in this case prompt action was possible since Beverley had a generous sponsor in the person of Sir Michael Warton. Two years later the gable was shored, slit along its base and screwed back to the vertical: an ingenious and effective remedy devised by a certain William Thornton of York.

Eighteenth-century churchmen took a utilitarian view of their buildings. Wren had composed a list of requisites for a cathedral. It was brief: 'Quire, Consistory, Chapter House, Library, Preaching-auditory' (*Parentalia*, 274). The requisites for a parish church were fewer still, a fact that can be understood from the contraction of many of the monastic buildings which were kept in use. Hence if money was available for anything beyond routine maintenance it was often spent upon internal improvements: the modernization of the choir (as at Ely in 1770), repaving (as at Bristol, York, Worcester and Lincoln), the installation or rearrangement of furnishings and fittings (such as the Inigo Jones screen at Winchester (1635–40)), the screen and gallery at Abbey Dore (1635), William Cosins' oak choir screen and stalls at Durham (1662), the organ (a late sixteenth-century case containing early seventeenth-century pipework), box pews, reredos and three-decker pulpit introduced at Tewkesbury in 1727–30; or ancillary buildings (the Wren library at Lincoln) and modest stylistic adjustments (such as the octagonal cupola added to the south-west tower at Bridlington in the eighteenth century, or the small dome raised over the crossing at Beverley in 1721).

9 Bridlington: church in 1852, with eighteenth-century cupola

Wren had pondered the origins of Gothic architecture. He concluded that 'it ought properly and truly to be named *Saracenic Architecture*, refined by the Christians'. This claim was based on the Islamic use of its leading characteristic, the pointed arch, before it was adopted by western builders. Some later commentators scoffed at this idea, and the origins of Gothic are still a matter of dispute. But Wren was a percipient man, and aspects of his theory have received support in recent years (Harvey 1968).

Early ideas aside, academic interest in the evolution of medieval architecture was not aroused in earnest until the second half of the eighteenth century, when antiquaries began to tackle the task of discriminating between the various styles. Among them were James Bentham, whose *History of Ely* appeared in 1771; John Carter, who produced *Specimens of Ancient Sculpture and Painting* (1786), *Ancient Architecture in England* (1795), and *History of Gothic and Saxon Architecture in England* (1798); and Francis Grose, author of *Antiquities of England and Wales*.

At the same time new work in great churches was increasingly made to match rather than clash with medieval idioms. Architects like Essex, Nash and Wyatt who were engaged to repair or modify cathedrals and abbeys began to bring a nascent appreciation of medieval construction to their duties. But neither the architects nor the antiquaries yet possessed any clear understanding of what the medieval idioms consisted. As James Essex admitted: 'There is no Stile or Architecture so little observed and less understood than that which we call Gothic, though it is not by any means so barbarous and inelegant as is generally supposed . . .' (cited in Pevsner 1972). So the language of ecclesiastical architects before *c.* 1820 was a pidgin-Gothic, spoken with a heavy Classical accent. An Augustan concern for order and dislike of medieval 'untidiness' persisted. At Ely the twelfth-century pulpitum was removed. At Salisbury Bishop Burrington enlisted James Wyatt to carry out improvements. Between 1787 and 1793 Wyatt presided over the destruction of medieval screen-work, porches, paintings, monuments and glass. Most of the medieval glass was removed and tipped into the city ditch. Surviving monuments were uprooted and paraded in straight lines. The thirteenth-century campanile was felled in order to tidy up the precinct.

Concurrently Wyatt undertook a punishing overhaul of Lichfield Cathedral. Lichfield had already suffered. During the Civil War the church was shelled, the central steeple was shattered, the roofs were stripped, and the church fell into ruin until decay was arrested by repairs in 1661–9. Now Wyatt removed the high altar 'to the further end of the long Lady-Chapel, and made the whole place snug for canons and their wives and retainers by walling up the arcades of the choir. . . . Everywhere he patched with Roman cement, chopping off sculpture and twisting in wire and tarred rope to make it hold.' At the west end – which Leland had described as 'the glory of the churche . . . that is excedynge costly and fayre' – Wyatt was 'specially lavish' with his cement, 'supplying even a whole row of kingly figures, grotesquely modelled upon old cores' (Cox 1897, 247).

At Hereford the western tower collapsed in 1786. Wyatt was called in by the dean and chapter. He deleted the western bay of the nave and removed the Norman triforium and clerestory, substituting creations of his own. Away to the west at St David's, which was also in shaky condition, Nash was commissioned to produce designs for a new west front early in the 1790s. At St Asaph the choir was rebuilt from *c*. 1780.

Wyatt's career as a restorer of cathedrals earned him the title 'the destroyer'. He expiated some of his sins with a comparatively respectful renovation of Henry VII's Chapel at Westminster, which was begun with the aid of a grant from the Treasury in 1807 and continued after Wyatt's death in 1813. Four years later another architect wrote:

> During the eighteenth century, various attempts, under the name of Gothic, have arisen in repairs and rebuilding ecclesiastical edifices, but these have been little more than making clustered columns and pointed windows, every real principle of English architecture being, by the builders, either unknown or neglected.

These words occur in a book by Thomas Rickman called *An Attempt to Discriminate the Styles of Architecture in England, from the Conquest to the Reformation*. Rickman continued:

> English architecture may be divided into four distinct periods, or styles, which may be named
> 1st, the Norman style,
> 2nd, the Early English style,
> 3rd, the Decorated style, and
> 4th, the Perpendicular English style.

Rickman's classification marked an epoch. His aim was the 'elucidation . . . of the real principle and essential differences of the styles of ancient English Architecture'. His method was systematic, involving a 'constant reference to buildings'. Under each style he examined the forms and characteristics of doors, windows, arches, piers, buttresses, sculpture, roofs, façades and porches. Rickman also identified some pre-Conquest churches, initially through the application of basic stratigraphic principles.

Rickman's ideas about the various period styles met with resistance later in the nineteenth century. Some of Rickman's successors, including Willis, Sharpe and Prior, disliked his system and offered classifications of their own. Francis Bond went even further and condemned the whole concept of a classificatory approach as 'mischievous'. Bond described Rickman's four phases as 'figments of the imagination'. He gave his reasons:

> Take a subject of primary and fundamental importance: that of the planning of the greater churches; there are not four, but only two periods of planning; of which the first, the period of the three parallel apses and of the periapsidal plan, ends with the twelfth century, while the later plans were all in use by that time. Or take vaulting as the criterion. Then the periods become five: that of the groined vault, the ribbed vault whether quadripartite or sexpartite, the vault with tiercerons and ridge ribs, the lierne

vault, and the fan-vault; the periods are not four but five, and do not coincide with the traditional Norman, Early English, Decorated and Perpendicular. If the very important matter of abutment be taken as a criterion, we are equally in difficulty. All the main methods of abutment had come into use by AD 1200. . . . Only to one, and that quite a subordinate member of the building, does the antiquated terminology apply, viz., to the fenestration . . .

(1905, xx)

It is difficult to disagree with this judgment. Classification is misleading not merely because it oversimplifies, but also because it depicts architectural history as a series of well-defined episodes, each a spurious entity, while according correspondingly less importance to the equally fictitious phases of transition which such a system necessarily implies. Viollet-le-Duc observed that medieval architecture was *always* in a state of transition. Nevertheless, it is significant that Rickman's 'antiquated terminology' is still used. There is general agreement that the four titles capture something of the artistic personality of the 'phases' involved, even if reason demands that we should concede the validity of objections and abandon the concept of phases in close discussion.

Here it is worth pausing to consider some of the factors involved in the production of a taxonomic framework for medieval architecture. Dr H. M. Taylor has pointed out that the architectural historians of the nineteenth century were fortunate in that

> . . . for the whole period from the eleventh to the sixteenth centuries there was hardly any repetition in the styles or fashions, whether in general plan or in details. It was therefore possible . . . to compile and publish detailed drawings of plans and architectural features grouped by styles, and to provide beside those drawings the dates that had been fixed for such of the examples as had been dated from written records. The degree of consistency of these dates served to establish the truth of the general principles stated above about a steady development and consistent use of styles, and the commonly accepted nomenclature and dating of the Norman and several Gothic styles in England became established in this way.

Taylor continues:

> . . . the detailed study of buildings in past centuries has by no means been limited to . . . typological studies . . . Indeed, much of the accurate association of written records with surviving fabric has depended on the extent to which the sequence of erection of parts of the fabric could be determined from a study of the fabric itself.

(1976, 4)

This must seem self-evident, but it is an axiom which has not always been honoured.

Some of the pitfalls involved in identifying a sequence of erection of parts have recently been exposed at Hadstock, in Essex, where the cruciform church of St Botolph has usually been regarded as a typical late Saxon building because it displays details and decoration which 'are acknowledged as belonging to the post-Danish period. From such features, here and elsewhere, the central-towered transeptal church-type has been dated to the tenth and eleventh centuries.' But investigations at Hadstock, above and below ground, have now shown that 'the three diagnostic features (decoration, [double-splayed] windows, and central tower) were all inserted into an earlier building, the plan of which had been determined at some earlier period' (Rodwell 1976, 69).

Hadstock is not a cathedral or an abbey, and it might be imagined that the greater churches would have been studied in such detail that problems of this nature would long since have been solved. But if we turn to two of our most famous cathedrals, York and Canterbury, we find that this is not always the case. At York, despite a succession of studies, it is only during the last decade that remains beneath the choir which have been known for 150 years have been elucidated. They formed part of a Norman cathedral of unusual design. A near-contemporary record, written by a man who knew both the cathedral and its patron, fixes the date of construction within the period 1070–1100. But because the design was unorthodox it did not tally with the conventional classification of early Anglo-Norman churches; hence several commentators (e.g. Willis and Sir Charles Peers) who tried to understand the scheme in terms of preconceived ideas about Norman planning were led astray. It may be that aspects of the Norman phases of some other cathedrals, such as the eastern arm at Chester (Burne 1962), the nave at Lincoln (Bilson 1911) and the transept and eastern arm at Rochester (St John Hope 1884; Fairweather 1929) are due for reappraisal.

At Canterbury evidence has been recorded by Mr Hendrick Strik and Mr T. Tatton-Brown which indicates that the late fifteenth-century central tower – the famous 'Bell Harry' – was the outcome of two separate campaigns. The tower was originally conceived as a simple lantern and afterwards doubled in height (Tatton-Brown 1978; cf. Urry 1965). Fragments of Archbishop Lanfranc's cathedral (built 1070–7) which are lodged within later elements of the building have also been examined. These include part of a staircase which belonged to the Angel Steeple (the eleventh-century central tower) and a sizeable shard of the northern transeptal apse which survives above the fan-vault of the 'Dean's' Chapel. The significance of this apse, which is strongly stilted, has either been missed or ignored in several recent articles on the church. Canterbury is our premier cathedral, but no comprehensive analysis of its fabric has appeared since Willis' pioneer survey of 1845 (Tatton-Brown 1978).

These examples lead to a broader issue, namely the extent to which a large medieval church may be regarded as 'factual'. Historic buildings are often loosely described as 'documents', but the constituent materials and features of a church are not factual in the sense that we would allow, say, of an inscription or a written record. Physical evidence must first be recognized, next recorded, and then correlated before it can be turned into history.

It will be useful to illustrate this process with a few examples. Written sources report that the central tower of the cathedral begun at Winchester in 1079 collapsed in 1107. Adjoining portions of the transept were affected by the disaster and they were rebuilt along with the tower. The extent of the repair is marked by a change from crude to more finely-jointed masonry in the vicinity of the crossing. This in turn indicates an improvement in standards of cutting and setting ashlar during the intervening twenty years. The correspondence between written and physical evidence is close.

More often facts must be coaxed from the fabric. Casual inspection of the nave at Winchester reveals it to be a Perpendicular transformation of its Norman predecessor; but the extent to which the elevation of the nave designed by William Wynford in 1394 is a reflex of the registers of its twelfth-century precursor is not overtly apparent to the newcomer without close attention to detail (Willis 1846, 66–74).

Evidence may be concealed within walls, above vaults and below floors. Until recently, for instance, there was no indication that York Minster originally possessed a pair of Transitional or Early English western towers; the remains of such towers were encountered by archaeologists working in advance of repairs to the cathedral in 1970 (Hope-Taylor 1971).

Operations necessary to arrest or prevent decay of the church fabric may obliterate evidence. Even careful renovation may lead to the loss or misrepresentation of an original feature or relationship. All the greater churches contain less evidence today

10 Beverley: putative twelfth-century masonry backing onto the north triforium of the thirteenth-/fourteenth-century nave

11 (right) *Winchester: nave, c. 1395*

than they did 150 years ago. Further, much of the potential total of evidence which survives is only accessible on rare or intermittent occasions: when scaffolding is up, when plaster or limewash have been stripped, during repairs to the roof, or when part of the pavement has been lifted. Entire chapters in the history of some of our cathedrals and abbeys have been written as an aspect of their renovation; but a corollary to this lies in the fact that a conscious effort has to be made to grasp such opportunities. A timber joint, or a foundation uncovered in an unexpected position, will not proclaim its own significance. Unless someone is on the spot who is able to detect and record the evidence, and who then makes it available to others, that evidence may be misunderstood or ignored.

12 York Minster: eleventh-century capital and shaft discovered 50 feet above the pavement during repairs to the fabric of the thirteenth-century transept. The capital originally formed part of the entrance to the southern transeptal apse of the church begun by Archbishop Thomas c. 1080, and was subsequently fossilized within the structure of the later transept. Romanesque features are latent within the fabric of many Gothic churches

42

Investigators

Architectural historians working in the nineteenth century set out to codify the formal principles of Gothic architecture. Thomas Rickman's role in this enterprise has already been mentioned. Another important antiquary was John Britton, who was born in Sodbury in 1771 and after various youthful adventures turned his attention to the compilation and publication of topographical studies. Britton described his first excursion, *c.* 1800:

> With maps, a pocket-compass, a small camera obscura (for the more portable and simple camera *lucida* was not then known), two or three portable volumes, an umbrella, and a scanty packet of body linen, &c., I commenced a walk from London, on June 20, and returned again to it on September 30. During that excursion, I visited Oxford, Woodstock, Stratford-on-Avon, Warwick, Kenilworth, Birmingham, Hagley, 'the Leasowes', and Church Stretton. Thence I made diverging excursions to Shrewsbury, Welsh Pool, and several other places within twenty miles of my residence, and returned through Ludlow, Leominster, Hereford, Ross, down the Wye to Chepstow, to Bristol, and Bath; thence to several parts of Wiltshire, and back to London. This long and toilsome, but eminently interesting and attractive journey, cost me only 11*l.* 16*s.* 9*d.*
> (cited in Eastlake 1872, 83)

Britton's most important studies involving the greater churches were his *Architectural Antiquities of Great Britain*, which appeared in five volumes between 1807 and 1818, and his *Cathedral Antiquities of Great Britain*, produced in six volumes between 1814 and 1835. Britton employed a number of artists and engravers to assist him, most notably Mackenzie and Le Keux who in the *Cathedral Antiquities* 'attained a perfection in their peculiar branch of art which had not hitherto been reached, and has since scarcely been surpassed' (Eastlake 1872, 85). These series provided what had previously been lacking: a reliable conspectus of the greater churches. When Britton died in 1857 the *Ecclesiologist* remembered that 'his elaborately illustrated works were among the earliest of the causes which led to that revived appreciation in England of medieval ecclesiastical architecture . . .' (XVIII, 70). Today Britton's works are of additional value because they record major ecclesiastical buildings as they stood prior to restoration later in the century.

Appropriately enough the titles of some of the other chief publications of this period convey a preoccupation with what might be called the grammar of medieval architecture: Pugin and Willson's meticulous *Specimens of Gothic Architecture* (1821); J. L. Petit's *Remarks on Church Architecture* (2 vols, 1841); Edmund Sharpe's *Architectural Parallels of the Twelfth and Thirteenth Centuries* (1848) and *Decorated Window Tracery in England* (1849); F. A. Paley's *Manual of Gothic Moldings*. During the middle years of the century Professor Robert Willis produced a series of brilliant monographs on English cathedrals, starting at Hereford (1841), then Canterbury (1845), Winchester and York (1846), Salisbury (1849; unpublished until 1973), Chichester and Lichfield (1861), Worcester (1863).

Architectural history became popular. John Britton grew wealthy on the proceeds of his topographical studies. J. H. Parker's important *Glossary of Gothic Architecture* was already in its fifth edition by 1850. The formation of the Cambridge Camden Society in 1839 stimulated further interest. The professed objects of the Society were 'to promote the study of Ecclesiastical Architecture and Antiquities, and the restoration of mutilated Architectural remains', but in fact there was at least as much theology as archaeology in the aims of the Society's ruling Committee. In 1843, just four years after its inception, the Society could muster '2 Archbishops, 16 Bishops, 31 Peers and M.P.s, 7 Deans and Chancellors of Dioceses, 21 Archdeacons and Rural Deans, 16 Architects, and over 700 ordinary members' (Boyce 1888, 10). This spectacular growth in membership was checked after an internecine struggle in 1845, but it is notable that the *floruit* of the Society in the 1840s coincided with a period of scholarly activity when more books of enduring importance on English medieval architecture were published than in any other decade of the nineteenth century.

The first significant archaeological excavation in an English church was occasioned by arson. Jonathan Martin, a tanner and Dissenting preacher, became convinced that he was 'a special instrument appointed by God to do great works'. In 1829, after an abortive attempt to assassinate the Bishop of Lincoln, Martin made his way to York, pasted a 'fierce denunciation' of the Church and clergy on the main door of the Minster and then set fire to the organ loft. The fire spread and did considerable damage to the eastern arm of the cathedral (Dickens 1866).

John Browne, a local art teacher and antiquary, persuaded the Dean and Chapter to allow time for an investigation in the area of the choir before repairs began. Browne duly disinterred the remains of the twelfth-century crypt, and went on to record details of another structure which lay below them. In 1840, after a second fire, he excavated in the nave. Browne also made large numbers of measured drawings of architectural details throughout the cathedral. It is no longer possible to accept some of the conclusions which Browne drew from his excavations (e.g. about the layout of the Norman nave, or the evolution of the transept), but recent excavations, again in conjunction with a major programme of repair, have confirmed the general accuracy and importance of the records he kept. Moreover, Browne's methods at York combined excavation with scrutiny of written sources and analysis of the standing fabric. It was the alignment of these methods of inquiry which formed the basis of Victorian attempts to reach an objective assessment of medieval architecture and has continued to do so down to the present.

Growth of concern for Gothic architecture was accompanied by a revival of interest in medieval liturgy. Indeed for some the two were regarded as being aspects of each other. After the upheavals of the Cambridge Camden Society in 1845 J. M. Neale wrote: 'I want to protest most strongly against forming an Architectural Society out of our ruins. People will ignorantly think that our religious views are given up, and our Architectural retained – as if the two were separable' (1910, 84). Pugin (1841) claimed that of all the styles Gothic was the only true Christian architecture. The Ecclesiologists looked upon the pointed arch as the 'necessary result of the teaching of the Church' (*Handbook* 1848, 16) and argued for the ultimate Christian 'reality' of early fourteenth-century Decorated architecture. Later on Sir G. G. Scott complained: 'So imperious was their law, that any one who dared to deviate from or to build in any other than the sacred "Middle Pointed", well knew what he must suffer . . .' (1879, 203).

The story of the Gothic Revival has been told elsewhere (Eastlake 1872; Clarke 1938; White 1962; Macaulay 1975) and lies beyond the scope of this book. However, one of the side effects occasioned by the wave of restoration and liturgical re-arrangement which swept the Church from about 1840 to 1880 was a series of disturbances to fabrics and sites which offered opportunities to antiquaries to examine such evidence as was being revealed. Local and national periodicals were filled with accounts of church investigations, surveys and architectural descriptions.

13 York Minster: excavations in the choir in 1829

Some of these accounts, particularly those dealing with the exposure of evidence which was subsequently destroyed or now lies concealed, have remained standard until the present day. Plans of all the cathedrals and many of the ex-monastic churches were drawn before the end of the century; few of the greater churches have been planned in such detail since.

At the same time there were losses. These can be divided into two categories: the destruction of medieval features in the course of restorations, and losses of information sustained when opportunities were missed or inadequately exploited.

Of the need for repairs to the greater churches during the nineteenth century there can be no doubt. We have already seen that some of them, such as Great Malvern and Pershore, were in tender condition, while a number of the cathedrals were due for extensive overhaul. But the nineteenth-century architects were not content merely to respond to problems of decay and instability. Aided and abetted by deans and chapters they practised a policy of restoration. 'To restore,' explained the *Ecclesiologist* in 1842, 'is to recover the original appearance, which has been lost by decay, accident, or ill-judged alteration' (I, 70). John Ruskin disagreed.

> Neither by the public, nor by those who have care of public monuments, is the true meaning of the word *restoration* understood. It means the most total destruction which a building can suffer: a destruction out of which no remnant can be gathered: a destruction accompanied with a false description of the thing destroyed.
>
> (1849; 2nd ed. 1956, 199)

For several decades warnings of the kind enunciated by Ruskin went largely unheeded. Medieval features ranging from corbels to entire buildings were sacrificed to the ideals of retrospective authenticity and liturgical theory. In fact few of the architects entrusted with the task of caring for the greater churches were imbued with the ideological motivations of the Ecclesiologists; when some of the worst excesses were reviewed at the end of the century (Cox 1897, 239–74) it was noted that:

> . . . two factors are mainly responsible for the mischievous treatment and spoiling of the interior of our minsters during the latter half of Victoria's reign . . . firstly, the playing at parish church with the whole of the cathedral (combined with the idea of rendering it a great preaching-house), and hence endeavouring to obliterate the proper division between quire and nave; and, secondly, an undue giving way to the rage for gigantic organ effects, an idea involving music-hall arrangements, where everything has to give way to the pervading influence of sound.

Many of the ex-monastic buildings *were* now parish churches, of course, and in the case of the cathedrals the parish church syndrome can be seen as a reaction against the tendency of eighteenth-century canons to cocoon themselves in their choirs to the exclusion of lay congregations. But this does not excuse and certainly does not explain all that was done. Nor did the changes meet with unanimous approval at the time. The consequences of ill-advised restoration were perceived by a commentator

47

14 (above left) *Malmesbury in 1864*
15 (left) *Howden: view of the church from the east in* c. *1910*

16 (left) *Ripon: west front, c. 1230–70; heavily restored in 1860s*
17 (below) *Romsey: apse of (?) pre-Conquest church revealed by excavation c. 1900*

in the *Saturday Review* in the 1860s. Provoked by works of an exceptionally punitive kind then in progress at Worcester he wrote:

> They are destroying the title deeds and credentials of art under the pretence of restoring. Thus they break up the very patterns which convey first principles, and give back in their place the bauble conceptions of the nineteenth century.

The period which saw the greatest restoring activity lasted from *c*. 1840 to 1880. In 1877 came the backlash when William Morris and other like-minded colleagues founded the Society for the Protection of Ancient Buildings. They announced:

> We think that these last fifty years of knowledge and attention have done more for their destruction (i.e. of ancient buildings) than all the foregoing centuries of revolution, violence, and contempt.
>
> (cited in Briggs 1952, 208)

It was no exaggeration.

In considering losses under the second category it is perhaps easy to adopt an over-censorious attitude to the efforts of antiquaries who were working without the benefit of any kind of established archaeological discipline. Soil was simply something to be shovelled out in pursuit of 'the plan', and there seems to have been only a dim appreciation of the importance of the immediate below-ground surroundings of a church. Even so, after allowances have been made it is a fact that the approach of Victorian (and for that matter some twentieth-century) antiquaries to the recovery of evidence buried in and around churches was sometimes surprisingly casual.

Willis' account of discoveries at Lichfield Cathedral, for example, was published in 1861 after he had

> ... paid only one brief visit to the Cathedral when only the south-west corner of the small Early English rectangular chapel leading from the apsidal chancel was exposed. That area is the most detailed part of his plan. The rest was apparently composed from information sent to him. A field plan of the foundations uncovered is in the Lichfield Joint Record Office. ... It differs from Prof. Willis's plan in important respects ...
>
> (Gould 1976, 9–10)

At Lincoln John Bilson searched for the layout of the first Norman cathedral. He 'came to the conclusion that comparatively small excavations would probably give ... fixed points for a definite plan'. Accordingly the trial excavations 'were only made in those places which were likely to furnish data for the principal lines of the plan ...' (Bilson 1911, 546). Near the end of his account Bilson wrote: 'The plan is a remarkable orderly and logical piece of work. Indeed it is due to the fact that it so closely conforms to the Norman type that we have been able to recover its main lines with comparatively little excavation' (1911, 553). There is circular reasoning here, and although the greater part of Bilson's exposition of the Lincoln plan seems convincing, on the evidence he presents, there are unexplained anomalies, particularly in the nave. (As a pendant to this it is interesting to compare the results of another set of 'comparatively small excavations' with which Bilson was associated, at the important Anglo-Saxon church of St Peter, Barton-on-Humber, with the results of a modern (1978) excavation on the same site. The excavators stated that they had found the remains of a rectangular building beneath the floor of the pre-Conquest tower. It is now clear that this building did not exist: its 'walls' were areas of a mortar floor, and its 'shape' was determined by the positions of the excavators' own trenches.)

Many medieval tombs were prised open during the eighteenth and nineteenth centuries. A few were disturbed because they lay in the path of building operations and had to be moved; a few more for purposes of identification. But most, one suspects, were opened out of plain curiosity. At Worcester King John had been inspected in 1754 and again in 1797. Early in the nineteenth century the Abbot of Cheltenham was opened up at Tewkesbury. The Elricke Tomb was opened at Wimborne in 1857, and three years later John Fitzalan was shown to the light at Arundel. Henry VII was examined at Westminster in 1869. In the same year the tomb of 'William Rufus' (but probably that of Henry de Blois) was opened at Winchester. The historian Ranulph Higden was disturbed at Chester in 1874, and in 1889 the bones of Oliver Sutton, Bishop of Lincoln (1281–99), were viewed in his minster.

Synthesis

Hand in hand with local and thematic projects went the task of drawing together the evidence provided by studies of individual churches and categories of detail into works of general application.

The process of synthesis was already well advanced by the third quarter of the nineteenth century. The years leading up to the First World War were outstandingly fruitful, with the publication of Baldwin Brown's volume on Anglo-Saxon architecture in his series *The Arts in Early England* (1903), Edward Prior's *History of Gothic Art in England* (1900), Francis Bond's *Gothic Architecture in England* (1905), Lethaby's *Westminster Abbey and the King's Craftsmen* (1906), and a series of monographs on specific aspects of church architecture, fittings, dedications and screens.

Today these Edwardian years have the appearance of a golden age in architectural history, but at the time Bond complained of a 'general neglect' of medieval architecture and regretted that 'Nowadays the students of our national architecture are few'. Bond thought of his own time as being distinguished by a 'blackness of indifference to the master art'. He looked back with nostalgia to the days when 'For a brief period . . . interest in this supreme artistic achievement was revived by Britton, Pugin, Petit and Willis, greatest of all' (1905, xvii–xviii).

The phase of synthesis continued between the wars, with contributions of both local and general application from such masters as Bilson, Clapham, Hamilton Thompson and Peers. By this time too the origins and development of Christian architecture were being considered in an international context.

The question of authorship in medieval architecture was also now re-examined. Scholars were no longer content to accept the doctrine propounded by certain earlier writers that 'the power of designing art in medieval times was common property, not merely very usual, but what could be demanded of any workman, and was existent in the masses of the people' (Prior 1905, 22). Indeed, studies by Lethaby, Douglas Knoop and G. P. Jones, Francis Andrews and Martin Briggs were beginning to show that the truth lay in the opposite direction. The evidence which they assembled indicated that the medieval master-mason could be every bit as individualistic, and his industry almost as hierarchical, as at any subsequent stage in history.

Despite this progress during the first half of the twentieth century the general pace of archaeological research in surviving churches slackened. Surface features such as glass, wall paintings, sculpture and iconography continued to attract expert attention, on an increasingly departmentalized basis, but rather less effort was put into the exploration and scientific analysis of fabrics and sites.

Four main reasons for this reduction in activity may be suggested. First, the spate of restoration which characterized the Victorian period had largely spent itself. The need for further major works was thus for the time being reduced. Many architects and churchmen were dismayed at some of the excesses of Victorian restoration, and this too served to inhibit new projects and hence to diminish the scope for fresh investigation. Naturally there were exceptions, but they were not always adequately exploited. At Norwich, for instance, the east end was altered in 1930–2 by the addition of a War Memorial Chapel. The Dean reported promptly upon the results

51

of an excavation which was carried out beforehand. Referring to 'early foundations' which were found at the east end of the cathedral he wrote:

> The manner in which the Norman apse stands on the earlier work almost proves that the earlier building was already ruined. *It is difficult to convey this clearly to any one who is not on the spot*, but it is almost certain that nothing was standing above ground when the Norman chapel was built.

(Cranage 1932, 123–4; italics mine)

Secondly, curiosity as to the evolution of churches and the typologies of their features seems largely to have been satisfied by the results of work in the nineteenth century, which as we have seen were being drawn together and served up in consolidated form during the first half of the twentieth. Whereas the Victorians had been compelled to start from first principles there was now, it seemed, a wealth of information and a widespread faith in its accuracy. Bond's warning that 'A great book can be a great evil' was not always heeded. Thirdly, after the First World War archaeologists turned their attention to the field: to prehistoric and Roman sites, to monastic remains, and particularly to castles. Previously the leading architects had been closely involved in the historical investigation of churches, but now the architectural and archaeological professions drew apart. Fourthly, churches in use were excluded from the Ancient Monuments Acts of 1913 and 1931 and hence were often assumed to be inaccessible for purposes of investigation. The need for extensive further research was apparently removed.

Conclusion

So far it has been possible to scan in a very superficial way the evolution of aspects of architectural history in England and Wales. Recent developments cannot be sketched with such ease.

Great strides have been made towards an elucidation of the organization, economy and methods of the medieval building industry, most notably by the late Dr L. F. Salzman in his book *Building in England Down to 1540* and by Mr J. H. Harvey who has given us a small library dealing with medieval buildings and the men who designed them.

There has also been an upsurge of material dealing with detail and parts. Much of it lurks in periodicals of restricted appeal and circulation, while a great deal more is being contributed by scholars based in the United States. Alongside the traditional art-historical and typological approaches to architectural history have sprung up new sub-literatures dealing with medieval technology, the structural behaviour of great churches, archaeological science, medieval geometry, liturgy and architecture, metaphysics and symbolism, and the problems faced by modern architects who have the sensitive and increasingly difficult task of caring for our greater churches and adapting them to meet contemporary needs without tarnishing further what Dr Bernard Feilden has aptly called the 'patina of history'.

The habit of harmonizing scientific investigation with repair, which had largely died out, has recently shown signs of revival. In particular there has been a welcome reconvergence of the methods of architectural history on the one hand and scientific archaeology on the other. Two enterprises deserve particular mention in this connection. These are the excavations which were carried out on the site of the Anglo-Saxon cathedral at Winchester between 1961 and 1969 under the direction of Professor and Mrs Martin Biddle; and Mr Derek Phillips' rescue excavations in and around the cathedral at York during the repairs of 1967–72. The former explored traces of a vanished pre-Conquest building; the latter examined the origins and development of a familiar standing church. Each in its way has been revelatory. Winchester has provided a reliable yardstick by which to measure the achievements and ambitions of Anglo-Saxon churchbuilders. Discoveries at York have transformed received doctrines about Anglo-Norman cathedral design, and remind us that entire and important phases in the evolution of a church may now be unrepresented in the standing fabric, or commemorated merely by fragmentary remains lodged in later work. Taken together the results of the two projects should act as a

18 Winchester Old Minster: foundations of northern apse of martyrium, *begun c. 971–4 to enclose St Swithun's grave. Notice channels for timber reinforcement*

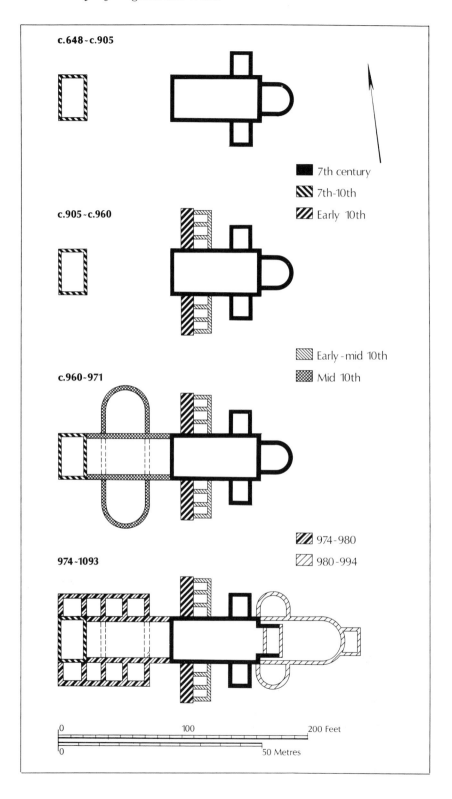

c.648 ~ c.905

7th century

7th-10th

Early 10th

c.905 ~ c.960

Early-mid 10th

Mid 10th

c.960 - 971

974 - 980

980 - 994

974 - 1093

0   100   200 Feet

0   50 Metres

caution to those who are still under the impression that everything worth knowing about the greater churches is already known. We have seen that systematic study of these buildings has been in progress for more than a century and a half, but that in general this study has been restricted to the visible (and accessible) parts of the standing structures. In consequence we remain under-informed about the origins of the great churches, our ideas about their structural development until *c*. 1200 are oversimplified, and liturgical layouts in earlier periods have been neglected. No other post-Conquest English or Welsh cathedral has been investigated in such detail as was possible at York between 1967 and 1972. What further reappraisals would follow from work on a comparable scale at, say, Beverley, Lichfield or Lincoln? At Lincoln, for instance, the sites of the major piers of the three-sided apse of St Hugh's east end (begun 1192) have never been established (Venables 1887), although several commentators have published plans which purportedly locate them (e.g. Bond and Watkins 1910; Clapham 1934, 90). A knowledge of the positions of these piers is crucial to an understanding of the vaulting system of St Hugh's choir.

Even today, however, habits acquired in the Victorian era can still die hard. At Ripon the seventh-century crypt underwent alterations as recently as 1974 without provision for adequate archaeological investigation. Britain has yet to see collaborative research on the scale which has been possible in a number of major continental churches.

Specialization in scholarship leads to the fragmentation of knowledge, which is a quick route to general ignorance unless ways can be found to build bridges between multiplying disciplines. The whole trend of architectural history has been towards the realization that the study of great churches is an interdisciplinary process, but recent progress has been so rapid that there is a real risk that it will outpace our capacity to digest the information and put it to good use. Architectural history began as a series of small springs which subsequently joined to form a major river. The river has now turned into a delta of proliferating channels of inquiry.

This is not merely a question of a glut of research. Architectural history spans what C. P. Snow has called the 'two cultures': the world of the humanities and the world of mathematics. A Gothic cathedral is at once an artistic and a technical achievement; a sacred image and an essay in statics. The fact that it may have been built by men who kept no distinction between the two is of little practical assistance to the modern scholar, who is unlikely to be bilingual, let alone fluent in the respective vernaculars of art history and applied engineering. For some the raw materials of architectural history are sculpture, mouldings, tracery, tooling, glass, iconography and liturgical history. But thrusts, stresses, wind-loads, mortar-mixes, and the dynamics of structures are not less relevant. Both cultures have their place

Fig. 3 (left) *Winchester: development of the Old Minster, c.648–1093, as revealed by excavation.* (*After Biddle & Kjølbye-Biddle*)

within the sphere of the discipline. Hopefully the way forward will be through lively discourse between the two.

A great church is rather like a small universe: it is capable of absorbing any amount of study.

3
Masters and Men

The gestures of an adult are those of a carpenter, the gestures of an infant are those of a mason.

Malcolm de Chazal

WHO BUILT THE great churches? Mathew Paris was in no doubt as to where the *credit* for building work lay; writing in the thirteenth century he contended that recent modifications to the church at St Albans should be ascribed to the abbot, since it was the abbot who had initiated the work. Some historians have taken him literally and have assumed that ecclesiastical dignitaries actively participated in the design of churches, but it is quite clear from illustrations elsewhere in Mathew Paris's work how things were organized. A drawing of *c.* 1250 depicts a king delivering instructions to his master-mason alongside a building site where craftsmen and labourers are engaged upon dressing and setting stone and operating machinery. Here we have the circumstances of a medieval building project in microcosm: a patron or client, an architect, and a workforce comprising craftsmen of different kinds.

But the concept of the medieval architect as an individual took some time to win acceptance. Edward Prior, for example, writing just after the turn of the century, observed: 'One is often asked who were the "architects" of cathedrals. The reply must be that the function of architect as designer of building, and determiner of its forms of beauty, did not exist in any personality' (1905, 58). The corollary to this allegation, that medieval clergy and craftsmen possessed some innate propensity for collective invention, is manifestly far-fetched, but it persisted for a considerable time and even today it is occasionally to be encountered in some guide-books of the less authoritative kind. Suffice it to say that there is now ample and clear-cut evidence to indicate that medieval cathedral and abbey churches were not, as a rule, designed by committees, and that the direct dictation of architectural schemes by ecclesiastical dignitaries was rare. Bishops, abbots and capitular bodies naturally took a close interest in the projects they commissioned, but they exercised their influence by proxy, through the selection of designers whose output or reputation conformed most closely to their taste or ambition. Cases are known in which high-ranking personalities concerned themselves with building operations: Abbot Hugh of Selby, for example, was described as *devotus architectus* and is recorded as having worked as a labourer; and St Hugh of Lincoln took his turn as a navvy. (St Hugh left behind a

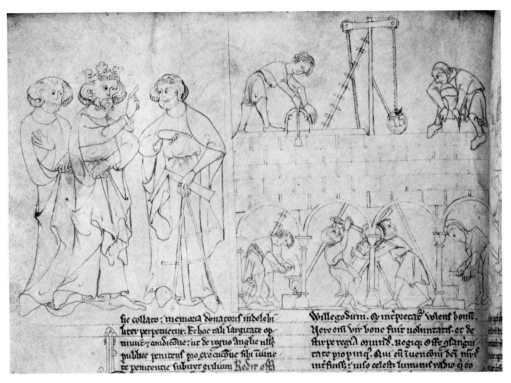

19 Matthew Paris' drawing, c. 1250, depicts a medieval building project in microcosm

hod which was venerated in the belief that it possessed supernatural powers.) But these are best explained as gestures of piety. Churchmen were certainly closely involved in the administration, and sometimes the lines of supply of building projects, but the real work of design and superintendence required exceptional ability and years of practical experience. It was almost always entrusted to a layman.

Masons formed the core of any medieval building crew involved in the construction of a large church. They were not alone, of course; carpenters were required to provide scaffolding, to co-operate with the masons in the provision of falsework, and to roof the building and fit it out; tilers and paviours were needed to roof and floor the church; glaziers to supply and fit the glass; marblers to embellish; plumbers to make it weatherproof; and plasterers to provide a finish. Metalworkers would have to be on hand to maintain tools and to manufacture new ones, while the various departments would be serviced by apprentices and labourers who would fetch and carry.

Key craftsmen frequently travelled long distances from one job to another. Masons working on the Cistercian abbey at Vale Royal, Cheshire, between 1278 and 1280 came from as far afield as Abbey Dore, Lincoln, Oxford, St Albans and Salisbury (Knoop and Jones 1933, 74). Unskilled workers were usually recruited locally. Accounts kept at York Minster in 1371, for example, reveal that the master-carpenter was one Philip of Lincoln, whereas the majority of the labourers (*operarii*) had surnames indicating an origin in the near vicinity (William of Goldsborough, Thomas of Clifton, John of Acomb, Roger of Otley). Philip of Lincoln's status reminds us that occasionally we find a master-carpenter in charge of a building project, but in most cases it was a well-qualified mason who was in overall control and who was responsible for the design. It was not uncommon, however, for a master-mason to have had experience as a carpenter. Gervase of Canterbury reports that William of Sens, a French architect who was engaged to rebuild the eastern part of the cathedral after a bad fire in 1174, 'was as a workman most skilful both in wood and stone'. In fact this is hardly surprising if we bear in mind that masons would have been directly concerned with such matters as the design and erection of falsework, and the manufacture of templates for mouldings and tracery.

Two words were commonly used to describe masons in the Middle Ages: *cementarius* and the Anglo-French *masoun*. These terms were used more or less interchangeably and covered a wide variety of semi-specialized branches of the craft, ranging from roughmasons, quarriers of various kinds and cutters through to the more expert setters and freestone masons (Knoop and Jones 1933, 81–9). Lines of demarcation were by no means rigid, however, and medieval accounts show that masons of almost all grades could transfer from one class of task to another, either by way of promotion or as the need arose. The importance of the quarrymen, too, should not be underestimated, for their role went well beyond the task of extraction. Stone was usually rough-dressed into convenient blocks prior to transportation, and in some cases a good deal of detailed work was carried out at the quarry as well. If the quarry was owned or rented by a cathedral or abbey then operations at the quarry could be under the direct control of the master-mason; if not, then templates or *moldes* might nevertheless be dispatched to the quarry for execution by others.

Direction

The men in charge of building projects were usually clearly distinguished from their subordinates. At Lincoln in *c*. 1240, for example, we find the chief mason Alexander designated *cementario magistro operis*, and the title 'master of the works' was regularly applied to medieval designer-supervisors. It is not to be confused with the term *custos fabricae*, for in large projects it was common for overall responsibility to be divided between the master-mason and an administrative official (*custos*). At monastic churches, such as Worcester and Durham, it was usual for the sacrist to act as administrator, while in secular cathedrals and collegiate churches a canon or vicar-choral might be selected. Part of the administrator's job was to collect and keep track of revenues which were earmarked for the fabric fund. This was not always easy. The income of a large church was derived from a wide variety of sources and it could be difficult to ensure prompt payment or claim from defaulters. Monastic finances could sometimes become hopelessly chaotic, and where mismanagement was gross it could starve a building scheme of the funds necessary to keep it going.

The other main task of the administrator was to audit and regulate expenditure on materials and wages. Here there was inevitably some overlap with the province of the master-mason, since it would be he who had responsibility for the estimation of quantities of materials and who had control of the workforce. In cases where the partnership was particularly close the administrator has sometimes been mistaken for the architect. Alan of Walsingham, for example, the sacrist at Ely in the 1320s, has been credited by some with the design of the great octagon which was erected after the collapse of the central tower in 1322. Elias of Dereham, a canon, has likewise been associated with the design of Salisbury Cathedral. Without doubt both men were very closely connected with these projects but it is not at all certain that they functioned as architects. Dereham, in particular, acted as an administrator for a number of prominent men, and it seems probable that it is in this capacity that we should regard him. Matthew Paris referred to Dereham as *incomparabilis artifex*. Knowing Paris' views on authorship this might appear to reinforce the view that Dereham had more to do with the instigation of building projects than with matters of design or site supervision. Alan of Walsingham's own Sacrist Rolls indicate that he was not the designer of the *novum opus* at Ely, although it was he who organized the clearance and preparation of the site. It was men such as Alan who created the conditions in which great churches could be built. Nevertheless, a handful of clerical builders have been identified (Harvey 1972, 81), although only two can be reasonably connected with the buildings discussed here: Robert of Holm Cultram, a carpenter, and Arnald of Crowland. It is significant that both were laybrothers. Arnald was in charge of works at Crowland from *c*. 1114, and was described as *cementario artis scientissimo magistro*. If we assume that Arnald was in his early thirties at the time it is just possible that he is to be identified with the mason Arnald who is recorded as holding property in Newark from the Dean and Chapter of Lincoln in the 1150s. If so, it would be interesting to know if he had anything to do with the improvements to the cathedral carried out during the episcopate of Bishop Alexander (1123–48); at any rate, the Arnald in question was dead by *c*. 1165, by which time the property had been redistributed.

Masons

Masons in the upper echelon of their craft were frequently well off, sometimes quite wealthy, and enjoyed considerable social status. Leading masons were often, though not necessarily, literate and numerate, and those reared in the shadow of great churches may have benefited from an education at ecclesiastical schools. There were three ways in which a mason might receive his practical education: he could be born into the craft and absorb the necessary skills, detailed knowledge and trade secrets from his family background; he could be apprenticed to a master for seven years; or he could be promoted from one of the lower grades.

The organization of masons was fluid. In the main it centred upon individual projects and contracts for which craftsmen and labourers would be engaged upon specific terms: either for a fixed period, or for the construction of some specific feature (such as a screen or chantry), or simply on a casual fortnightly, weekly or daily basis. Building accounts which survive from the thirteenth century onwards show that there could be considerable fluctuations in the size of a workforce engaged on the erection of a great church. To a large extent the size of the workforce depended on seasonal factors, but it would also reflect the nature of the work in hand, an interruption in supply or finance, or the labour requirements of another major building project in the region under a more influential patron. Nevertheless, major campaigns of building might lead to the establishment of a semi-permanent construction organization in which skilled craftsmen could expect continuity of employment for several years at a time, and where a master-mason might spend a large part of his career. Sometimes a master-mason was engaged for life. In 1359, for example, a contract was made between the Dean and Chapter of Hereford and John of Evesham; in return for his work on the cathedral (which may have included the design of the fan-vaulted Chapter House which was destroyed in 1769) Evesham was to receive a wage of three shillings per week, a daily ration of bread and accommodation at a favourable rent. The contract included provision for disability payments in the event of ill-health. Evesham was skilled as a mason and as a carpenter, and one of his duties was to give tuition in these crafts to others (Capes 1908, 230–1). In addition to 'set piece' projects and long-term contracts such as this, master-masons might also be called upon to act as consultants for existing churches, to make structural surveys and to advise on restoration work.

On site the life of masons centred on the lodge. In essence the masons' lodge was simply a shelter for indoor work carried out at the bench. The permanence of the lodge would depend upon the scale of the campaign and the size of the building involved. Very large churches such as York Minster and Westminster possessed semi-permanent working quarters, whereas smaller churches might run to no more than a temporary lean-to, or even a tent. The lodge is not to be confused with the tracing-house or *trasour*, which was the drawing-office used by a master-mason to design and produce the templates or moldes for mouldings and architectural details. *Trasours* are known to have existed at Ely, Exeter, London St Paul's and Westminster, and two such cathedral drawing-offices survive (there is another at Queens' College, Cambridge): at York (Harvey 1968) and at Wells (Colchester and Harvey 1974, 214). At York the *trasour* is located in a room above the Chapter House Vestibule, while at Wells the drawing-office occupies a room above the north porch and is reached from the triforium. Both rooms are partially floored with plaster-of-paris, which enabled the master-masons to etch in designs for mouldings and tracery at full size, using square and iron compasses. Once finished with these figures could be rubbed out and the surface used over again.

The master-mason presided over the lodge. In addition to his professional site duties he was responsible for the conduct of his workforce. A lodge usually had its own set of rules, and it would be the task of the master to see that these were observed. On 31 October 1370, for example, Master Robert de Patrington and twelve other masons came before the Dean and Chapter at York in order to swear to observe regulations which detailed the length of the working day in winter and summer, the time available for eating and drinking and penalties for slackness. Newcomers were to be given a week's trial in which to prove their competence. Working hours and breaks were ruled by a bell or clock; most monastic houses and cathedrals had acquired a clock by the end of the thirteenth century.

The churchbuilders' year was divided into two periods. Outdoor construction went ahead between March and October, when a typical working day might run from between 5.00 and 6.00 in the morning until 7.00 or 8.00 at night. Breaks of half an hour were commonly allowed at breakfast time and later in the day, plus an hour at lunch. In very hot weather a siesta was permitted after lunch. During the winter the raw edges of the unfinished building would be bandaged over with bracken or straw and a large part of the workforce would be laid off. It was very necessary to protect the structure in this way since lime mortar hardens slowly and is susceptible

20 York Minster: tracing-house, c. *1450–60*

21 Tracing-house: detail of designs incised in plaster floor

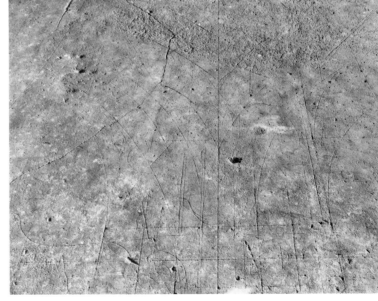

to contamination; failure to take such steps to keep the wall-cores dry and safe from frost could lead to serious structural problems later in the life of the building. Winter work would be largely confined to the lodge or the tracing-house – the tracing-house at York was provided with a fireplace – where a nucleus of masons would work through the dark months preparing detailed components in readiness for the following season. Complicated mouldings and in particular architectural sculpture took rather longer to produce than more straightforward components, and we may imagine that in the case of intricate schemes such as the Chapter House at Southwell

22 Southwell: chapter-house entrance, c. 1295

and the Lady Chapel at Ely the winter period provided a useful opportunity for the carvers to keep pace. In midwinter work in the lodge might begin before dawn, by candlelight.

This strenuous regime was relieved by many one-day holidays marking such important points in the ecclesiastical calendar as saints' days, patronal festivals and octaves, as well as the ritual turning points of the seasonal cycle. Skilled men were paid for some holidays, and before certain principal feasts the workforce might be permitted to knock off early on the preceding day.

Pay was generally good by medieval standards. Wages were normally allocated by time (day, week or fortnight), although piece-rates were sometimes paid (Knoop and Jones 1933, 112). On some sites there were also perks: allowances for clothing, tools and rations of food or drink. Key craftsmen might receive a robe, accommodation and food, in addition to a regular wage or annual stipend.

Pay leads us to the question of masons' marks. A mason's mark is simply a symbol, a kind of geometrical autograph which has been scratched onto the surface of a stone by the mason who dressed it. This method of indicating work done became normal practice in England during the twelfth century, and from *c*. 1200 until the sixteenth century the wall surfaces of many major churches abound with incised symbols. Masons' marks vary a good deal, not only in their complexity but also in the frequency with which they appear. On the continent it appears that a mark would be assigned to a newly-qualified apprentice by his master, but there is no definite evidence to indicate the authority on which marks were issued in England and Wales and their distribution is noticeably uneven. According to Salzman, 'Their practical purpose must have been to identify the work of an individual mason for the information of the paymaster.' Salzman stated that marks seldom appear on tracery or carved stones and concluded that since the authorship of such detailed work would be known to the master-mason additional information would not be required. Salzman thought that the irregular distribution of marks on plain ashlar was suggestive of men who were on piece-rates or possibly 'casual labourers who were not known to the master and whose work it would therefore be desirable to check' (Salzman 1967, 127). This makes sense, but it must be pointed out that some marks appear regularly on work that was in progress for several years, that in certain buildings (e.g. Exeter) up to five marks have been recorded on one stone, and that in others (e.g. Beverley) marks do occur on tracery. It seems logical to assume that banker marks were associated with piece-work, although we have already seen that it was more usual for masons to be paid by time than by task. Possibly some kind of quota system was involved, or marks could have been used in conjunction with a particular method of supervision. Banker marks are used to this day in some cathedral stoneyards, but since the seventeenth century the practice has been to incise them on the reverse or bed of the stone, not on the face.

Tools which are well adapted to a particular function tend to change very little over the years. Many of the implements which were used in the construction of

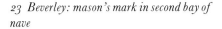

23 *Beverley: mason's mark in second bay of nave*

24 *Gloved mason at work with mallet and chisel (detail of interior spandrel of St William's tomb, York, second quarter of fourteenth century)*

medieval churches are closely paralleled by the equipment used by masons today and equally resemble the tools used by Roman artificers.

Nowadays the tools of a builder tend to fall into two categories: hand tools with specialized functions, which are often the personal property of the craftsman; and tools of more general usage, which belong to the contractor. Whether this division existed in the medieval period is not clear, since tools in the former class would be jealously guarded by their owners and would not appear in medieval equipment inventories. In this category we may place the master's square and compasses, and just possibly certain types of chisel. On the whole, however, most of the items needed for building were provided in a general equipment pool, and consequently their whereabouts had to be periodically checked. Such lists have survived for projects at Exeter, Durham, York and elsewhere, and from them we can gain a fairly clear idea of the character and variety of the tools which were in use. Even objects of the supposedly 'personal' kind, such as compasses, are sometimes mentioned. The main tools of the mason were the stone-axe and the chisel. Among the tools listed in the masons' lodge at York in 1399 were sixty-nine *stanexes* and ninety-six *chisielles ferri*, suggesting that these two items were very roughly of comparable importance in the business of dressing and finishing stone. This impression is confirmed by medieval illustrations which depict masons at work. The stone-axe, or its near relation the adze, was essentially a percussion tool, being used to strike off fragments from the block and to rough-dress the stone. The axe could also be used for fair-faced work, as it was throughout the first half of the twelfth century, and in sensitive hands it could

65

be used for shafts and elementary mouldings. Chisels were used as finishing tools. Their purpose was to dress the stone to a smooth surface and to iron out any irregularities left by the axe. Modern masons use a succession of tools for this purpose (pitcher, draught, punch, claw, bolster) and it is possible that the total of ninety-six iron chisels mentioned at York at the end of the fourteenth century was composed of smaller numbers of chisels of different categories. Alternatively, it may be that some of the tools which feature in the repertoire of the modern mason were originally employed at the quarry.

The basic chisel consisted of a simple metal shaft broadening to a flat blade at the working end. It was easy to keep sharp and relatively easy to make, but from the beginning of the thirteenth century (in some areas the end of the twelfth) its use for fine work was widely superseded by the claw-chisel. This possessed a comb-like toothed blade which produced a characteristic rippled effect on the surface of the stone. It was nothing new. Roman masons had used it extensively, and there are now signs that builders working in Northumbria during the Anglo-Saxon period occasionally employed it. The claw-tool enabled a faster rate of work, and was particularly efficient for dressing the harder limestones; it seems to have been used less on coarse, granular sandstones. It has been suggested that English masons were taught to appreciate its merits by Saracen craftsmen. At any rate, its reappearance coincided with the end of a period of great crusading activity, and came during the Early English era when standards of precision in stone cutting were rising. Although the claw-tool was commonly used to finish stones in the Middle Ages, it is hardly ever used for this purpose by masons working today. Instead it is used in the penultimate stages of dressing a block, or for surfaces which are not meant to be seen; the final finish is achieved with the broad-bladed bolster.

The marks left on a stone by a claw-tool bear a superficial resemblance to those produced by a drag. The drag, which occurs both as a kind of toothed hammer-axe (Salzman 1967, Pl. 10b) and as a species of plane in which serrated blades are set in a block of wood, was used extensively in France by medieval masons. For some reason it does not seem to have found favour in England. This may have been because English limestones are on the whole harder than French varieties and hence were less suited to treatment by the drag; however, the techniques of English and French masons differ in a number of respects, and the apparent failure of the drag to achieve popularity in English lodges may have been simply a matter of national preference. The choice of tool would be dictated by the texture and type of the stone in use, and the standard of finish could vary according to the position of the stone in the completed building and according to whether or not it was intended to carry plaster. Many medieval churches, particularly in the Romanesque era, were plastered inside *and out*, and a coarse masonry surface was often desirable as a means of keying the plaster to the fabric. Thus while tooling can be very helpful as a general guide for dating, it is best considered in the context of local practice and in connection with the particular circumstances of individual buildings.

At the quarry robust tackle would be needed. An inventory made at the limestone quarry of Stapleton, Yorkshire, at the end of the fourteenth century lists picks, *weges ferri* (each weighing 10 lb), *pulyngaxes* (hammer-axes), *gavelokes* (crowbars), *kevelles* and *mallea* (iron hammers). Wedges (for splitting the stone from its bed) and levers for manoeuvring large blocks were always needed. Other heavy-duty implements included the *blokker* (broad axe) and another kind of axe known as the *dolobrium*. For the handles of tools ashwood was preferred. All this hardware required constant maintenance; tools used in connection with stone quickly became blunt, and on the larger ecclesiastical building sites a complete department could be kept occupied in keeping these various implements in trim.

Carpenters

In the medieval building industry as a whole masons were well outnumbered by carpenters and joiners. The Anglo-Saxon words *getimbran* (to build) and *getimbro* (buildings) indicate where the emphasis lay in the pre-Conquest period. We have seen that master-craftsmen of the calibre of John of Evesham and William of Sens could be skilled workers in both wood and stone, and it was not unknown for a master-carpenter to be put in overall control of a building project. Carpenters usually had their own lodge on a building site and had their own rules and craft organization.

Responsibility for the construction of Edward the Confessor's abbey at Westminster, probably begun *c.* 1045–50, seems to have been shared among three men: Leofsi Duddensunu, Godwin Gretsith (both masons), and Teinfrith, who is described as 'church-wright'. If one of the masons was acting as co-ordinator or administrator then here we meet the 'big three' of a major church campaign, the church-wright or master-carpenter being on the same plane as his mason colleague. This is very much as we would expect, for the carpenter's contribution to the building of a large church went far beyond the provision of scaffolding and accessories. At York in *c.* 1080 an enormous quantity of prefabricated oak reinforcement was installed in the substructure alone, while the achievements of Gothic masons in matters of vaulting have often distracted attention from the role which was played by carpenters in actually putting the vaults up.

Nor was the carpenter's contribution always temporary. Most early Anglo-Norman churches were unvaulted in their clear spans and hence were roofed or ceiled with wood. The painted ceiling above the nave at Peterborough probably dates from the 1220s, but gives a good idea of Romanesque idiom. Timber never lost its appeal among English and Welsh builders, and even when stone vaults became a commonplace timber structures were often preferred. In 1243 Henry III issued instructions that his new chapel at Windsor should be provided with a high wooden roof which was to resemble the new roof recently completed at Lichfield (Harvey 1961). A timber vault was added to the presbytery at St Albans in the fourteenth century, and in the 1390s a wooden vault was erected over the new presbytery at Arundel. At about the same time the transept at York was revaulted in wood. In the fifteenth century the tradition of flat ceilings was maintained at St David's while at Wymondham the parishioners modified the nave of the monastic church and supplied oak roofs embellished with angels. The habit of vaulting with wood persisted after the Reformation, as for example at Winchester, where a wooden vault was erected over the crossing late in the 1630s to a design by Inigo Jones.

Timber structures were nearly always prefabricated. Roofs were usually framed up in the forest or on open ground near the site prior to assembly *in situ*, each component being marked to indicate its eventual place in the structure. This technique called for close co-operation between the master-mason and the master-carpenter, and the fact that it was not unusual for an elaborate roof to be framed up well before the walls of the building were ready to receive it suggests that the full particulars of a design could be settled in detail and committed to parchment or paper in advance of construction. But this did not always happen. Instances of extemporization are known, and carpenters were sometimes invited to provide solutions where the ingenuity or nerve of the master-mason failed. The original design of the Chapter House at York provided for a vault, but while construction was in progress the master-mason seems to have thought better of it (the span is close to 60 feet) and a timber roof was commissioned instead. The result was a remarkable

25 (below) *Peterborough: nave ceiling, c. 1225*
26 *Peterborough: detail of nave ceiling*
27 (right) *St David's: nave ceiling, c. 1480*
28 (right centre) *Wymondham: nave roof, c. 1450*
29 (far right) *Wymondham: roof bracket in north aisle, c. 1450*

pyramid structure of three receding stages which among other things is a *tour de force* of prefabrication techniques.

Accurate construction requires accurate measurement. At York measuring rules called *metroddes* or *metwands* were in use during the fourteenth century. A fifteenth-century poem entitled *The Debate of the Carpenter's Tools* mentions *compas*, *lyne* and *chalke*, *skantyllyon*, *rewle* and *squyre*. The *skantyllyon* was apparently some kind of adjustable instrument, but its comments in *The Debate* are restricted to insulting the *persore* (boring tool):

> Soft, ser, seyd the skantyllyon,
> I trow your thryft be wele ny done;
> Ever to crewyll thou arte in word,
> And yet thou arte not worth a tord:

The *lyne* and the *chalke* are more helpful:

> I schall merke well upone the wode,
> And kepe his mesures trew and gode . . .

Other tools mentioned in *The Debate* include the *shype ax* and *brode ax*, *adys* (adze), *wymbylle* (drill, which promises to 'crepe fast into the tymbyre'), *groping-iren*, *chesyll*, *pleyn*, *gowge*, saw and whetstone. The *brode ax* states 'the pleyn my brother is' which suggests that it was used as a finishing tool (Hazlitt 1864, 79–90). Mention of the saw

in *The Debate* reminds us that medieval illustrations and building accounts make it perfectly clear that sawn planks were available. Saws varied from the specialized handsaw and framesaw through to the larger double-handled specimens; these were worked near to the vertical by pairs of sawyers, with the timber either propped on trestles or placed over a saw-pit. A drawing by the thirteenth-century architect Villard de Honnecourt indicates that water-driven saw-mills were in existence, or at least in mind on the continent by *c.* 1230 (Hahnloser 1972, Taf. 44).

Glaziers

Glass was used in important ecclesiastical buildings almost from the earliest days of the Anglo-Saxon Church. Eddius Stephanus, the biographer of St Wilfrid, reports that in 669 or shortly after Wilfrid renovated the church at York and put glass in the windows. We are told by Bede that at about the same time Benedict Biscop summoned glaziers from Gaul to assist in the completion of the new monastic church at Monkwearmouth. In the following century we hear of the installation of glass in the windows of the cathedral at Worcester during the episcopate of Bishop Wilfrid (717–43). The use of window-glass in the Anglo-Saxon period was not restricted to cathedrals, or even to ecclesiastical buildings (Harden 1961, 54). Excavations beside the pre-Conquest crypt at St Wystan's church, Repton, under the direction of Professor Biddle, have yielded quantities of Anglo-Saxon coloured window-glass with clipped, or 'grozed' edges. It is reported that facilities for the manufacture of cylinder-blown glass, probably dating to the ninth or tenth centuries, were revealed in Radford's excavations at Glastonbury Abbey in the 1950s (cited in Harden 1961, 53), and window-glass has since been discovered at excavations of pre-Conquest churches at Escomb, Co. Durham, Brixworth, Northamptonshire, and the Old Minster, Winchester. At Hadstock original wooden window-frames have survived in the double-splayed windows of the pre-Conquest nave.

Glass became progressively more important as an ingredient in church fabrics as time went on. The windows of Romanesque churches were usually small, with wide-angled splays to compensate for the narrow apertures. From the twelfth century the trend was towards thinner walls and larger windows. At first the windows were still pierced through the wall individually, but during the thirteenth century windows were steadily enlarged until they began to coalesce. The invention of bar-tracery made it possible to reduce the area of intervening masonry even further, and in the fourteenth and fifteenth centuries entire façades and transept ends came to be composed of translucent glazed walls.

This increase in the sheer area of glass available for decoration offered a great challenge to the glass painter, but it does not always seem to have led to a corresponding improvement in the technical quality of the glass itself. Now that Anglo-Saxon window-glass from a number of sites is available for comparison with later Gothic material it can be seen that in certain respects the glass of the post-Conquest

Canterbury: 'Becket's Crown', 1179–84

Crowland, from the south-east

Wells: Lady Chapel and retrochoir viewed from presbytery

Oxford: vault of choir, *c.* 1480–1500

Nun Monkton: west end of nave

Ely: lantern, *c*. 1328–40

Ely

30 Gloucester: choir, remodelled 1337–57; east window glazed c. 1347–50

era was inferior. Saxon glasswrights produced high soda-lime glass of lasting quality. Between the tenth and twelfth centuries there seems to have been a gradual
change of practice. Forest-glass, so called because of the use of potash as an additive,
was manufactured in increasing quantity and eventually superseded the high soda-
lime variety. The change appears to have been in progress around the millennium,
for fragments of both types were recovered during excavation of the Old Minster at
Winchester. Soda-glass was still in production in the twelfth century, however, since
it was used in the glazing of Archbishop Roger's choir at York (c. 1170). Forest-glass
was less durable than high soda-lime glass, as the potash used in its manufacture was

too alkaline and in certain conditions caused it to split and shell off in layers. Despite its shorter life-expectancy, however, forest-glass was used throughout the Gothic centuries. The disuse of soda-lime glass may have been connected with a scarcity of materials (coastal salts), coupled with the technical difficulties of achieving purity in the face of growing requirements for a mass-produced item.

Clear and coloured glass were manufactured in medieval England, but the best coloured glass was produced abroad and was imported from Normandy, the Rhineland and the Low Countries. The technique of making glass by the spun crown process may have been acquired by the Normans when they captured Corinth in the middle of the twelfth century; at any rate, Normandy became one of the chief producers of coloured crown glass. Large windows were composed of numerous small pieces of glass which were held together in the fashion of a mosaic by strips of lead with grooved edges (*calmes*). The working design for a window was prepared at full size, and each piece of glass was cut to correspond with its place on the master-plan: cutting was accomplished by cracking the glass with a hot iron; the edges were then trimmed with a grozing-iron (*groser*). Colour-impregnated glass (known as 'pot-metal') was available for the basic colours. Details had to be painted on using specially prepared pigments. (Enamel techniques of painting on glass did not come into regular use until the end of the medieval period.) Next, the glass was refired to a temperature sufficient to fuse the paint with the surface of the glass. The finished pieces were then reassembled, using lead calmes and solder. When fitted, the completed panels were held secure in the window by wrought-iron saddlebars. In large windows these bars served a dual purpose, since during construction they helped to steady the mullions before the tracery was complete, and strengthened the window thereafter.

The design, assembly and installation of stained-glass windows thus required extensive liaison between master-mason, glasswright and ironworker. However, while certain churches, such as Chichester, retained a resident glazier (Salzman 1967, 175) it seems to have been common practice to subcontract the manufacture of important windows to independent firms of glasswrights. In 1339–40 William de Bramptone was engaged by the Sacrist at Ely to provide glazing for the lantern of the octagon, then nearing completion. Bramptone appears to have been a merchant of glass as well as a glazier (Chapman 1907, 57), but in addition to supplying new glass he also made use of glass which had been salvaged from older windows in the cathedral. However, the task of painting the glass was entrusted to one Walter the painter, who was occupied with the work for nearly ten months and received a robe in addition to his stipend at the end of it. The account is of special interest for the fact that it itemizes the outlay on the materials which were used: silverfoil from a London goldsmith, vermilion, *orpiment* (a gold pigment), and white lead bought in from Cambridge. Taken together with Walter's stipend, expenditure on painting was slightly in excess of the material and labour costs of glazing. Among many other glasswrights of whom we have some knowledge one may mention Master Robert de

Verreour, who glazed Ivo de Raghton's great west window at York and who had an extensive practice (Harvey 1975, 171), and the Coventry-based John Thornton junior who was responsible for the design of the east window of Great Malvern Priory early in the 1450s (Knowles 1959, 274). Firms of glasswrights were often family concerns, and the cartoons used in the designs of windows were frequently filed away and reused, or handed on from father to son. William Bramptone had his son with him at Ely in 1340; a John Brampton is found working as a glazier at St Stephen's Chapel, Westminster, nine years later, and as Master of the Glaziers' Company in 1373.

The increase in window sizes during the thirteenth century meant that there was greater scope for the embellishment of floors. Prior to *c.* 1150 there would have been little point in creating highly finished floor designs since normally there would have been insufficient light by which to admire them.

31 Great Malvern: east window, glazed c. 1450

32 Great Malvern: east window, the mocking of Christ

Tilers

Floors were composed either of stone paving slabs or of tiles. Mortar and plaster 'floors' are sometimes encountered in Anglo-Saxon churches, but it is not clear if these always represent the real surfaces or were merely used to bed paving which was subsequently removed for use elsewhere or broken up for hardcore. Medieval builders were thrifty, and usable materials were seldom abandoned. Marble pavements were favoured by churches which could afford them (such as Canterbury and London St Paul's), but after *c*. 1220 there was an increasing preference for tiles.

The English tile industry seems to have grown up in the thirteenth century, although both plain and decorated tiles were used sporadically long before this, and on the continent St Bernard was denouncing decorated floors in the 1120s: 'How may we revere the images of the saints with which the very pavement, trodden by the feet, abounds? Often someone spits on an angel's face, and often the countenance of one of the saints is stamped on by the feet of the passers-by. And if these images are not sacred, why not omit the fine colours? Why adorn what will soon be made filthy?' (*Apologia ad Guillelmum*, trans. Harvey 1972, 225). (It is not clear from St Bernard's remarks whether he was referring to inlaid floor tiles of the (later) Chertsey type, or mosaic tiling (as at Modena), or carved and painted stone (as at St Omer). Habits have not changed all that much since St Bernard's day; over 1000 pieces of chewing gum were recently removed from the pavement of the transept of one of our larger cathedrals.)

There were several categories of tile. Tiles of differing shapes and colours could be interlocked into mosaics, as at the east end of the corona at Canterbury (Eames 1968, 4). Contrasts of colour could be obtained by applying lead glazes either direct to the earthenware body of a tile or as an overlay to a white slip, producing brown and yellow respectively (Eames 1968, 2). The colour range could be extended by using glazes containing additives such as manganese and copper. Quite often coloured mosaic tiles were embellished further by the impression of linear designs. These ranged from simple foiled and geometrical patterns to more complicated representations of animals, heads, foliage and stylized architectural forms and details. Line-impressed tiles survive *in situ* in some parish churches, and loose survivors have been found at such churches as Bangor, Bolton Priory, Holm Cultram and Lichfield. An important pavement of this type dating from the 1330s still remains, though somewhat rearranged, in Prior Crauden's Chapel at Ely.

A more ambitious technique involved stamping the unfired earthenware quarry with a design and filling the hollow area with white clay. The surface was then cleaned in order to sharpen the contrast between the darker and lighter clays, glazed and fired. The development and production of inlaid tiles seem to have owed a good deal to the enthusiasm of Henry III, who commissioned pavements of this kind at his palaces at Clarendon and Westminster. The sumptuous thirteenth-century tiles produced at Chertsey Abbey depicting the legend of Tristram and Isolde rank

33 Westminster: inlaid tiles of chapter-house floor, c. 1259

among the supreme achievements of medieval tile design anywhere in Europe. Inlaid tiles in a closely-related tradition are still to be seen in the Chapter House at Westminster Abbey, another scheme which arose from the patronage of Henry III, where the pavement was laid in the 1250s. It combines geometrical ideas with vigorous representational scenes, and contains an inscription (now damaged) which reads: *Ut rosa flos florum, sic est domus domorum* . . . ('As the rose is the flower of flowers, so is this the house of houses'). Pavements of inlaid tiles are also recorded in the new cathedral at Salisbury at this time, and shortly afterwards in the Chapter House there.

Artistically the inlay technique was highly satisfactory, but it required impeccable craftsmanship and close supervision during production. Consequently means were sought of developing a technical short cut to the manufacture of polychrome tiles. During the fourteenth century an industry grew up in the Chilterns which specialized in the production of tiles carrying designs which, though resembling inlaid products, were in fact achieved by stencilling a superficial layer of white clay onto the body of the tile. These tiles were more economical to make than inlaid varieties, for they were mass-produced and achieved great commercial success. However, the stencilled designs often lacked the clarity of inlaid tiles, and whereas the latter wore evenly under foot a stencilled surface could be scuffed away more rapidly. (An interesting modern analogy to this search for a cheaper alternative to a quality product is to be found in the development of patterned carpets on which the design is printed rather than woven. Like the Chiltern tiles, the printed carpets have captured a large market.)

Inlaid tiles were not entirely superseded. In the fifteenth century there was a substantial output of them in the West Midlands and in Wales. An inlaid pavement of this kind survives in the presbytery at Gloucester, and conveniently includes a dated tile which reads 1455. Tiles of related design also occur in the presbytery at St David's, while in the Priory Church of Malvern a wall faced with inlaid tiles was built to enclose the sanctuary; here too there are dated tiles: 1453 and 1457 (Eames 1968, 23).

It is not clear how the medieval floor-tile industry was organized. Harvey has suggested that tileworks and potteries functioned as independent industries (1975, 139), but excavations at several kiln sites have produced evidence which points to the likelihood that floor-tiles, roof-tiles and pottery were at least sometimes manufactured by the same concern (Keen 1969, 146). This would have made good commercial sense, since to a degree the various technical processes involved (clay extraction, preparation, mixing of glazes, kiln operation) would have been common to all three products. Kiln evidence also shows that it was not unusual for itinerant tile-makers to meet an order by building a 'one off' kiln on the site itself. This would have been particularly logical in the case of a large ecclesiastical building which was situated outside the economic transport range of an established factory, and would account for the appearance of identical stamp-designs in tiles of different fabric at churches, such as Great Malvern and Lenton, which are 80 miles apart.

Metalworkers

Tile-kilns presented a fire risk, and hence along with smithies and bell-furnaces they were often located near the perimeter of the site. The amount of metal which went into medieval churches is sometimes underestimated. Much of it is hidden, and hence only comes to light during repair work or alterations. In addition to the saddlebars of windows it was often the custom to stiffen arches with metal and to thread long strips of wrought-iron through walls or inside towers as a means of reinforcement. Ferrous strengthening of the latter kind was apparently used in the Chapter House at Westminster (Lethaby 1925, 103–5), and certainly in both the first and second stages of the central tower at Salisbury (Forsyth 1946). At Westminster eight 30 foot wrought-iron ties were also used in the open, to restrain the

Chapter House vault. Annulets of brass or copper were sometimes used to secure shafts to piers, and metal cramps were always needed to anchor pinnacles, gargoyles and other exposed or precarious features. Nails were required in quantity and produced in many delightful varieties: gullet-nails, lat-nails, bord-nails, flornayles, sherplings, water nayles, lednayles, tynnales, and large, medium and small spikyngs. Metal strapping, often highly elaborate, was applied to doors (which also required locks and latches), while iron grilles were often installed at the entrances of chapels and chantry tombs, and even, as at Arundel, across main spans.

34 Canterbury: St Anselm's Chapel, wrought-iron grille, c. *1333*

For special projects craftsmen might be called in from outside. This happened at Beverley in the 1060s, when German metalworkers were employed to fashion the gold, silver and bronze *pulpitum* which was commissioned for the new presbytery by Ealdred, Archbishop of York (1061–9). In 1291 William Farringdon, a London goldsmith, supplied images which were donated to the church at Durham (Harvey 1975, 90), while at Westminster the effigies of Henry VII, his wife and Margaret his mother were cast in bronze by the Florentine artist Pietro Torrigiano.

Roofing was the province either of the tiler (working with wooden shingles, ceramic tiles or thin sandstone flags) or the plumber. Lead was in regular use for roof covering throughout the medieval period, although for small features, such as bell-cotes and cupolas, tin or copper was sometimes used. In 801, for example,

Alcuin donated a hundred pounds of tin for the purpose of roofing the *domuncula cloccarum* at York; it has been estimated that this gift would cover about seventeen square feet (Harrison 1960, 237). Dr Lawrence Butler has pointed out that the great expanses of lead roofing which sheltered such churches as Beverley, Ely and Lincoln were the visible expressions of ecclesiastical wealth as much as was the gold and silver work of the shrines inside. They represented a triumph over the practical difficulties of extraction and transport, and over the physical problems of covering a large surface area at a high level. Except near the mines, lead was a status symbol.

Bell-casting was a specialized, and by its nature an itinerant craft, although those who practised it often worked in other areas of the metal trade as well. Master John of Gloucester cast four bells at Ely in 1342, and it is evident from his expenses as well as his name that he and his men were brought in from outside (Chapman 1907 II, 114). Bells were cast in pits, with an adjacent furnace to heat the copper and tin which went to make bell-metal. The inner and outer sections of the mould (known as the core and cope) were made of unfired clay, often with an admixture of sand, horsehair and dung (Greene 1977, 12). As the bell was cast the inner surfaces of the mould would be scorched and hence sometimes survive as semi-fired shards. If a series of bells was to be cast it was sometimes the practice to cast the largest first, and then to cast each succeeding bell within the space left by its predecessor, rising up the scale. Tuning adjustments were achieved by filing or chipping away metal inside the lip of the bell until the desired pitch was obtained. The sound made by a bell is complicated, but medieval bellfounders seem to have been mainly concerned with the pitch of the 'strike note', and do not appear to have been much interested in the tuning of the 'hum note' (which should sound an octave below the strike note) or the principal overtones. Bells were used to regulate the monastic day, and played an integral part in liturgical ritual. Until the fourteenth century they were generally chimed, and hence did not need any complicated method of hanging, but thereafter experiments were made with quarter- and half-wheel systems of ringing and bell-frames grew correspondingly more elaborate.

Bells were in use throughout the Christian Anglo-Saxon period. Mention has already been made of the ninth-century bell-cote at York, while Crowland is alleged to have possessed a ring of seven bells in the century before the Conquest. Bells could be hung in the central tower, as at Melbourne and Southwell where twelfth-century galleries for ringers overlook the crossing, or in a western tower if the church possessed one or a pair, as at Beverley. Free-standing bell-towers were not unusual. London St Paul's, Llandaff, Tewkesbury, Westminster and Worcester were all provided with campaniles, and there was one at Salisbury until James Wyatt destroyed it in the eighteenth century. Rochester possessed two, of which one remains (Gundulf's tower of *c.* 1080 was fitted with bells in the twelfth century). There are other survivors at Evesham (built to contain twelve bells on the eve of the Dissolution) and Chichester (*c.* 1410–40). In some cases free-standing bell-towers may have been constructed as a safety measure, or because of the practical difficulty

35 Beverley: tread-wheel crane above vault of central crossing

of hoisting large heavy bells into an existing tower (especially over a central crossing) without weakening the vault in order to admit them. At Exeter the medieval bells were hung 'antiphonally' in the two transeptal towers; the cathedral eventually acquired eight bells, four to each side.

The sites of bell-casting pits vary. There was a natural wish to cast bells as close to their final position as possible, in order to reduce the distance they would have to be carried, and instances are known of casting taking place within the naves of churches. On the other hand bell-furnaces, like kilns and smithies, posed a fire risk, and they were sometimes relegated to the cathedral yard (as at Lincoln), to the monastic outer courtyard (as at Norton Priory, Cheshire) or close to the precinct wall (as at Durham).

In addition to other specialized interior craftsmen, such as plasterers, carvers, imagers, marblers and painters, there would also be a reservoir of semi-skilled and unskilled labourers. The numbers of these men fluctuated from week to week, according to the requirements of the work in hand. It was they who pushed the wheel-barrows (in use in England before the Conquest), carried the hods, mixed the sand and lime in mortar-pits, dug foundations, soakaways and latrines, removed spoil, and dragged the sledges and trolleys which were used to transport loads of stone about the site. Operators were required for machines. Two *magna ingennia* (presumably cranes) are mentioned at Winchester in 1409, for instance (Kitchen 1892, 211). Machinery (lifting gear, large wheels, etc.) required maintenance; in the fourteenth century the monks at Lindisfarne were buying hog's lard as a lubricant for moving parts.

79

Conclusion

We have seen that a pre-Renaissance cathedral or monastic church was the outcome of processes of design, execution and co-ordination which were at once distinct and yet inextricably intertwined. They were separate in that, as today, a variety of specialized and individual tasks was involved; they were unified in that a project would be under the direction of a master who was simultaneously a designer, a logistician, and an experienced craftsman, often in several media. This mating of the imagination with technical ability meant that the superintendence of medieval churchbuilding operations was essentially seamless, involving few of the rigid lines of demarcation which craze the pattern of the modern building industry. It cannot be assumed nowadays that architects are accomplished bricklayers, joiners, sculptors or engineers; nor can it be assumed that those who do possess these qualifications would be able to determine the design of a large building in all its details, prepare the necessary working drawings, undertake day-to-day supervision on the site, and steer the scheme through the thickets of contemporary planning law. This last point is of course an anachronism – medieval designers were unfettered by codes of practice, building regulations and the opinions of amenity societies – yet leaving it aside this was the scope of the master-builder's role and the extent of his achievement.

Not all writers on the subject have found this easy to accept. Francis Bond, for instance, took the view that

> When the Parthenon was built, or Santa Sophia, or Amiens Cathedral or Salisbury, even if the architect had gone through the 'shops', as the British engineer still does, he would have too much to do with planning, design, drawings and superintendence, to work at the buildings to any considerable extent with his own hands. The more he used his hands, the less time he would have to use his brains.

(Bond 1905, 2)

Up to a point this may be fair comment; we can easily imagine, for example, the *magister operis* working in his heated tracing-house wearing a clean robe on some cold, wet afternoon, while the rest of the crew is outside, damp and perhaps resentful at the master's status and privileged surroundings. At least one medieval observer remarked acidly that master-masons did not get their hands dirty. But Bond's contention that handwork and brainwork are somehow mutually exclusive is puzzling, not to say patronizing, and reflects the trend of disengagement between practice and theory which has been in progress since the seventeenth century. The *cementarius* became *magister cementariorum* because, among other things, he had used his hands. Modern architecture is mathematically predictive and to a degree bureaucratic, whereas the basis of the medieval master-mason's ability as a designer lay in his working contact with materials and his first-hand experience of using them.

4

Resources

*On al þis yuele time heold Martin abbot his abbotrice XX
wintre and half gaer and viii daeis, mid micel suinc, and
fand þe munekes and to gestes al þat heom behoued . . . and
þoþ wethere wrohte on þe circe, and sette þarto landes and
rentes, and goded it suythe, and laet it refen, and brohte
heom into þe neuuae mynstre on Sancte Petres maessedai
mid micel wurtscipe;*

Peterborough Chronicle

THE RESOURCES WHICH went into medieval churchbuilding may be considered in three categories: resources of craftsmanship; material resources
and supply; and resources of patronage (chiefly cash, encouragement,
influence and, above all, a determination to build). Of these three a glimpse of the
first has already been provided in Chapter 3, while the second is self-explanatory and
is examined in the second part of this chapter. Before this, however, we shall look at
the question of patronage, in part because it is logical to begin with the instigation
and funding of church projects, but more particularly because the subject of patronage cannot easily be divorced from matters of invention, craftsmanship and materials. Whether the patron was an individual, such as a king or a bishop, or a corporate
body, such as a chapter of canons, there would be a direct concern on the one hand
with the identity, qualifications and ideas of the principal craftsmen, and on the
other, at a more prosaic level, with the source and cost of the ingredients of the
building.

Influences

An artist is usually the product, not the maker of his times. If we consider the realm
of music it is no coincidence to find that the harmonic methods employed in the late
compositions of the fifteenth-century composer John Dunstable reveal a Renaissance preoccupation with Time, that Beethoven lived in an age of revolutions, or
that Elgar's career accompanied the closing years of the British Empire. It is often
said that great artists are ahead of their times, but this is rarely the case; more usually
the artist perceives his present with a greater clarity than his fellows, the majority of
whom are often to be found living in the past. George Orwell wrote *1984* in 1949 not
through inspired guesswork but by extrapolating forwards from the circumstances of

his own day. Even William Blake's visionary mythology, incomprehensible to most of his contemporaries and to many people since, was totally of its age.

But of all artists it is the architect who is the most 'epoch-centred', for he can only operate with the approval, or at the very least the acquiescence, of those for whom he works. His art, moreover, is distinguished by an inescapability which is unknown in other spheres. It cannot be left unheard like a poor sonata, or unread like an ill-written poem. With a building the choice is between maintenance and demolition.

The relationship between an architect and his client or patron is thus a matter of unusual interest. Patronage is itself potentially creative, for by selecting a particular designer the patron is already exercising some kind of preference for a style, an idiom, or the prospect of innovation. It has often been pointed out that the most outstanding phases of architectural activity have been closely connected with the outlook and temperament of particular regimes. In the aftermath of the Norman Conquest came a momentous revolution in the scale of English churchbuilding, while in the first half of the twelfth century it was not by chance that the artistic (as opposed to structural) essentials of Gothic emerged in the Ile-de-France during the period of Capetian ascendancy. In much the same way influence was exercised intermittently by the English monarchy, either through the active encouragement of individual schemes, as in the case of Henry III or, as at the court of Richard II, or by Henry VI and his uncles, by the creation of a *milieu* in which artistic endeavour might prosper.

It has been suggested in the preceding chapter that medieval churchmen took little direct part in the process of designing large churches. Prelates or senior monastic officials could, of course, be highly specific in detailing the requirements of the buildings they commissioned (or for that matter explicit where iconographical schemes were desired), but translation of those needs into defined space was a matter for the master-mason, who would naturally be mindful of the constraints of cost, materials and the nature of the site. A close analogy for this process of interaction between architect and ecclesiastic is available from our own time: the late Sir Basil Spence stated that his design for the new cathedral at Coventry was in many respects compelled by the liturgical and practical needs which it was intended that the building should fulfil. Yet no one would contend that the cathedral which was finished in 1962 is the invention of Anglican clergy; the building is an interpretation of what was asked for, and like its medieval predecessors it owes its form primarily to an architect's perception of function, expressed within the limits of economic possibility.

Some patrons, like Archbishop Walter de Gray (1215–55), who initiated ambitious projects at Beverley, Ripon, Southwell and York, seem to have regarded building almost as a recreation. Men of de Gray's calibre could influence building in several ways. Sometimes it is likely that liturgical needs were presented as abstract problems for which the master-mason was invited to find a practical or cost-effective solution (one wonders if the eastern cross-aisles at churches such as Romsey and Old

Sarum originated like this); on other occasions the basic elements of the scheme were dictated to the architect direct, often expressed in terms of an admired building somewhere else. Both processes left room for originality, however, and it would be a mistake to regard the medieval master-mason merely as some kind of architectural amanuensis. Henry III was deeply concerned with the rebuilding of Westminster Abbey (*c.* 1245–72), and all evidence goes to show that it was he who was determined that the new work should be abreast of contemporary architectural developments in France. Yet although his first master-mason, Henry de Reyns, was well versed in the detail and technology of Amiens and Sainte-Chapelle, he was also given the freedom to blend specifically English traits into the scheme, such as the extensive use of Purbeck and the centrally-planned Chapter House.

Other patrons seem to have been less exacting about matters of style, confining their efforts to the very necessary business of raising funds. Sir Alfred Clapham (1934, 20) pointed out that few of the great cathedrals and abbeys begun in England during the generation after the Conquest display any close kinship with the former continental churches of the prelates and abbots concerned. Here and there we do find a building which seems to reflect the origin or background of its patron. For example: the church begun at Hereford by Bishop Reynelm (1107–15) probably incorporated a pair of eastern towers. This arrangement was rare in continental-Norman buildings but Reynelm was a Lorrainer by upbringing, and towered façades were a feature of the architecture of that region. Hereford provides a further interesting example of this kind of apparent association: William of Malmesbury reported that Robert, Bishop of Hereford (1079–95), another Lorrainer, constructed a church which resembled Charlemagne's palatine chapel at Aachen. The building in question is almost certainly the chapel which still exists as a ruin in the garden of the Bishop's Palace (RCHM Hereford I, 115). Drawings which were made before the destruction of the chapel in the eighteenth century suggest that this was a building in the tradition of the German *Dopel-Kapellen* (that is to say, two-storeyed church in which the upper level served as a gallery to overlook an open, central space). In both instances it would seem that the buildings reflected the taste of their patrons, but whether this was the outcome of detailed specifications issued by Robert and Reynelm, or the work of master-masons brought in from abroad, it is impossible to say.

A rather different case has been put forward in respect of Robert Grosseteste's alleged involvement in the designs of the painted ceiling at Peterborough and the so-called 'crazy vaults' over the western portion of the eastern arm at Lincoln (Nordstrom 1955). Before his appointment as Bishop of Lincoln in 1235 Grosseteste had already acquired a reputation as one of the leading experimental scientists of his day. Roger Bacon was his star pupil. Grosseteste specialized in optics, and Nordstrom has suggested that the works at both Peterborough and Lincoln reflect this interest. In the case of Lincoln the chronology of the building alone almost certainly rules out Nordstrom's theory, but the idea does serve to raise the question of the extent to which medieval scholars and master-masons communicated with each other. Harvey (1972, 88) has argued that by the thirteenth century 'a high proportion of the significant architects were literate', and it seems more than probable that there would have been many opportunities for discourse between lay craftsmen and ecclesiastical academics. But whether the results of these conversations ever found their way into buildings is another matter, for it is now clear from Mr François Bucher's survey of medieval plans and working drawings that the design techniques of medieval builders were purely utilitarian; they rested upon practical, constructive geometry, not upon academic theory (Bucher 1968). Doubtless there were instances of collaboration (we have the example of Cluny III for one: Conant 1963), but there is no reason to think that scholarly participation was ever particularly extensive or influential.

A much more likely source of ideas would stem from opportunities for travel afforded to a master-builder by his patron. Even at the formative stage in his career it would not be unusual for the young mason to work abroad, or at the opposite end of the country from his place of apprenticeship. Later on the very nature of his professsion would require travel: to distant quarries, to buildings specified by patrons as exemplars or to churches where the master was retained as a visiting consultant. The rapidity with which architectural ideas could spread over long distances is a sure indication of the extent to which masons travelled, observed and sketched what they saw. Prelates and other ecclesiastical dignitaries were frequently on the move, royalty incessantly so, and this brought the patrons into contact with a wide variety of architectural ideas, achievements and mistakes. The patrons knew what they liked, and they knew what they wanted to avoid.

Finance

In the realm of funding the patrons, often quite literally, had the greatest contribution to make. Continuity of finance was as important as short-term success. The additive character of nearly all our great churches is largely due to the fact that religious establishments were on the whole unequal to the task of maintaining the momentum of fund-raising over long periods. Hence the majority of churches were rebuilt piecemeal, and even when resources were sufficient to enable uninterrupted progress it was not often that they were available on a scale which would permit work to outpace the advance of fashion. In the twelfth and particularly in the thirteenth centuries stylistic ideas tended to develop faster than individual buildings. Uncertain funding could lead to spasmodic progress, as at Selby and Romsey where the frequent changes of idiom in the naves suggest a fitful cash-flow. A reduction in funds might compel some simplification of detail towards the end of the project, or lead to temporary abandonment. Even a scheme with royal backing such as Westminster was not immune from financial problems: by the time of Henry III's death in 1272 the project was in difficulty, and work on the nave was suspended for over a century.

84

36 (right) *St Albans: nave; eastern bays* c. *1100, western bays on north side* c. *1220–30*

Funds for building were accumulated in a variety of ways. Always welcome was the major grant or legacy from an individual. Thomas of Bayeux, Archbishop of York (1070–1100), rebuilt the Minster largely out of his own endowment. A century later Archbishop Roger de Pont l'Evêque donated a large sum for the rebuilding of the church at Ripon. Walter de Stapledon, Bishop of Exeter (1308–26), contributed handsomely towards the reconstruction and decoration of his cathedral. He also commissioned what was by all accounts a sensational set of accessories for the sanctuary. Not all patrons were so extravagant. Late in the fifteenth century Oliver King, Bishop of Exeter (1492–5), initiated the rebuilding of Bath Abbey, but for reasons of cost he decided to restrict the new work to the area of the former Norman nave. The new church was not completed until late in the sixteenth century. Income from individual benefactors was rarely adequate or intended to cover the cost of outright rebuilding; more often gifts and legacies were made for a specific purpose, such as the renewal or addition of individual features, or to prime the pump for a larger campaign. At Howden

> Bishop Skirlaw was good to the people;
> He built them a School House
> And raised them a Steeple.

Skirlaw died in 1406 and bequeathed funds for 'the construction of a bell-tower at the church of Howden,' and totally rebuilt the parish church in his native village. Then there were the smaller presents, sufficient for a window, a porch or an item of furniture. William Lorynge, a canon at Wimborne, for example, donated a great bell to the Minster late in the fourteenth century (this was recast in 1629), while at Great Malvern the fifteenth-century stained glass windows virtually amount to a directory of the local families who made much of the glazing feasible. Examples of this lesser

37 Howden Minster: tower begun using funds contributed by Robert Skirlaw, Bishop of Durham (1388–1405)

kind could be multiplied almost indefinitely. Motives were mixed. Great buildings offered the prospect of enduring prestige for those who made them possible; it was also held that contributions to church projects could offset the consequences of misbehaviour and assist the passage of the soul, an idea that the Church assiduously encouraged. Rivalry between different ecclesiastical establishments may have been an additional spur to building in certain cases. Yet behind it all one senses a pride in what was done, an enthusiasm and affection for the structures. Welcome as it was, spontaneous generosity could not always be relied upon, particularly where a long-term scheme was intended. Land was the basis of the medieval economy, and progress in the enlargement of churches was usually proportional to the extent of their estates and interests. Tolls, rents, leases and dues went far to subsidize the construction of churches and to maintain them thereafter. Generally speaking, during the twelfth century it was the Benedictine houses which were most richly endowed. This is reflected not only in the imperial scale of such churches as Bury, Norwich, Peterborough and St Albans, but also in the size of some of the churches belonging to smaller monastic establishments. The twelfth-century secular cathedral at Lichfield, for example, seems to have been no larger than the Benedictine priory church at Leominster (which was but a (revived) offshoot from the mother house at Reading), and in terms of length it would have fitted within the nave at Winchester.

Wealth accumulated with time, however, and as the assets of the secular cathedrals and collegiate churches increased so funds could be attracted to rebuild in a more ambitious manner. Hence while a number of Benedictine houses had to remain content with their long Norman naves, after *c.* 1200 churches such as Lincoln, Hereford, Exeter and Lichfield were in a position to put extensive new works in hand. At Lincoln we find grants of property and land being made to the fabric fund in large numbers during the thirteenth century. These ranged in size from substantial estates down through parcels of a few acres to single strips. Documents drawn up at Lichfield during the last quarter of the century reveal that property rents were being channelled into the building fund. One of these concerns Thomas Wallace, 'master of the fabric', who in 1274 gave the annual rent of ten shillings from his tenement in Bacon Street 'to be received at the regular terms from the tenant or tenants by the said custodian for 2 candles for the altar of B.V.M. costing 3s; and for 1d to be given to each of the Vicars in the said Church every year on the donor's anniversary; and the remainder for the fabric' (Savage 1924, 265). Wallace was probably in charge of work on the nave or west front of the cathedral at the time. Another mason, Nicholas de Eton, appears among the witnesses to the grant.

There were also resources of ecclesiastical character to be tapped. In 1174–5 Gilbert Foliot, Bishop of London, diverted half of the Whitsun offerings due from every church in the diocese to the fabric fund of St Paul's. Reginald, Bishop of Wells (1174–91), primed the fabric fund for the rebuilding of the 1180s with proceeds from vacant benefices. A steady income from appropriated churches was important, and

38 Lichfield: nave, c. 1265–90. Notice the device of the 'spherical triangle', used here to confer unity between clerestory and triforium

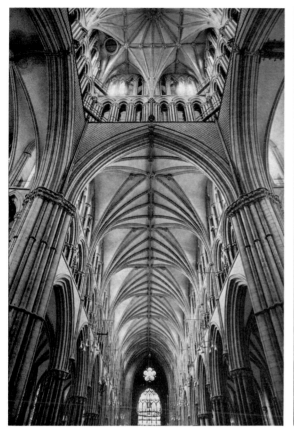

39 Lincoln: central tower and nave   *40 Westminster: south tribune of nave, c. 1260*

when works were beset with financial difficulties it was not unusual for additional churches to be appropriated in order to meet the shortfall. The sale of indulgences brought in funds for building works, and sometimes this technique was augmented by the formation of special confraternities of donors for limited periods. Confraternities were organized at Winchester (1202: retrochoir and Lady Chapel), Lincoln (1205: St Hugh's Choir) and Worcester (1224: choir and retrochoir). Masses were sung for those who subscribed, and membership conferred such additional advantages as the right of burial in the consecrated ground of the church irrespective of the circumstances of death (Graham 1945, 73).

Churches which housed attractive relics could do very well from the offerings of pilgrims. Canterbury derived a substantial income from the shrine of Thomas Becket; Worcester prospered on the proceeds of offerings at the shrines of Oswald and Wulfstan; Hereford on Thomas Cantilupe; and the remodelling of the eastern arm at Gloucester was much assisted by contributions from visitors to the tomb of Edward II. At Norwich the cathedral authorities shrewdly placed collecting boxes beside some of the principal altars. In the case of royal projects further sources of support were sometimes available: grants from the treasury, fines, fees and dues. Last but not least were gifts in kind: particularly timber, the use of quarries, the render of transport services, and wayleaves for the carriage of stone and timber.

Natural resources

Medieval England was well endowed with the materials necessary for building great churches. Good freestone was to be had from the great belt of Jurassic rocks which curves across the country from Lyme Bay to Yorkshire, and from the ribbon of magnesian limestone which outcrops on a line extending northwards from Nottingham. Timber was on the whole plentiful, though good specimens of favoured species grew scarce towards the fifteenth century. Lead was mined in Yorkshire, Derbyshire and Somerset, tin in Devon and Cornwall. There were important centres of iron production in the Forest of Dean, the Sussex Weald, the Forest of Rockingham, Weardale and the Lake District. Alabaster was available in the Trent valley, and clays suitable for the manufacture of paving tiles were to be found in many localities.

Transport was the problem. The cost of moving stone, timber or lead in bulk for any distance across country could be astronomic, and while most churches were close to the sources of a proportion of the raw materials they needed, it was unusual for an abbey or cathedral to be supplied entirely from its near vicinity. Until *c.* 1100 the difficulty posed by transport was often overcome by salvaging reusable materials (chiefly brick, tile and cut stone) from redundant Roman buildings. (The word 'redundant' is chosen with care, for Roman buildings remained in use, though often patched up and altered many times over, throughout the Middle Ages.) We have already seen that a high percentage of the most important Anglo-Saxon churches were situated in close relation to places of former Roman occupation. The convenience of access to second-hand building materials cannot have been the principal reason for this pattern, but it may have been a factor which was sometimes taken into account. Roman buildings in towns such as Canterbury, Leicester, Lincoln and Dorchester, and in military bases such as Chester and York, provided Anglo-Saxon builders with what in effect amounted to construction kits for churches. In some cases it may be that entire arches and columns were dismantled and brought to the site for reassembly. At Hexham, for example, the builders of Wilfrid's church in the 670s made use of Roman masonry, presumably acquired from the nearby Roman depot of Corbridge (where an arch that is claimed as Roman is embodied in the parish church). Later on, during the first half of the eleventh century, Abbot Ealdred of St Albans scavenged Roman bricks from the site of Verulamium in order to build a new church.

By no means all important Anglo-Saxon churches were located near Roman sites, however, and Professor Jope has shown that building stone was being quarried and transported for considerable distances in the later Anglo-Saxon period (Jope 1964, 91–118). A number of quarries are mentioned in the Domesday Survey of 1086

41 *York Minster: fallen column of headquarters building of Roman legionary fortress, found beneath the south transept of the cathedral during repairs in 1968. This part of the* principia *was probably demolished around 800*

(Darby 1977, 287). Nevertheless, in the generation after the Conquest continued use was made of old materials at certain churches. Archbishop Thomas' men at York, for instance, collected large quantities of ashlar and rubble from the former legionary fortress (or the *colonia*) for the new cathedral begun *c.* 1080. Anglo-Norman builders soon began to prospect for natural sources of suitable stone, however, and from *c.* 1080 new works were generally supplied from quarries. But the practice of reusing stone (and recycling old mortar) never ceased entirely; at Malmesbury, for example, it is reported that King John permitted the monks to take stone from his castle when he had it demolished.

The example of the Old Minster at Winchester teaches us that important Anglo-Saxon churches could be quite large. By *c.* 1000 the Old Minster measured 241 feet in length, but it was probably typical of many pre-Conquest major churches in that it owed its eventual size to a process of accretion rather than to the ambitions or visions of any single designer. In other words, Anglo-Saxon churches grew large in small stages. It is likely that the problem of supply was one of the factors which inhibited Anglo-Saxon builders. Reginald of Durham, who wrote in the twelfth century, recounted that those who had seen the two towers of the pre-Conquest cathedral at Durham were not only impressed by the great scale of the work, but also doubted that a comparable structure could be built anywhere else, since the necessary

91

resources 'could hardly be assembled in one place from the surrounding area' (Raine 1835 I, 29). This is very revealing, for it pinpoints one of the major differences between pre-Conquest and later medieval builders. As much as anything else it was logistical superiority which enabled the great churches to be imagined and built. Anglo-Norman churchbuilders and their Gothic successors overcame the problem of supply in two ways: by the use of water transport, and by prefabrication of components.

Wherever possible stone was carried by water. The cost of transporting a load of stone several hundred miles by ship or barge might compare competitively with the price of an overland journey of thirty miles or less. Thus we find stone from Beer in Devon being sent to London in the fourteenth century, while consignments of magnesian limestone from the Yorkshire quarries of Thevesdale, Stapleton and Huddlestone went as far afield as London St Paul's, Rochester and Exeter. In the case of Huddlestone it is interesting to notice that the cost of transport for the short overland journey from the quarry to the inland port at Cawood on the Ouse could add to the expense of extraction by as much as sixty per cent. The accounts of Walter Frost, *custos operum* at Winchester Cathedral Priory in 1532–3, reveal the purchase of a load of 20 hundredweight of gypsum from Paris (*plaster de Parrys*). The cost of purchase, and the river and sea journey to Southampton amounted to 3s 4d. The twelve-mile road journey from Southampton to Winchester came to the same amount (Kitchen 1892, 218).

Much of the stone used in the fifteenth-century rebuilding of Great Malvern Priory was taken from Highley, twenty-two miles away to the north, and rafted down the Severn to Clevelode, three miles from the church. The limestone quarries at Barnack were owned by the Benedictine monks of Peterborough, who built a special quay at Gunwade and exported the stone along the fenland waterways to Crowland, Ramsey, Ely and Norwich. Cross-channel shipments of the excellent limestone quarried at Caen in Normandy feature regularly in medieval building accounts. Canterbury, Norwich, London St Paul's, Westminster and Shoreham were among the churches which received it in quantity, but use was also made of Caen stone on a more limited scale, as in Salisbury and Draper chantries at Christchurch. In 1538 Cromwell's agents visited the priory and noted 'a chaple and monument curiosly made of Cane stone preparyd by the late mother of Raynolde Pole [i.e. Cardinal Pole] for herre buriall, wiche we have causyd to be defacyd and all the armys and badgis clerly to be delete' (Wright 1843, 232). However, churches in parts of the south-east and East Anglia were at a disadvantage in that they lay in areas largely devoid of reasonable freestone, and against these long-range transactions we must also set the instances where stone was acquired from quarries which were closer to hand.

In some cases stone was virtually on the doorstep, as at Lincoln, where in 1223 the Dean and Chapter were granted permission to take stone from the castle ditch, and at Exeter, where some stone was acquired from a site on the outskirts of the city. More usually the quarry (or quarries, for many churches were supplied from several sources) was further afield. In the thirteenth century masons at Lichfield made use of stone from a quarry at Hopwas which the canons bought from Margaret de Eccleshall for 20 shillings (three miles from the cathedral): Pershore used stone from Bredon Hill (four miles); Exeter from Silverton (seven miles); Wells from Doulting (eight miles); Beverley (in the twelfth century) from North Newbald (ten miles), and later on from the Tadcaster district; York from Thevesdale (eleven miles for a crow, over seventeen along the combined land and water route which was taken). At St David's stone was acquired from nearby cliffs at Caerbwdy and Caerfai, while the canons of St Asaph took stone from Pont-yr-allt-goch on the River Elwy. The magnesian limestone used at Selby in the twelfth century was apparently floated in from Monk Fryston (eight miles) along a canal specially constructed for the purpose. The large blocks of millstone grit which are to be seen in the walls of Howden Minster also arrived by water, although in this case the stone was reused, perhaps several times over, and may have been procured from a Roman source. Here it is worth adding that several medieval waterways were in fact Roman canals which were dredged out and made serviceable again in the Middle Ages.

A nearby supply of stone could be a mixed blessing, for it was a convenience which might lure builders, or more probably the ecclesiastical authorities who had to foot the bill, into using materials which were not entirely suitable. The friable sandstones employed at such churches as Carlisle, Leominster and Lichfield have charm, but they have not worn well. The failure of certain types of stone to resist decay has

42 Lincoln: flying buttresses

43 *Ely: Lady Chapel, 1321–50; east window c. 1375. The richly-carved interior is worked in chalk*

sometimes led to extensive refacing and replacement of detail, as at Worcester, or to the methodical cutting back of a wall-face to a plane where the stone is sound, as at Durham. (This last practice is still recommended in some quarters.) During the last hundred years it has often been the custom to substitute sawn stone for injured masonry. This lacks the subtle irregularity of medieval tooling, and as a result considerable areas of wall-surfacing at churches such as Lichfield, Hereford and Melbourne have acquired a staring monotony. Sir George Gilbert Scott described the condition of Chester Cathedral in 1868 as that of 'a mere wreck . . . a mouldering sandstone cliff' and went on to apologize for the fact that the 'frightful extent of the decay forced upon me, most unwillingly, very considerable renewal of the stonework' (cited in Briggs 1952). This dilemma faces many ecclesiastical architects today.

Chalk was used extensively by churchbuilders in the areas in which it naturally occurs. When crushed or rammed it made a sturdy foundation (as at the Old Minster, Winchester); it was often used as rubble in wall-cores, or cut for internal facings, and it could be burned to produce lime for the manufacture of mortar. Chalk is tractable, and hence appealed to carvers, but it was seldom used externally on account of its inability to resist the weather. Only the harder varieties could be used outside, as at Dunstable where the elaborate west front of the priory church is built of the tough chalk from nearby Totternhoe. Chalk is also relatively light, and this made it a popular material for the construction of the webs of vaults. Even lighter is tufa, a

94

44 Durham: Galilee, c.1170. When first erected the monolithic 'marble' columns originally stood free, in pairs

cellular calcareous stone, which was employed for vaulting purposes at, among other places, Bishop Robert's chapel, Hereford (*c.* 1080), the new choir at Canterbury (after 1177) and the Elder Lady Chapel, Bristol (*c.* 1220–30).

Marble does not occur naturally in England or Wales, but certain types of fossiliferous limestone can be polished to a glossy finish which resembles marble, and these were widely used in the Middle Ages both for architectural purposes and monumental sculpture. A large proportion of English 'marble' was won from the coastal quarries on the Purbeck peninsula, in Dorset. Purbeck marble appears in English churches as early as the third quarter of the twelfth century: at St Cross, Winchester, in the 1160s, and in the Galilee Chapel at Durham (*c.* 1170–5). The craze for marble reached its climax in the thirteenth century, when scarcely a major church was built which was not trimmed with Purbeck. The convenience of water transport facilitated its use in churches which could be approached by boat: Exeter, Salisbury, Chichester, Boxgrove, Westminster, Ely, Lincoln, Beverley, York. Purbeck was the leading centre of production, but other ersatz marbles were extracted at Petworth, Alwalton, Frosterley and Eggleston.

Medieval quarries were not as a rule very deep or individually extensive, although where a preferred stone was to be found, as at Barnack, the workings might proliferate and eventually come to cover many acres. Some of the greater churches either owned or leased quarries, and where this was the case it was possible for the stone to be extracted and dressed at the quarry according to instructions issued by

95

the master-mason in charge of the building programme. Prefabrication helped to keep down the costs of transportation, and a good deal of detailed work (string-courses, corbels, plinths, mouldings, shafts) could be produced in this way, cut to templates which were designed by the master-mason and sent to the quarry. The results of the technique of standardizing components can be seen very well in the nave at Durham, where the great cylindrical piers are composed of pre-cut blocks of identical size and form. Quarry-dressing was additionally advantageous for the reason that certain types of freestone tend to harden on exposure to the atmosphere, and hence are more easily worked while they are still relatively soft and 'sappy'. Not all churches either owned or had direct access to quarries, however, and pre-cut stone was sometimes purchased from a quarry which was run as an independent commercial enterprise, or from a stone-merchant. Quarrying and building were closely allied crafts, and some masons were quarry owners. Henry Yevele, for example, supplied stone as well as worked it, and in certain circumstances the price agreed for a job could be inclusive of materials, which the mason would undertake to provide. Thus at Hereford a contract of *c.* 1412 between the Dean and Chapter and Thomas Denyar, a local mason, concerning the construction of the cloister, stipulated that Denyar should supply the stone (Capes 1908, 232).

The greatest building resource of the Middle Ages was timber. The achievements of medieval masons distract attention from the fact that timber was the premier material in use in the secular sphere, while in campaigns of churchbuilding timber was needed not only for the frames of roofs, ceilings, screens and stalls, but also for structural reinforcement, shoring, piles to compensate for doubtful ground, shuttering for 'cast' flint rubble masonry, scaffolding, temporary partitions, centring, site huts, ladders, barrow runs and machinery.

Different types of timber were assigned to these various purposes. Oak was regarded as pre-eminent for virtually all permanent structural work. Alder, ash and poplar were liked for scaffolding. Conifers were also used: in 1371 the Dean and Chapter at York were buying *firspars* for use as scaffold-poles, and the Sacrist's Roll at Ely for the financial year 1325–6 records the purchase of *sparris sapienis*. Ash was slightly flexible and hence was preferred for the shafts of tools. Elm seems to have been held in low esteem, although it was often chosen for piling (along with beech and alder) and it sometimes appears in buildings (Rackham 1972).

The medieval carpenter liked to visit the wood in person and select timber of scantling and posture which, after any necessary trimming, would correspond with the size and form of each member required. This practice was cost-efficient because it minimized waste and avoided the labour charges which arise when large trees are cut up into subsidiary components. As a result trees of every age might be used, ranging from saplings to mature timber. Timber was acquired from woodland rather than plantations, and although a big church could devour substantial quantities of timber it seems that efficient techniques of woodmanship ensured the replacement of what was felled. In 1234, for example, Henry III donated a hundred oaks to the canons at Chichester, and two years later fifty more, plus a further hundred to the abbey at Gloucester (Salzman 1967, 240). It is estimated that the fifteenth-century roofs of Norwich Cathedral contained about 680 oaks. Consumption on this scale could not have been sustained through the Middle Ages without sensitive methods of woodland management which provided for regrowth through coppicing and suckering (Rackham 1976, 20–2, 74–5).

Only in circumstances where very large timbers were required do problems seem to have arisen. Salzman has pointed out that usable timber much over thirty feet in length was unusual (1967, 238). This appears to be reflected in the spans of the greater churches, which rarely exceed 33–44 feet in the clear and more usually fall in the region of twenty-six to thirty-two feet. Only eight per cent of the churches discussed in this book boasted spans of thirty-six feet or more. The widest included York (forty-five feet), Ripon (forty feet), Ely, Lincoln and Canterbury choir (all thirty-nine feet). This applied to vaulted and unvaulted churches alike, partly because the width of a vaulted Gothic church was often determined by the layout of the wood-covered Romanesque building which preceded it, but also possibly because of difficulties which would have been encountered in scaffolding larger spans and roofing the vault. Timbers of exceptional length could be found if the need arose, as must have been the case at York *c*. 1090 when Archbishop Thomas' master-carpenter came to roof the forty-five foot nave, and at Ripon a century later. The roof of the chapter-house at York (after *c*. 1280) contains four double ties, each of which is seventy feet long. However, the problems encountered some fifty years afterwards by Alan of Walsingham in his famous quest for timbers fifty feet in length which would be suitable for the angle posts of the octagon under construction at Ely suggest that resources of outsize timber were becoming depleted by the early fourteenth century (Salzman 1967, 238–40). Necessity is the mother of invention, and it is interesting to notice that the earliest surviving example of a hammer-beam roof which can be dated with confidence was completed in 1325; this is the roof of the Pilgrim's Hall at Winchester (Harvey 1972, 135). The principle of the hammer-beam had been known for at least a century, since there are sketches which anticipate the system in Villard de Honnecourt's album (Hahnloser 1972, Taf. 34), but it may be that the development of the idea in fourteenth- and fifteenth-century England was prompted at least in part by a desire to circumvent the problems of a shortage of large-size timber.

5
Technology

Opposite him, the other side of the model of the cathedral on its trestle table stood the chancellor, his face dark with shadow, over ancient pallor.

'I don't know, my Lord Dean. I don't know.'

He peered across the model of the spire, where Jocelin held it so firmly in both hands. His voice was bat-thin, and wandered vaguely into the large, high air of the chapter house.

'But if you consider that this small piece of wood – how long is it?'

'Eighteen inches, my Lord Chancellor.'

'Eighteen inches. Yes. Well. It represents, does it not, a construction of wood and stone and metal –'

'Four hundred feet high.'

William Golding: *The Spire*

THIS CHAPTER EXPLORES some technical aspects of the process of building a large church in the Middle Ages. The topics or steps are introduced in order, beginning with questions to do with the scientific *milieu* in which the churches were constructed, then turning to the preparation of designs, and rising from the foundations to the roof.

It is important to understand the nature and limitations of the evidence that is available for study. Hundreds of large medieval churches survive, but contemporary written descriptions of the ways in which they were planned and built are scarce. On the other hand, medieval illustrations of building sites, depicting machinery, masons' tools, scaffolding and falsework, are relatively plentiful. Where they can be examined in juxtaposition with accounts for labour and materials, and with the buildings themselves, a fairly clear picture of the building process emerges. What we lack are facts about medieval design methods, and above all about how the master-mason approached and solved statical problems.

Until the fifteenth century master-masons rarely wrote text-books: their knowledge and experience were accumulated and handed on in practice. Hence there is nothing to compare with Theophilus' discussions of bell founding, metallurgy, glass making, wall painting and organ building in the realm of large-scale engineering. The descriptions that were written, such as Gervase's chronicle of works at Canterbury between 1175 and 1184, or Abbot Suger's enthusiastic memoir of the rebuilding of St Denis in the 1140s, tend to be the products of interested onlookers or active patrons, and therefore to be non-technical in their vocabulary. Where Suger discusses the co-ordination of the plans of the new and old work at St Denis he reports that this was done with the assistance of 'geometrical and arithmetical instruments', but he does not explain what these instruments were, or how they were used. Likewise, Suger stresses his own role as prime mover of the work at St Denis, although he does not trouble to mention the name of his master-mason.

The conceptions of medieval builders on statical matters present us with even greater difficulties. Modern engineering science provides methods of analysing the achievements, and sometimes the failures of medieval builders from a practical viewpoint. The subject of medieval building technology has received close attention in recent years, notably from Mr John Fitchen (an architect) in his book *The Construction of Gothic Cathedrals*, which deals chiefly with methods of vault erection, and from Dr Jacques Heyman (an engineer) who has shown that limit theorems originally developed for steel-framed structures can be adapted for the analysis of masonry.

Heyman's methods can establish, in statical terms, what it was that the medieval builder actually did. What they do not do, and hitherto have not been intended to do, is to establish what the designer *thought* he was doing. The modern commentator takes risks if he attempts to describe what was essentially a technological achievement in the language of twentieth-century science. It would be anachronistic to insist that the designer of St Hugh's Choir at Lincoln late in the twelfth century, or of the nave vault at Sherborne in the fifteenth, thought in terms of thrusts, loadings or a skeleton of forces. It is possible that some of the theories to which medieval builders subscribed would nowadays be dismissed as nonsensical. This might not matter. As Sir Christopher Wren observed: 'If the butment be more than enough, 'tis an idle expense of material.'

Part of the story of English medieval architecture concerns a search for means of reducing the level of this 'idle expense'. It can be traced in the gradual whittling down of wall-thicknesses, the systematic exploitation of cavities and voids, the enlargement of windows and the attenuation of piers. These developments were the work of empiricists. Their successors, the gentlemen architects of the seventeenth century, viewed them with disdain and looked back beyond Gothic achievements to the Roman concept of architecture as an intellectual pursuit. The contrast is evident not only in matters of style, but also in the technological principles which underlay and informed invention. Medieval architecture, once it had sloughed off its Romanesque bulk in the twelfth century, was dynamic, experimental and often adventurous, whereas a good deal of neoclassical architecture is decidedly 'nonstructural'.

But if the gentleman architect orientated his ideas by the compass of a liberal education, the nature of the relationship between master-builder and scholar in the centuries from, say, 1100 to 1500 is much less definite. Medieval scholars knew something about statics. They called it the 'science of weights' (*scientia de ponderibus*).

As far as we know, however, the master-mason made no attempt to capitalize upon these researches. Indeed, he anticipated them. Yet at the same time 'what was intellectualized by the philosopher had its own humble reality in the lodge. Most notably it was the shared belief that geometry was both the aesthetic and technical basis of the universe' (Kostof 1977, 79). Since number was abstract, there was a plane of contact between the practical geometry which was used by masons as an everyday tool in the composition and realization of designs, and the symbolic geometry, with its harmonic and numerological connotations, which was contained in compends of Augustine, Boethius, Gerbert and Isidore, available in some cathedral and monastic libraries. Proportional relationships permeate a great church, as they do for example in the nave porch at Beverley or the west front at Peterborough, because they were used to assist its construction and to ensure artistic success, but they could also be appreciated at a metaphysical level. As Kostof has put it (1977, 80), masons' geometry was 'the vernacular of the same language that was used by the intelligentsia'.

Architects and scholars

The twelfth century was an age of intellectual enlightenment and architectural revolution. It was the time when western Europe acquired texts on mathematics, astronomy, medicine and philosophy from the Arabs, who in turn had had them translated from the Hebrew, Syriac or Greek. Spain, Sicily and other areas bordering the Mediterranean became the lending library of Europe, making accessible the works of Ptolemy, Aristotle and Euclid.

The process of copying and translating classical texts began to accelerate rapidly after *c*. 1125, but scholars from northern Europe had begun to probe the rich vein of Arab learning well before this. Walcher, a prior of Malvern who was in England before 1091, was familiar with the astrolabe, and was taught to reckon in degrees, minutes and seconds by a Spanish Jew (Haskins 1971, 313). Thomas of Bayeux, Archbishop of York (1070–1100), had studied at Liège and went on to complete his education in Spain where, it was said, he 'learned things which could not be learned elsewhere'. By the middle years of the eleventh century the monastic school at Ripoll in Catalonia had accumulated 246 volumes, including many scientific texts. Catalonia was accessible to northerners before the reconquest of Spain, and its scholars were in touch with their counterparts in Lorraine. When Count Guifre, founder of Saint-Martin-du-Canigou, died in 1050 the news of his death was taken as far as Aachen and Maastricht, though apparently not into Spain (Whitehill 1941, 8).

In the twelfth century such Englishmen as Adelard of Bath (who brought back a translation of Euclid's *Elements* in the 1120s), Robert of Chester and Daniel of Morley were in the forefront of the movement to acquire and disseminate Greek texts and Arab commentaries. Their work was often conducted with the assistance of Jewish interpreters. Words like alcohol, algebra, alkali, almanac, alchemy, azimuth, cipher, nadir, tariff, zenith and zero, which were received raw into our language, testify to their efforts, and indicate some of the areas in which the impact of the New Learning was greatest.

Some writers have visualized a direct connection between this New Learning, in particular the infusion of Euclidean geometry, and the birth and development of Gothic. Harvey, for instance, has argued that improvements in techniques of design and surveying occurred as a direct result of contacts between master-builders and the 'very first generation of western scientists' (1972, 94). The time-scale of Gothic development appears to reinforce this contention. The structural essentials of Gothic – whereby churches were systematically vaulted, and the forces of the vaults were collected (rather like rainwater) at specific points in the building, to be transmitted outward and down by an exoskeleton of buttresses – parallel developments in the world of scientific thought.

Heyman (1966, 250) has argued that the mastery of engineering technique was 'maintained with complete authority for only a short period, in a very limited region: for about 144 years in France'; between the start of work on the new choir at the Abbey church of St Denis in 1140 and the collapse of Beauvais in 1284. Thereafter, Heyman argues, the lessons which had been learned took on an almost ideological significance. They still worked, of course, but the functional reasons behind their formulation seem to have been gradually forgotten. This appears to provide an important insight into the process by which the lessons had been grasped in the first place.

45 Lincoln: tierceron vault of nave, c. 1227–40

Nevertheless, compare Heyman's analysis, and particularly his dates, with the views of the late Erwin Panofsky:

> During the 'concentrated' phase of this astonishingly synchronous development, viz., in the period between about 1130–40 and about 1270, we can observe, it seems to me, a connection between Gothic art and scholasticism which is more concrete than a mere 'parallelism' and yet more general than those individual (and very important) 'influences' which are inevitably exerted on painters, sculptors, or architects by erudite advisers. In contrast to a mere parallelism, the connection which I have in mind is a genuine cause-and-effect relation; but in contrast to an individual influence, this cause-and-effect relation comes about by diffusion rather than by direct impact. It comes about by the spreading of what might be called, for want of a better term, a mental habit – reducing this overworked cliché to its precise Scholastic sense as a 'principle that regulates the act' . . .
>
> (Panofsky 1973, 20–1)

Panofsky calls attention to the 'tight little sphere' of the zone around Paris during the critical period, to the shift of intellectual training from the Benedictine monastic schools to urban cathedral centres and universities, and to what he interprets as signs of the rising status of the professional architect:

> After Hugues Libergier, the master of the lost St-Niçaise in Reims, had died in 1263, he was accorded the unheard of honour of being immortalized in an effigy that shows him not only clad in something like academic garb but also carrying a model of 'his' church . . . Pierre de Montereau . . . is designated on his tombstone in St-Germain-des-Près as 'Doctor Lathomorum'; by 1267, it seems, the architect himself had come to be looked upon as a kind of scholastic.
>
> (1973, 26)

One wonders what some future generation will make of the tombstone of 'Duke' Ellington. Excellence in a non-academic sphere brings its own accolades, some of which may take the form of sincere parody. (The analogy between the virtuoso jazz musician and the 'serious' performer on the one hand, and medieval technology and science on the other is worth some consideration. Many gifted jazz composer/performers have been unable to read or write a note of music in conventional notation, while many competent musicians reared in academies are unable to extemporize with much fluency, or to compose.) Nor do one or two swallows make a summer: the examples of Libergier and Pierre de Montereau would seem to be insufficient to establish the *dynamic* connection between universities and master-builders which Panofsky envisaged. Nevertheless, a third commentator has insisted that while a distinction was drawn in the Middle Ages between the practice and theory of geometry, architects (as opposed to masons) were obliged to master both. This knowledge, it is argued, and the 'metaphysical framework from which it was inseparable, could be acquired in cathedral and monastic schools only' (Simson 1956, 34, n. 35).

These views differ in emphasis, but they all converge on one claim: that Gothic building science and design owed some kind of debt, directly or indirectly, to the New Learning of the twelfth century, and in particular to the new position which had been reached by geometry.

There must have been close contacts between builders and schoolmen. Master-masons, especially those working on ecclesiastical jobs in centres of learning such as Oxford and Canterbury, or, at a less exalted level, places like Crowland and Malmesbury, would have mingled with scholars almost as a matter of routine. Medieval architects certainly dined with aristocrats and royal officials. Many of the patrons whose taste counted were men of learning.

The real issue centres not on whether there was dialogue between master-builder and scholastic, but upon the question of what it was that the master-mason of the twelfth or thirteenth century could learn from the academic that he did not already know. Were there 'essential facts' about geometry, draughtsmanship and proportional systems which could only be acquired in cathedral schools, and which acted as a kind of yeast to trigger off the Gothic process; or could it be, as Haskins thought (1971, 330–1), that there was a reservoir of practical expertise which may be considered independently from any theoretical contribution?

Outside the cloister geometry was above all else regarded as a practical science. Gower, writing in 1390, defined geometry as the process 'through which a man hath the sleight of length, of brede, of depth, of height'. English master-masons unquestionably saw themselves as heirs to the Euclidean tradition, as for example in the fourteenth-century Regius Poem and the Cooke MS, the former existing under the head of *Constituciones Artis Gemetriae Secundum Euclydem* (Knoop, Jones and Hamer 1938). Lydgate, in his *Troy Book*, written between 1412 and 1420, described the preparations which were made for Priam's City of New Troy. The account opens with a search

> For swiche werkemen as were corious,
> Of wyt inventif, of casting merveilous;
> Of swyche as coude crafte of gemetrye,
> Or wer sotyle in her fantasye;

(II. 491–4)

But Lydgate admitted:

> I can no termys to speke of gemetrye,
> Wherfore as now I muste hem sette a-syde;
> For douteless I radde neuer Euclide,
> That the maister and the founder was
> Of alle that werkyn by squyre or compas,
> Or kepe her mesour by leuel or by lyne;
> I am to rude clerly to diffyne
> Or to discrive this werk in euery parte,
> For lak of termys longyng to that arte

(II. 522–60)

In the *Knight's Tale* Chaucer (d. 1400) described the construction of the stadium in which Palamoun and Arcite were to hold their contest for the hand of Emelye:

> And shortly to concluden, swich a place
> Was noon in erthe, as in so litel space;
> For in the lond ther nas no crafty man,
> That geometrie or ars-metrik can,
> Ne portreyour, ne kervere of images,
> That Theseus ne yaf him mete and wages
> The theatre for to maken and devyse.

Such extracts present a popular view of the designer/architect and his methods in the later Middle Ages. It is decidedly hazy. Lydgate's 'lak of termys longyng to that arte' reminds us of the mystery which surrounds the surveyor and his theodolite in the mind of the modern layman.

Nor are the scholars particularly forthcoming. During the critical period of technical development – i.e. *c.* 1140 to 1270 – references to masoncraft and design in academic treatises on geometry and arithmetic are rare. Building operations are often mentioned in poems, narratives, chronicles and sermons and they are depicted in illustrated manuscripts, but they are not as a rule discussed within the 'strictly scientific framework'. This is not altogether surprising. The New Learning was not a

46 Peterborough: detail of nave ceiling, c. 1225, depicting geometrica, *one of the four Liberal Arts*

matter of instant revelation. It is an oversimplification to claim that the world of thought was placed upon a strictly scientific footing by the first generation of western scientists. Scholars worked for over a century to translate the principal Greek and Arabic sources into Latin, and the process of assimilation took rather longer. Experimental science was a phenomenon of the thirteenth century. Nevertheless, if architects were as beholden to cathedral and monastic schools for a decisive portion of their scientific education as some have insisted, even for a short period, one would expect some kind of reciprocal indication that this was the case.

Such indications are rare, and the occasional exceptions are revealing. At about the same time as Abbot Suger was presiding over the start of work at St Denis (1140) a Spaniard named Dominicus Gundissalinus was following the example of an Arab author, Alfarabi, by attempting to classify the various sciences. In his *De Divisione Philosophiae* Gundissalinus adhered to the Aristotelian distinction between theoretical and practical sciences. The theoretical group included mathematics, physics and metaphysics. The practical sciences consisted of government, ethics and what has been translated as 'family government', itself subdivided and including the mechanical arts which in turn included masoncraft (Crombie 1953, 37).

A little later Michael Scot, a British author and translator (Haskins 1924, 272–98), produced a classification of science which was closely based upon the work of Gundissalinus. In it Scot partitioned knowledge into a group of three theoretical sciences and a group of three classes of arts (*practica*). The subsidiary categories in each group were arranged to correspond. Thus the second category of *practica*, which included carpentry and masoncraft, mirrored the theoretical science of mathematics. Scot 'thus envisaged some definite connection between the theoretical and practical sciences, but he never explained what this might be . . .' (Crombie 1953, 42). Scot died abroad in about 1235. Masoncraft, though related to mathematics in principle, is accorded the importance of no more than a toe, and a small toe at that, of a very large creature. Most of Scot's contemporaries ignored masoncraft altogether in the course of compiling their classifications.

However, it seems that Scot was no mere armchair scholar. While at the court of Frederick II of Sicily he undertook an experiment to calculate the height of the heavens *per geometriam et arismetricam* (a pre-echo of Chaucer's 'crafty man/That geometrie and ars-metrik can'), using a church tower as a point of reference. His results for the sky are not clear but, unbeknown to Scot, Frederick had the height of the tower fractionally reduced and then invited Scot to repeat the experiment. Scot's technique of measurement was evidently sensitive, for it is reported that he detected the change (Haskins 1924, 290, n. 110; cf. Hahnloser 1972, Taf. 40).

If we look at the subject from the masons' viewpoint we find a similar notional correspondence between *theoretica* and *practica*. Euclid was cited as a patron scientist. The designation *magister* and the distinctive robe of the architect, visible for example on the graveslab of the fifteenth-century master-mason William of Wermington at Crowland, mirrored the hierarchy of the academic world.

But although the applied geometry of the master-mason might resemble academic geometry, the steps involved in its production, and the objectives in view, were different. Medieval design techniques avoided the need for mathematical reasoning. The master-mason was not concerned with theorems or proofs; he had no cause to demonstrate the scientific validity of his methods in any other way than through the stability of the structures he created. This is well illustrated in two pamphlets published by the German mason Matthew Roriczer late in the fifteenth century: *Buchlein von der Fialen Gerechtigkeit* (1486), and *Geometria Deutsch* (*c*. 1488). Roriczer was a cathedral architect. His pamphlets are interesting not merely because they illuminate aspects of his geometrical technique, but also for the fact that he published them at all, thereby breaking the tradition of craft secrecy which until then had shrouded the design methods of master-builders and was sternly enjoined in masonic Ordinances.

Roriczer's methods were entirely practical. He shows such procedures as how to construct a triangle and a square of (approximately) the same area; how to find the circumference of a circle; and how to develop the design of a pinnacle by the manipulation of squares. Calculation did not enter these methods: all was done with square and compasses. Both pamphlets have been examined and discussed by Dr L. R. Shelby, who comments:

> . . . whatever may have been the relationship between Gothic architecture and scholasticism, when medieval master masons did write books, they certainly did not reveal that penchant for systematic literary organization characteristic of scholastic treatises. . . . Medieval masons did not teach from books, but rather from memory and from experience in the techniques of the craft. When they did decide to describe some of these techniques . . . they had no established literary forms to follow. Consequently, it appears that they wrote as they taught – by piling up one description after another of the particular rules and procedures of the craft . . .
>
> (Shelby 1972, 411)

Roriczer wrote his booklets late in the fifteenth century, towards the end of the Gothic era, but we may be equally sceptical about any significant connection between academicians and builders at the beginning. The fact is that many of the technical innovations and refinements which have been attributed to the New Learning had already made their appearance individually before the end of the eleventh century. It is clear from the results of recent work done at Norwich (Fernie 1976), for example, that sophisticated canons of proportional geometry were being used by Anglo-Norman architects in the 1080s and 1090s. The influence exerted by Vitruvius upon twelfth-century builders has often been exaggerated. This is not because Vitruvius was little known, but because his work was familiar, and had been so since the ninth century (Frankl 1960, 88–9). Tips on how to strengthen a wall with wooden ties, or how to set out a right-angle using a 3:4:5 triangle were known, if not well known, in tenth-century England. The author of the *Anonymous Life of St Oswald*, probably a monk of Ramsey who wrote between 995 and 1005, referred to Oswald's preparations for the construction of a new church in 969:

> . . . he searched diligently for masons who would know how to set out the foundations of the monastery in the correct fashion, using the straight-edge, triangulation, and compasses . . .
>
> (Raine 1879, 434)

The principles of scale drawing were known to the draughtsman who produced the diagrammatic plan of the monastic complex at St Gall, Switzerland, in about 820 (Horn 1966).

The *structural system* which was invented in the twelfth century and perfected in the thirteenth was new, but the means which were used to produce it were not. The pointed arch was on view to western travellers in Spain, Sicily and the Middle East during the eleventh century, and this may have stimulated the European Gothic aesthetic (Harvey 1968). But Gothic *structure* went beyond plain aesthetic preference because it demanded a radical rearrangement of the anatomy of a church, which in a sense was turned inside out. The experiments may have been provoked or facilitated by the fresh intellectual climate, but they were made feasible by a body of practical experience which had been accumulated by Romanesque master-builders.

The scholars who probably came closest to dealing with issues of relevance to the operations of Gothic builders were the mathematicians who studied the 'science of weights'. One man in particular concerned himself with a wide range of statical problems, some of which paralleled topics which had recently been under empirical investigation in the lodges on ecclesiastical building sites. His name was Jordanus Nemorarius.

Jordanus' *Elementa* and his *De Ratione Ponderis* may be regarded as the growing edge of a statical tradition which went back to the Hellenistic mathematical tradition of Archimedes, Euclid and Ptolemy (Moody and Clagett 1952, 3). Jordanus Nemorarius has sometimes been identified with Jordanus of Saxony, who was Master General of the Dominican Order from 1222 to 1227. However, this identification seems doubtful (Moody 1952, 121–2), and it is more probable that Jordanus Nemorarius was teaching mathematics in Toulouse sometime after 1229, and that previously he had taught at the university in Paris. He was thus a contemporary of Villard de Honnecourt, and his career coincided with a number of important building projects, including Amiens and Salisbury. Jordanus tackled such matters as the descent of weights along diversely inclined planes, elasticity, the strength of beams, and the directional analysis of force (*virtus*). His works were known and studied in the sixteenth century, when 'the discussion of Jordanus' theorems, and the frequent utilization of them without acknowledgment, testify to the continuing influence and vitality of the medieval science of weights in early modern times' (Moody and Clagett 1952, 20). Jordanus may thus be looked upon as one of the forerunners of modern statical science, a science which has for the most part supplanted the empirical methods which were used by master-builders in

Jordanus' own day. But there is no reason to believe that either Jordanus or any of his pupils attempted to apply their research to the problems of large-scale building. Indeed, by the time that Jordanus came to write his treatises on weights the main elements of the Gothic structural system had already been invented. Whatever the possibilities of any underlying 'principle that regulates the act', and the parallelisms are certainly striking, one could not wish for a clearer illustration of the gulf which intervened between thirteenth-century theoretical science and empirical technology.

Measurement and design

The apparent persistence of prehistoric units of measurement, without significant variation, into the medieval period and, in those parts of the globe as yet unaffected by the cerebral metre, to the present day, might be seen as a further indication of unbroken threads of practical tradition to which the medieval builder was heir. These threads appear to wind through many nations. It has been claimed, for example, that the Royal Persian Cubit of 25.2 inches (640 mm) reappeared in the Arabic Empire as the 'hashami Cubit' of 25.26 inches (649 mm), again, as a sub-multiple, as the Frankish Foot, and ultimately as the French Pied du Roi of 12.789 inches (324.8 mm) (Skinner 1967, 44). The so-called 'Northern Foot' of the Indus civilization (13.2 inches/335.3 mm) is said to have been used in medieval England, along with the Greek Common Foot (12.47 inches/317 mm) and the Roman Foot (11.65 inches/296 mm) (Skinner 1967, 93). However, it may be that some of these claims are due for reappraisal.

All these units derived in one way or another from a single standard: the human body. The cubit, for example, is normally taken as the length of the forearm, measured from the elbow to the tip of the middle finger. My own personal cubit is 18.4 inches, just 0.26 inches shorter than a cubit based on the Athens variant of the Greek Foot. It is interesting to notice that two of the favourite modular units used by Anglo-Norman builders, 4 feet 8 inches and 7 feet (Imperial), work out as multiples of the Greek Cubit (1 Greek Cubit = 1½ × the Greek Foot of 12.47 inches). If the Athens variant is used (12.44 inches/316 mm) the errors in translation into the Norman modules are extremely small. However, where a medieval building is concerned it is often difficult to be sure that any particular unit was in force at the time of its construction, since precision of the kind described above is far greater than normal site tolerances would permit. Mr Derek Phillips (1976, 7) has pointed out that errors in setting out, construction and taking measurements must be allowed for in a calculation to determine an ancient unit of measurement. It may also be necessary to take into account the extent to which parts of a building have shifted since it was built, or the effects of restoration or repair. At Durham, for instance, a two-inch thickness of masonry was shaved off areas of the exterior in the nineteenth century.

Dimensional accuracy was needed in various walks of medieval life, particularly in the cloth trade. Uniformity of linear measure in England was achieved, at least notionally, by the introduction of the Statute Yard of 36 inches during the reign of Edward I. We need not suppose, however, that all craftsmen adjusted the units with which they were accustomed in order to conform with an iron bar which was in the possession of the king. Nevertheless, the strict enforcement of standards could cause difficulties. In 1421 a mass meeting of weavers and fullers was convened at Salisbury, occasioned by anxiety that 'their striped cloth must conform to the statute of measures, despite their demonstration, with the help of three cloths, one raw, one partly fulled, and one completely fulled, that such cloth could not be six quarters wide' (Bridbury 1975, 48–9).

Builders needed dimensional standards to regulate such things as setting out, the curvature of vault-ribs, the angles of buttresses and the prefabrication of timber roofs. But this does not mean that the medieval architect or his men worked from dimensioned plans, or that, where dimensions were specified, the same units were in force in all parts of the building. The level of exactitude depended on the nature of the work in hand: a trench-filled foundation might be set out to the nearest foot, the plane of a wall to within a couple of inches, a section of tracery to less than 0.2 of an inch. Units, depending as they almost always did upon a human standard, often varied. 'Personal' modules and regional units sometimes appear side by side, or even, one suspects, in playful combination.

Mouldings, bosses, vault-ribs and other details were cut to templates (usually of oak, or sometimes pricked through outlines drawn on canvas) which were prepared by the master-mason or one of his close associates. If decoration or further embellishment were called for the cutter would usually be free to work on his own initiative, provided he kept within the limits which were prescribed. The more precise the work, the more likely it would be that the craftsman would work by eye rather than by rule.

Where plans and elevations were concerned it seems that schemes were worked out on a basis of relative proportion rather than with linear measurement, which is the norm today. Vitruvius expressed the principle thus: 'Proportion is a correspondence among the measures of an entire work, and of the whole to a certain part selected as standard' (III.i: Morgan 1960, 72). Medieval churchbuilders are sometimes accused of inaccuracy when the dimensioning or setting out of their structures does not conform to the standards of modern linear measurement. A more relevant test would concern the degree of *proportional* accuracy, which lies rather within the completeness of the geometrical theme. Linear accuracy is in any case very difficult to achieve, even today, when it is based on geometrical setting out.

Proportional systems varied from region to region. The two chief systems employed in Europe during the Middle Ages were based on the square (*ad quadratum*) and the triangle (*ad triangulum*), but there is growing evidence for diversity of practice and flexibility in application. Whatever the ruling figure, the principles which determined the development of a design remained broadly the same: starting with one primary module, such as a bay span or width, the architect could generate all other elements in the scheme by the application of numerical rules, learned by rote, and through steps of constructive geometry. For this purpose the master used straight-edge, square and compasses. Compasses appear as an attribute of the architect as early as 2113–2096 BC in one of a series of illustrations on a stela depicting the construction of the great Ziggurat of Ur. (Sumeria also provides an early example of an architectural plan: a statue of Gudea, Prince of Lagash, *c.* 2170 BC, now in the Louvre, shows a king sitting with a drawing-board bearing the plans of a temple on his knees. The plans include a graduated scale (Skinner 1967, 20; Pl. IV)). Compasses or dividers were used to signify the act of creation or measurement long before Blake borrowed the image in the eighteenth century. They occur, for example, on the thirteenth-century ceiling at Peterborough (representing *Geometrica* of the quadrivium), and in a window of the south clerestory of the nave at Great Malvern Priory in the context of the Creation of Heaven and Earth (Rushforth 1936, 149–52, with other examples).

According to a study undertaken by Mr B. G. Morgan (1961, 55) the arms of the ordinary masons' square appear to have given a length relationship of $1:\sqrt{3}$ (i.e. 1:1.732) and imply a triangle of 90, 60 and 30 degrees. Other ratios, such as $1:\sqrt{2}$ ($\sqrt{2}$ = the coefficient of the diagonal of a square), 1:1.618 (1.618 = the coefficient of mean and extreme ratio: the 'Golden Section'), and 1:1.555 (the relationship of a side to the height of an equilateral triangle), could be obtained without difficulty and with accuracy by manipulation of square and compasses. These ratios pervade the proportions of many large medieval churches. Morgan has pointed out that some masons' squares, as they are depicted on funeral monuments, appear to be slightly tapered. Morgan's investigations suggest that these modified squares could have been used to summon up the Golden Section directly.

Discussion of these relationships in mathematical terms obscures the fundamental simplicity of the methods by which they were obtained, since part of their attraction lay in the fact that all the principal elements of a design could be automatically indicated and interrelated without recourse to calculation. The proportions were aesthetically proven, and it is very likely that some of them held an appeal for the patron on account of their symbolic and harmonic connotations.

Very few architectural working drawings of the Middle Ages have come down to us in England. Diagrams of water supply systems do survive, at Christ Church cathedral priory, Canterbury, and Waltham Abbey, the former dating to the twelfth century, but neither could be regarded as project drawings in an architectural sense. This paucity of evidence has led some scholars to doubt that such drawings ever formed a regular stage in the medieval design process. The ground-plan, it is alleged, was developed mentally by the master-mason and then set out at full scale on the site itself. This fallacy has been convincingly challenged by Harvey (1972, 101–2), but it is worth reiterating that a working drawing is an ephemeral thing. Many architects' drawings for important buildings of the nineteenth century have already been lost.

The high fatality rate of medieval drawings made by men who were working outside the sphere of archives and libraries, often on reusable surfaces such as plaster or parchment, or even on walls, as in the Galilee at Ely (Pritchard 1967, Figs 46, 48; cf. Anderson 1875) should be no cause for surprise.

Yet even where drawings do survive, as they do in some numbers on mainland Europe (Bucher 1968), it is not always clear how we should interpret them. The Reims Palimpsest and Villard de Honnecourt's album, for example, show that ground-plans, elevations in orthographic projection and vaulting diagrams were being made in north-eastern France at least as early as the first half of the thirteenth century. But how these drawings were actually used, or at what stage in the design process they were produced, is not explained.

The Reims Palimpsest, a series of architectural drawings dating from the middle years of the thirteenth century, exposes the methods of at least one draughtsman. His instruments were simple: straight-edge compasses, dividers, pen. Dr Robert Branner, who studied the drawings in detail, found no evidence for any 'overall geometric or proportional system controlling the disposition of the major elements'. The drawings suggested rather 'an excellent eye that could easily adjust to the scale and propriety of each design' (Branner 1958, 15, 19). In 1963 the origins of Gothic draughtsmanship came under further scrutiny from Branner, who argued that the habit of using small-scale drawings for design purposes originated in the first part of the thirteenth century. Where drawings on parchment were concerned Branner speculated that the instruments involved were probably at first the same as those which were used to trace profiles, such as the small compass and small ruler, but adds: 'Between 1100 and 1200 these were refined considerably, if the development of profiles of ribs and imposts is a criterion. Further refinement must have been necessary to permit their use on parchment . . .' (Branner 1963, 146, n. 40). This may be so, but sophisticated draughting instruments for use on parchment had been available in the west, in monastic scriptoria, since the seventh century. The *Codex Amiatinus*, for example, which was copied in Northumbria in the 690s, contains an illustration of a monastic scriptorium equipped with a selection of draughting instruments. Ancestors to some of these had been used in the Iron and Bronze Ages to assist in the development of ornamental patterns on metalwork (Lenerz-de Wilde 1977). Until the advent of Gothic and the increasing elaboration of architectural detail in the twelfth century it would not have been necessary to call upon those resources. But this is no reason to suppose that project drawings were not used before the thirteenth century. A building such as Durham could scarcely have been constructed without some preliminary delineation. Robert Mason's working drawings for the Norman church at St Albans (1077–1115) might have been of a very different order of complexity from those which were prepared for, say, Wells or Ripon a century later. Standards of accomplishment and execution had risen in the meanwhile, but the basic proportional methods, and the array of instruments, were much older.

However drawings were actually prepared it is important that we should try to view their use in the context of a medieval building operation. To do this it is necessary to shed preconceptions. The medieval architect had no facilities for the easy production of multiple copies of his drawings: a master-plan or elevation would thus have been a precious thing for the duration of a project, and highly vulnerable to loss or obliteration afterwards. A drawing of this kind could scarcely have been exposed to the wear, tear, mud and rain of site use. It would be a work of reference, a point of departure.

Since project drawings would be unsuitable for regular use on site, other methods had to be found, first, to communicate details of the scheme to those whose job it was to execute them, and second, to translate the design to full scale. Two factors controlled the nature of these methods: they had to be fairly simple, and they had to circumvent any need for calculation. Whatever the educational attainments of a master-mason might have been, there is no doubt at all that the majority of his *operarii* would have been illiterate and innumerate which does not mean that one cannot count, only that one is unaccustomed to *reasoning* mathematically. Hence modular units (rods or cords), grids, marker pegs and manipulative geometry could be used, whereas calculations to determine their positions could not.

For a building which was begun *de novo*, as many of the great Anglo-Norman churches were, the first step would be to indicate the positions of the foundations and strip footings on the ground; the exact positions of walls and arcades could only be surveyed when the substructure was complete. This could be done by reducing the entire scheme to a skeletal framework of lines, which could be realized on the site by manipulative geometry and then expanded to suit the layout of the superstructure, which theoretically would already be represented within them. These steps mirrored those used in the production of a project drawing. They could be dictated on site with little difficulty or fuss, and could govern virtually all the elements of a design at any magnitude (see for example Fernie 1976).

A series of architectural drawings incised on the roofs of the north and south aisles of the cathedral at Trogir, on the Dalmatian coast, provides a glimpse of the ways in which such drawings could be used. In effect the roofs were exploited as full-scale drawing boards. All the drawings were made at 1:1, and a number of them can be directly related to alterations and additions which were being made to the cathedral in the fifteenth and sixteenth centuries. Some of them seem to have been used for making templates, while others seem to have been intended to assist in the solution of technical and artistic problems. What is particularly interesting, however, is the fact that there is independent written evidence to show that the roof designs were used to *supplement* scale-drawings (Gibson and Ward-Perkins 1977).

Substructures

To a modern engineer the characteristics of the substructure of a building would be a sure guide to the competence, or optimism, of the man who designed it. The same conclusion could not be drawn from a medieval cathedral or abbey. Builders who performed dazzling feats of structural engineering above ground did not always tend to the foundations upon which the success of their efforts ultimately depended. In some cases it is almost as if the masons were deceived by the apparent 'weightlessness' of the structures they had created, as though in some way gravity had not been exploited but defeated.

It is impossible to generalize about medieval foundation-craft. Clapham, for example, stated that 'Early Anglo-Norman building varied remarkably in its structural stability, for while the principles of secure foundations were evidently understood, their application was often neglected' (Clapham 1934, 117). Commentators point to a long list of collapses which took place during the twelfth century and argue that many of these were due to defective substructures.

At this distance it is rarely easy to determine the exact mode of failure in a medieval building, particularly if the building in question, or the relevant part of it, is no longer there. Disaster or damage could be provoked in any one of a number of ways: differential settlement of the foundations, a changing water-table, the imposition of eccentric loads during construction, mortar failure, or by several factors acting in combination, perhaps promoted by an Act of God in the form of an earth-tremor (as at Lincoln in the twelfth century), a lightning strike (as at Durham in 1429) or a freak gust of wind (as at Crowland in 1254).

At least seventeen per cent of the buildings listed in the Gazetteer suffered collapses or severe structural distress at some stage in their history. It is noticeable that many of these falls concerned towers, and that in a number of instances the mishap occurred either while work was still in progress or soon afterwards. Thus the central tower at Abingdon fell in 1091, that at Winchester in 1107, and that at Beverley (during the remodelling of an earlier tower) in about 1200. A western tower fell at Gloucester in about 1170, and another at Worcester about five years later.

But the twelfth century had no monopoly on failure. Dunstable lost two towers in the 1220s. Collapses are recorded at St David's (1220), Lincoln (1237) and Ely (1321), all towers, while Bury, Evesham, Norwich, Ripon and York lost spires or towers at various times before the Reformation. Nor did the damage end there: the catalogue of collapses is almost as long for the post-Reformation era. At Tewkesbury the spire fell, with sinister timing, on Easter Day 1559. The spire at Wimborne fell in 1600, the central tower at Selby collapsed in 1690, and the steeple at St Paul's was giving serious cause for concern in 1663. At Chichester the central tower fell in in 1861, while the north-west tower at St John's Chester collapsed twenty years later. Some of these failures can be attributed to post-Reformation neglect, or to the removal of parts of structures which contributed to the stability of the whole. But a proportion of the earlier falls was precipitated by Gothic builders who were engaged upon the modification of an existing building, or who added new work without regard for the limitations of an existing substructure. These earlier substructures,

47 *Chichester: central crossing and transept arm after fall of tower in 1861*

which were usually Norman, are of great interest, for it emerges that at least some Anglo-Norman architects could be both flexible and imaginative in their response to the differing soil conditions and topographical characteristics of individual sites.

The eleventh-century foundations below the central crossing at Lincoln, for example, appear to have been narrower than the *walls* of the contemporary church at York. The difference was that at Lincoln it was possible to carry the foundations down into contact with bedrock, a procedure which was also adopted at such churches as Durham and Lichfield. At Blyth the foundations were placed upon a spread of natural gravel. Artificial platforms of rammed gravel or chalk were sometimes used, while it was normal practice to construct strip footings and to include ties beneath entrances to apses and chapels. At Selby, where the water-table is high, the church begun *c.* 1100 was erected upon a raft of oak timbers, perhaps in the (correct) expectation that the timber would last indefinitely in the anaerobic surroundings. Piles were often used in wet or marshy conditions.

On a number of sites the Anglo-Norman builders also had to contend with the remains of Roman buildings, the presence of an earlier church, or both. Earlier churches were often kept in use until work on the first phase of the new cathedral or abbey was complete. This ensured continuity of worship. At Winchester, for example, the monks entered the eastern arm of their new church on 8 April 1093; demolition men moved in to deal with the Old Minster on the following day.

Roman buildings could pose a threat to a new church, especially if they had been well built (as they often were) or lay on a different alignment, since a later structure

114

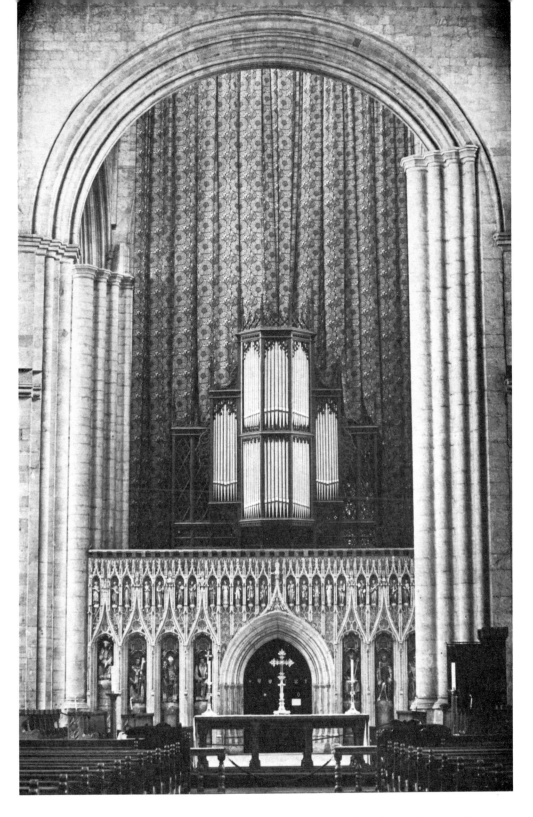

48 Ripon: central crossing, c. 1175–80; alterations to south-west and north-east piers, c. 1460

could break its back upon an earlier wall running below. Roman remains cluttered sites to a greater or lesser degree at Rochester, where the Roman London to Canterbury road (Watling Street) formed the north side of the close; at Gloucester, where the cathedral lies partly within the walled area of the Roman city; perhaps at Worcester, and certainly at Chester and York where the cathedrals stand within the *enceintes* of former legionary fortresses. The church at Dorchester may occupy a salient in the Roman fortifications of the town, while at Lincoln the east end of Bishop Remigius' church (1072–92) was pressed hard up against the curtain wall of the upper *colonia*, an arrangement which caused problems when the canons decided to extend their church in 1192, and further embarrassment when the revised fortification had to be breached when the Angel Choir was started in 1256. At Exeter the cathedral stands near major Roman buildings, while similar factors affected sites at Southwell, Westminster, Holy Trinity York, Southwark and perhaps Wimborne. Roman sites did have their compensations, however, since they offered a ready supply of building material, good for wall-cores and foundations if not for fair-faced work.

In normal circumstances the internal structure of a medieval foundation is inaccessible except on occasions of drastic repair or alteration. Fortunately it is no longer necessary to speculate on the potential abilities of Norman builders where substructures are concerned, since the recent extensive repairs carried out at York Minster provided an opportunity to examine and record the foundations of the eleventh-century church in detail. The results of this investigation are to be published in the near future by Mr Derek Phillips. What follows here is thus no substitute for the full scientific account, and depends mainly upon the two short notices which have so far appeared in print (Hope-Taylor 1971; Phillips 1975); see also the chapter by Dr Eric Gee in *A History of York Minster* 1977.

When the Norman cathedral at York was begun in about 1080 its builders were faced by two problems: first, the intended site was already occupied by the remains of redundant Roman buildings; and second, the ground was of varying load-bearing capacity. The Roman walls were often at some depth from the eleventh-century ground surface (the visitor can judge this for himself in the new Undercroft), and they presented an additional hazard in that the new church was laid out on an alignment which differed from that of the Roman grid by about 45 degrees.

One way to overcome the threat presented by an obstacle was to jump it with an underground arch. Such arches are commonly encountered beneath medieval buildings. Soft-spots could also be bridged thus, although it was more usual to dig them out and pack the void with a consolidated mass of rubble and mortar, or to drive in piles (Salzman 1967, 83–5). At York, however, the Norman master mason decided upon a solution which incorporated a system of timber reinforcement.

The existence of a mesh of oak timbers beneath the eastern part of York Minster was first noted by John Browne in 1829, and was considered again by Sir Charles Peers in 1931 (*Antiq J* 11, 113–22, with plan), but it was not until the excavations in

49 York Minster: central crossing during repairs. Notice Roman wall on different alignment to cathedral; eleventh-century nave wall reused as stylobate by builders of thirteenth-/fourteenth-century piers; and modern reinforcement for substructure of central tower

50 York Minster: cavities left by decayed reinforcement timbers in the substructure of eleventh-century west wall

1967–72 that the extent of the system became apparent. It now seems that timbers were deployed according to a pattern throughout the substructure. Although Phillips has asserted that 'this approach to the problem of providing foundations with stiffness in the vertical plane in ground of varying load-bearing capacity is typically Norman' (1975, 25), the builders' intention in including the timbers is not obvious. The wooden grid could scarcely have been intended as a measure of permanent reinforcement, since timber, unless it is in water, is liable to decay. Anglo-Saxon and Norman builders must have known this. For full details and an explanation of the substructure at York we must await the definitive publication.

It is interesting to notice that technical ingenuity was being exercised on the threshold of the Gothic era. What is equally interesting is that later, Gothic architects did not always make such thorough provision for their own work, but elected instead to rely upon earlier substructures. This was the case at York, where we are told that 'the great early Norman church . . . was found to be supporting much of the weight of the present Minster' (Phillips 1975, 27). An account of the fall of the central tower at Beverley around 1200 contains the comment that the masons responsible for the work – which apparently involved the improvement of an earlier tower – were more interested in aesthetic effect than in stability. It is intriguing to find that the word *stabilitatis* was actually used by the historian, who stated that the builders were on the point of adding a spire when the tower collapsed, apparently because the foundations were inadequate (Rains 1879, 345). However, the historian was also convinced that the masonry of the superstructure itself had been seriously overloaded. In this, as we shall see, he might have been mistaken.

Superstructures

Broadly speaking, a stable church is a building in which the forces it exerts, or to which it may be subjected, lie enclosed within its fabric. These forces may be considered under the two main heads: *loads*, such as the dead weight of the fabric itself, or the variable 'live' load exerted by wind pressure; and *thrusts*, which concern the forces exerted by arches, vaults and some types of roof.

The thrust of an arch, for example, has both a vertical and an outward component. The ideal arch (from the point of view of stability) would mirror the line traced by a chain slung between two points, where every link is in tension; if this system is inverted all the voussoirs of the arch will be in compression and the thrust line will lie within the thickness of the masonry. Failure will occur if the line of thrust cannot be enclosed within the fabric.

The master-builder had three main materials at his disposal: timber, stone (dressed or used as rubble) and mortar. Chains or wrought-iron bars were sometimes used to reinforce walls or towers, as at Salisbury in the thirteenth and fourteenth centuries, or to restrain 'live' portions of the fabric during construction, but for the purpose of this discussion the potential contribution of metal to medieval structural systems will be discounted. Brick, too, will be ignored, although it was used on a large scale at St Albans late in the eleventh century, and after *c.* 1300 it was employed quite extensively by churchbuilders in eastern England, where it often appears in the webs of vaults.

Timber has been described as a material of almost universal nature: 'If suitably selected, timber is able to resist all stresses inherent in buildings: torque, compression, bending and extension . . .' (Hewett 1977, 175). Stone, or at least the good freestone preferred by medieval builders, is immensely strong in compression but weak in tension. Heyman (1966, 251) points out that a column formed of medium sandstone can be loaded to a height of more than a mile before crushing will occur at the base. Cross-sectional dimensions are thus theoretically irrelevant, provided the structure is not subjected to eccentric dead loads.

However, this statement holds good only for solid masonry, and medieval churches were rarely solid in the sense that the walls, piers and larger buttresses were formed of through-coursed stonework. Walls and piers generally comprised a skin, of greater or lesser thickness, formed of cut stones, which enclosed a core consisting of rubble and mortar. The importance of the skin could vary a good deal according to

51 Blyth: masonry and capital of c. *1090*

the type of structure. In true rubble buildings, erected in the Roman *opus incertum* tradition (Vitruvius 11.8), the facing was no more than a veneer and contributed next to nothing to the integrity of the wall. In Gothic churches, on the other hand, the walls were often much thinner than those of Romanesque buildings, the faces were composed of larger stones, cut with precision and laid with tight mortar joints, and correspondingly less importance was attached to the core which acted as a kind of dry padding. The characteristics of many walls lie somewhere between these two extremes, but it is worth pointing out that the change, or at least the emergence of a choice, came about within a single lifetime. Early Anglo-Norman rubble work is summed up at Blyth, begun in the 1080s in a style which was already obsolescent: roughly-dressed stone, wide mortar joints, unsophisticated capitals with elementary volutes. The fabric was meant to be concealed by plaster, and areas of walling at the east end of the nave still bear a white overcoat with counterfeit masonry joints picked out in red. This is a world away from the building operations carried out under the auspices of Roger, Bishop of Sarum (1107–42), in which the stones were cut and laid with such exactitude that William of Malmesbury mused how entire walls might have been fashioned from a single stone.

Stone, whether cut to shape or used as rubble, was almost invariably used in combination with mortar. Medieval builders used lime mortar, which they produced by adding water to a mixture of quicklime (calcium oxide) and sand. The water and lime combined to produce calcium hydroxide (hydrated lime), which then set as the surplus water was lost by evaporation. In this state lime mortar was very weak, with a poor compressive strength and negligible tensile strength. However, a second stage followed: the set mortar hardened as the hydrated lime reacted with atmospheric carbon dioxide, forming calcium carbonate. In medieval buildings this process could be slow, partly because there is little carbon dioxide in the atmosphere, but more particularly if the thickness and character of the wall were such as would impede the rate of progress of carbon dioxide into the core. The mortar at the face was carbonated first, and this acted as a barrier which inhibited further diffusion into the interstices of the structure (Wolfe and Mark 1976, 468–9). Excavations near the church of St Peter Northampton, in 1974 (Williams 1977) revealed three Anglo-Saxon mortar-mixing pits. These were lined with basket work which radiocarbon determinations have dated to the eighth century. Some of the mortar residue was uncarbonated. It is equally possible that appreciable quantities of mortar within the walls of some large churches have still not reacted fully with carbon dioxide. The slimmer walls of Gothic churches were more efficient from this point of view, since although the joints were tighter, sometimes less than one-eighth of an inch, the cross-sectional areas of mortar were reduced. (One wonders, incidentally, if some putlog holes were deliberately left open to act as ventilators, and thereby to accelerate the process of hardening.)

Since the initial setting process occupied days or weeks, whereas carbonation might take months or years, the medieval builder had to assemble his churches in such a way as to avoid asking more of his structure than could be provided by set but uncarbonated mortar. Masons often worked fairly slowly, particularly on towers, taking care to add no more in a season than that which could be accepted in safety by what had already been erected. (We have already seen what the consequences of carelessness or haste might be.) Where a faster rate of progress was required, a system of reinforcement could be introduced, either on a temporary or a permanent basis. Lastly, as Fitchen (1961, 3) has emphasized, solutions to all the main engineering problems encountered by medieval builders had to be found in terms of compression. The aim was to produce a self-equilibrating structure.

This idea was the objective of builders of both vaults and roofs. In Britain the outer roof was invariably formed of wood, framed together according to a system of triangulation, and bearing a weatherproof skin of lead, shingles or thatch. Subsidiary triangles were sometimes introduced into the system the better to resist wind loads, which in the case of a large, high church could be considerable. If the church was vaulted it was almost always the practice to dissociate the roof from the structure of the vault, in order to free the vault from the effects of live loads. The feet of rafters were normally jointed into wall-plates, mounted on the walls at either side and tied across at intervals in order to resist any tendency to spread. A good roof was thus largely a self-restraining structure, unless it was of an experimental kind like the Ely octagon (Quentin Hughes 1955). However, much depended upon the types of joint which were used to frame the structure together (Heyman 1976; Hewett 1977).

If the church was to be vaulted it was customary to build the roof first. The roof then acted as a protective canopy while work on the vault proceeded. The tie-beams could be used as gantries, for mounting cranes, or as members from which to sling platforms which dispensed with the need for elaborate timber scaffolds built up from the ground.

Medieval vaults may be divided into two main groups: (1) vaults in which forces were dispersed, and (2) vaults in which forces were concentrated. The former category concerns the semi-cylindrical barrel-vaults, which exercised continuous planes of thrust and consequently demanded continuous abutment to ensure their stability. In the latter group, which for convenience we may call Gothic vaults, although their essentials were invented and tested by Romanesque architects, the surface of the vaults was divided into intersecting cells. The boundaries or creases of the cells were reinforced with masonry ribs, which routed the main thrusts to 'collection points' at intervals along the clerestory walls.

Various suggestions have been put forward to account for the development of the structural ribbed vault, which appeared in England at Durham at the end of the eleventh century. It is often said that the search for a means of comprehensively covering a church in stone originated with a desire to minimize the effects of damage by fire. Fires, it is true, were frequent visitors at medieval churches. Yet it is hard to believe that the Gothic structural system originated with a fire prevention measure. The immunity of stone vaults to flame may have been an added attraction, but this can hardly be the whole story.

The semi-cylindrical vault was prone to splay at its feet and required extensive (and therefore expensive) abutment. It was thus unsuitable for covering large spans, and incompatible with the requirements of height and light which seem to have been idealized by twelfth-century patrons. The ribbed-vault, on the other hand, permitted both, and since the scale of internal supports could be substantially reduced it enabled the creation of more spacious interiors. Further, the rib offered prospects for new forms of artistic invention, later to be exploited by English architects in patterns of increasing complexity which culminated in the remarkable pendant vaults of the Tudor age.

However, in *c*. 1100 much of this was still beyond the horizon, and Harvey has questioned the idea that vaulting developments were central to the origins of the Gothic style at all: '. . . it is not primarily hidden techniques of structure which constitute a style, but its appearance . . . the reason for the sudden popularity of Gothic . . . its leading feature, immediately noticeable and full of symbolism, the pointed arch with its visible heavenward thrust and dynamic qualities which impressed the onlooker *on sight*' (Harvey 1968, 88). But the crucial early vaulting experiments could scarcely have been carried on by medieval architects as private ventures. Further, the ribbed vault is appealing for the same reasons that Harvey seems to reserve for the pointed arch. There is a profound contrast between the quality of the emotional impact generated by vaulted Durham and timbered Peterborough; the timber ceiling presses down, or at best feels inert, whereas the vault is literally charged with latent energy. It is also a fact that the pointed arch was a decided *structural* asset if it approximated to an inverted catenary (see Fig. 4, opposite). It is

52 *Selby: eastern arm after fire in 1906*　　　53 *Selby: repairs in progress after fire in 1906*

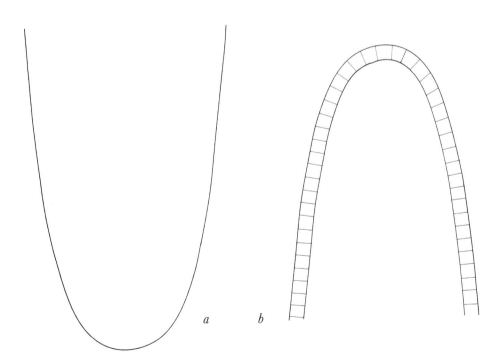

a　　　*b*

Fig. 4 (a) Catenary curve; (b) Masonry arch taking the form of an inverted catenary, in which every voussoir is in compression

123

this tight embrace between structural efficiency on the one hand and aesthetic success on the other that is the fascination and wonder of Gothic.

But how was it all achieved? We have seen that in matters of design the medieval master-mason had no cause to depend upon the science of academics. By the same token we must asume that the medieval builder had no means of calculating the behaviour of the churches he produced. Nor, apart from the curious text by the sixteenth-century Spanish architect Rodrigo Gil (*c*. 1500–77), is there any sign that he attempted to do so. Rodrigo Gil, who was architect to Segovia Cathedral from *c*. 1525 and later *maestro* at Salamanca, described how the sectional dimensions of vaulting ribs ought to be worked out from the side of a bay; he gave a geometrical procedure for determining the thickness of a buttress, and discussed the thrusts delivered by the ribs of the vaults (Kubler 1944, 135–48). The reasoning behind Rodrigo's rules has been questioned (Heyman 1968, 188, n. 43), and while the rules may indicate that some architects were casting about for a scientific framework within which to place their work at that time, Rodrigo Gil was dead before the problem of the parallelogram of forces was scientifically solved (Heyman 1966, 249–50). The squabbles at Milan late in the fourteenth century, when outside experts were called in to advise upon the construction of a new cathedral, reveal an obsession with ideology rather than with what we would regard today as questions of engineering. One dispute centred not upon the question of how high the church ought to be, but within what geometrical figure it ought to be inscribed. During another debate it was stated that a pointed arch delivers no thrust (Ackerman 1949). Nevertheless, the cathedral was eventually finished and still stands.

The alternative idea, that medieval building technology advanced by trial and error, leaves much unsaid. The boundaries of structural possibility could only be mapped through the observation and analysis of error, which at full scale would be precisely what the architect would have wished to avoid.

Of course only the major catastrophes were recorded by monastic historians. Details of day-to-day site mishaps have not come down to us, unless some additional drama was involved, such as the scaffolding accident which crippled William of Sens at Canterbury in 1178 and sent him back to France an invalid. Incidents of this kind must have been common: the buckling of a buttress, the failure of a rib or web, the distortion of centring, the unsuitability of a particular type of stone. Such setbacks would have been monitored, the problems isolated and the rules adjusted accordingly.

Heyman's essays on the behaviour of Gothic churches contain several recurring themes. First, Heyman points out that the level of stress in the greater part of a medieval church was low; so low, in fact, 'that strength of the material is only of secondary importance' (1967–8, 16). Secondly, Heyman calls attention to the natural tendency of a masonry structure to crack, 'hinge' or deform in order to accommodate itself to a given set of circumstances. An excellent illustration of this characteristic is to be seen at Selby, where the misshapen condition of the ground arcade in the eastern bay of the nave indicates rapid settlement in the vicinity of the central tower while the church was being built. It is clear that the settlement ceased during the twelfth century because when the builders came to add the clerestory they were able to compensate for the distortion. Unsightly though it is, the cracked arch is proof of the propensity towards flexibility which is inherent in masonry structures. Thirdly, Heyman demonstrates that it is stability, rather than strength, which is the overriding criterion in Gothic design (1968, 184–5). Stability depends upon proportion, which, as we have seen, was central to the medieval design process. From this observation Heyman goes on to suggest that models could have been used to 'check the stability of the whole or of any part of the real structure, since questions of stability, depending as they do upon relative proportions, *can* be scaled' (1968, 185).

Use of models could go some way towards explaining the astonishing rapidity of Gothic development. (It is part of Heyman's thesis, as an engineer, that the era of structural development was over before 1300.) Could it be that the masons' lodges of the twelfth and thirteenth centuries were, in effect, experimental laboratories? Was this the significance of the effigy which showed Hugues Libergier 'not only clad in something like academic garb but also carrying a model of "his" church . . .'? There is no doubt that medieval architects did make models of projected buildings. Models were produced for demonstration purposes, for clients, and some (e.g. models made of the *triburio* in Milan late in the fifteenth century) were created in order to settle matters of ordinance. They would also have been useful in estimating quantities and foreseeing procedural snags during construction on site.

54 Beverley: deformation of vaulting rib in nave, probably caused by settlement of the southern arcade

55 Beverley: detail of 'hinge' (cf. Pl. 54) revealing remains of oyster-shell packing inserted by mason when the vault was built

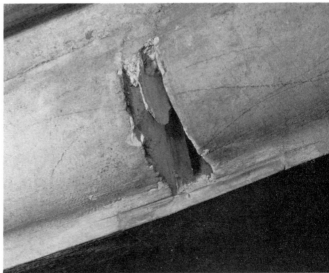

56 Salisbury: reinforcement arch to brace tower, added c. *1420*

However, virtually all the medieval church models of which we have knowledge were made of wood. This would not have been a suitable material for a model designed to test the behaviour of a masonry structure. The models mentioned in the Regensburg guild ordinances (Frankl 1960, 141) were formed of clay and loam, and would have been equally useless. The possible exception, a massive model of S. Petronio, Bologna, was made of brick and plaster; this would surely have been relatively stronger than any full-size counterpart.

57 *Beverley: roughened masonry at exterior of northern clerestory of nave. This was prepared to receive a flying buttress which was never built. Modifications to a structural system were often made while work was in progress*

58 *Bristol: north choir aisle, c. 1300–30. In this unusual design the thrust of the vault over the central aisle is transmitted across the outer aisles via a series of masonry bridges. The result is a 'hall church' in which the three aisles are roofed independently, more or less at the same height*

If models were not used for the resolution of statical problems, then how was the Gothic structural system worked out? The structural system was not only good, it was often *very* good, and this raises the additional question of how it was that the architect knew when he was succeeding. The flying buttresses at, say, Boxgrove are thick and crude. They suggest caution on the part of the architect, who seems to have put them up in the 1230s. Those at Lichfield are lean and elegant; but it is a functional elegance, for according to Heyman (1966, 263–4) they can resist a large range of thrust, between 3 and 100 tons: '. . . the flying buttress will adjust itself, automatically and exactly, to resist any value of thrust, live or dead, within that range' (1966, 263).

There are other instances of Gothic fortuitous ingenuity. The thin Gothic wall, consisting of two skins of tight-jointed masonry enclosing a rubble core, was in many ways an ideal structure, since to a degree the two faces could move independently, the dry core acting almost as a kind of lubricant. This permitted local deformation and adjustment without leading to the general distress which might affect a monolithic structure. Likewise, flying buttresses are often to be found simply propped against the clerestory wall, rather than bonded into it, as at Beverley (nave) and Lincoln (choir). Natural hinges of this kind abound in Gothic structures.

The fan vault, in which the ribs are all of the same curvature and are spaced at

60 *Bath: fan-vault above nave, first erected c. 1530, rebuilt in the 1860s*

61 *St Bartholomew Smithfield: wall passage*

equal angles with one another, combines the structural advantages of the dome and the cross vault (Howard 1911, 2). It was suitable for small or large spans and it was easy to prefabricate because the ribs and panels were cut from single stones. Economy, too, is suggested in the wall-passages and galleries which permit us to tour the upper levels of Gothic churches: these corridors turned the great churches into self-scaffolding structures while building work was in progress, they reduced the weight of the walls, and they provided ready access to remote portions of the fabric for purposes of maintenance or in times of emergency (Fitchen 1961).

Yet it would be a modern assumption to claim that all these devices were deliberately incorporated for engineering reasons, or even to claim that some of them are devices at all. On the other hand, it is not too far-fetched to suggest that it is *possible* that they were so incorporated. The master-builder spent his career looking at, touching, listening to, building and pulling down masonry structures. Every crack, fissure and movement would claim his attention, and his diagnosis of their significance would probably be good.

Nor should we forget that there were everyday objects and circumstances which paralleled the Gothic system. For the flying buttress there was the wooden prop placed to restrain the hayrick or the leaning barn wall. For the strength inherent in the curved shell of the vault there was the resilient hen's egg. Even the parallelogram of forces had an approximate analogue (albeit in negative) in the team of two oxen pulling a plough. It is unlikely that anything in this farmyard world would have suggested a specific structural idea, but it did offer empirical indications of the ways in which forces act and structures behave.

59 (left) *Gloucester: fan-vault above cloister, c. 1390*

6

Functions

And I John saw the holy city, new Jerusalem, coming down from God out of heaven, prepared as a bride adorned for her husband.
And I heard a great voice out of heaven saying, Behold, the tabernacle of God is with men, and he will dwell with them, and they shall be his people, and God himself shall be with them, and be their God.
And God shall wipe away all tears from their eyes; and there shall be no more death, neither sorrow, nor crying, neither shall there be any more pain: for the former things are passed away.
And he that sat upon the throne said, Behold, I make all things new. And he said unto me, Write: for these words are true and faithful.

Revelation 21: 2–5

That this abuse and profanation of that holy place hath growen onlie by the neglect and sufferance of the Deane and Chapter in tymes past. . . . Where vpon Sundayes and all festival dayes the boyes and maydes and children of the two neighbouringe parishes presently after dynner come into the Church, there they playe in such manner as children vse to doe till darke night, and hence cometh principally that inordinate noyse, which many tymes suffereth not the preacher to be heard in the Quyre.

Report . . . as to the
profanation of St Paul's
Cathedral, 1631.

FORM, AS FRANCIS BOND pointed out, is an expression of function. Both in their outline and internal arrangements the greater churches reflect this truth. To consider the design of a church without giving thought to the uses to which the building was put is to approach the subject backwards; medieval churches evolved in response to liturgical needs, not primarily as exercises in architectural virtuosity.

The functions of a great church cannot be summarized easily. As the opening quotations suggest, they fall across a spectrum which extends from the spiritual to the secular. The extract from Revelation, which was read during the medieval rite of dedication, suggests, in that context, that a symbolic correspondence was perceived between the whole Church and the church building. At the other extreme, the indignant memorandum on the 'delinquents' who 'misdemeane themselves . . . in time of Diuine Seruice' at St Paul's reveals that although the nave of the old cathedral was not designed as a playground, that nevertheless is how it had come to be customarily regarded. Ranged between the metaphysical and the mundane there were many functions, therefore, some of which the church fulfilled through its existence or appearance, some which the building was shaped or adapted to contain, and some which it acquired.

Above all else the medieval church was a theatre for the liturgy. Worship was more or less unceasing in the greater churches, with emphasis on the twin tasks of praise to God and intercession for the souls of the departed. The monastic timetable was formidable. A Benedictine monk or Austin canon might spend sixty per cent of his waking life in church. The routine of the secular cathedrals was not quite so arduous, but the liturgical arrangements within the buildings, although they often differed in matters of detail, were broadly comparable.

There was nothing immutable about medieval liturgy. The idea of a standardized Western liturgy was only realized at the Council of Trent in the sixteenth century (i.e. after the Dissolution of the monasteries in England and Wales). A drive towards uniformity had been in progress since the eleventh century, but during that period, and even more so in the era which preceded it, there was considerable variation in

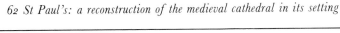

62 St Paul's: a reconstruction of the medieval cathedral in its setting

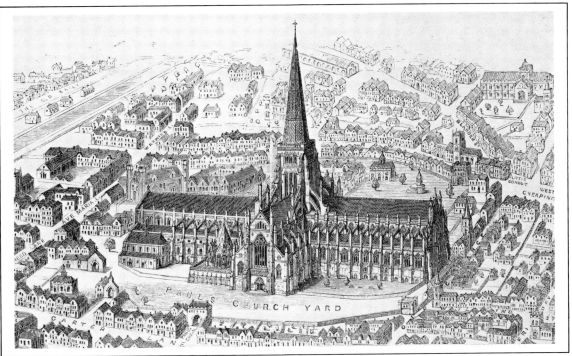

liturgical custom. Some of the sharpest regional differences had been settled by Carolingian reforms, but discrepancies persisted. Moreover, at a local level they could be exaggerated by the interpolation of extraneous material such as dramatic sequences and processions.

This diversity is suggested in the varied planning of great churches. It is not claimed that architectural variations were wholly determined by liturgical factors, but rather that liturgical considerations were among the strongest impulses to influence taste and guide invention. A number of national and regional traits in English Gothic planning, such as the flush east end, the craving for length and the fashion for outsize Lady Chapels, may be described in modern jargon as 'design solutions' for liturgical requirements. The subject of the architectural setting of the liturgy is thus best looked upon as an evolutionary process, not as a rigid pattern which remained settled in all its aspects throughout the Middle Ages.

Some idea of the extent and pace of this metamorphosis may be gained by comparing the ritual arrangements of pre-Conquest major churches with those of the buildings which succeeded them in the twelfth and thirteenth centuries. Here one must enter the caveat that a large number of major Anglo-Saxon churches have yet to be detected, let alone explored. We are for example ignorant of the layouts at Beverley, Chester, Crowland, Dorchester, Hereford, Lincoln, Wells, Worcester and York. Fragments of plans are known from Cirencester, Peterborough, Hexham, Rochester and Romsey, and a bare outline at North Elmham. Among the churches of which something is known, two, St Augustine's Canterbury and Glastonbury, have not been fully published at the time of writing, while two more, Sherborne and Winchester, lay in adjoining dioceses and hence might not present a representative picture. The investigations undertaken by C. C. Hodges at Hexham in the 1890s and 1900s were unsystematic, and there is disagreement about the significance of his results (Bailey 1976). The crypt at Ripon offers little indication of the arrangement of the upper church to which it belonged originally. However, the remains of what may have been the late Saxon cathedral at Exeter have recently been revealed by archaeologists, while even as this chapter is being written an announcement has come from Lincoln which reports the discovery of the church built there in 628 by the missionary Paulinus. So the picture continues to clarify. Nevertheless, in the absence of facts from a larger number of representative sites, valuable information about ritual arrangements can be gleaned from documentary sources, and this both accords with and is supplemented by the evidence which is available from excavations and from churches of lesser status which survive to this day. It must be admitted that the literary evidence is often ambiguous, but it is noticeable that confusion or controversy tends to be greatest when commentators attempt to use it in the cause of detailed *architectural* reconstructions of lost buildings. Here we are concerned only with the schematic recreation of liturgical layouts.

Pre-Conquest churches differed in functional terms from those of the later period in two ways. First, the Anglo-Saxon monastery or cathedral often consisted of an assemblage of compartments, each with its own ritual function, whereas in churches of the later Romanesque and Gothic eras these functions were collected within the shelter of a single large building. The second contrast arises from the degree of emphasis which was placed upon the extremities of the church. After *c*. 1050 it was the east end of the church to which greatest liturgical importance was attached; the nave was regarded as an assembly area, a space for additional altars, and as an avenue for processions. The nave was usually the last portion of the church to be built, and even a church which lacked one, as did some of the Benedictine abbeys when progress was slow west of the crossing, could function for a time without any serious liturgical ill-effects. In pre-Conquest churches, on the other hand, strong liturgical emphasis was often placed upon *both* ends of the building. We might generalize by describing early churches as additive and (potentially) dualistic, in contrast with later churches which were architectonic and tended towards a single area of focus. Before going on to consider the functions of Gothic churches it will be useful to examine the arrangements of some pre-Conquest buildings in greater detail.

The additive church

Important Anglo-Saxon churches were often flanked by one or more pairs of lateral annexes or *porticus*. These subsidiary compartments were grouped alongside the central body of the church and could be multiplied or deleted as the need arose. This process is clearly witnessed in the growth of the monastic church of St Mary, Deerhurst, in Gloucestershire, where an interdisciplinary study undertaken by Dr Lawrence Butler, Professor Philip Rahtz and Dr Harold Taylor has led to the elucidation of six main stages in the pre-Conquest evolution of the building. The first church was a simple rectangle with a small annexe projecting to the west. Then came the addition of a semi-circular eastern apse, followed by the construction of a cluster of flanking eastern *porticus*. Next it seems that the church was considerably heightened, since detailed inspection and analysis of the fabric has shown that the upper stages were secondary to the original ground-storey. At a later date the easternmost chapels were probably removed, and the semi-circular apse was rebuilt to a polygonal plan. Finally, the line of flanking *porticus* was extended westwards, providing a row of lateral chambers in series. The principal side chambers were of two storeys (Taylor 1977).

Split-level planning was not unusual in Anglo-Saxon churches. Multi-storey *porticus* are suggested by Eddius' description of Wilfrid's church at Hexham, and were possibly described by Prior Richard in his account of the church as it stood in the twelfth century. Taylor (following Verdier 1954) has suggested that at the pre-Conquest cathedral at Canterbury the altars of St Gregory and St Martin were located on the first floors of the lateral towers which Eadmer tells us existed there (Taylor 1969b, 112). Alcuin, writing of the construction of a new church at York in

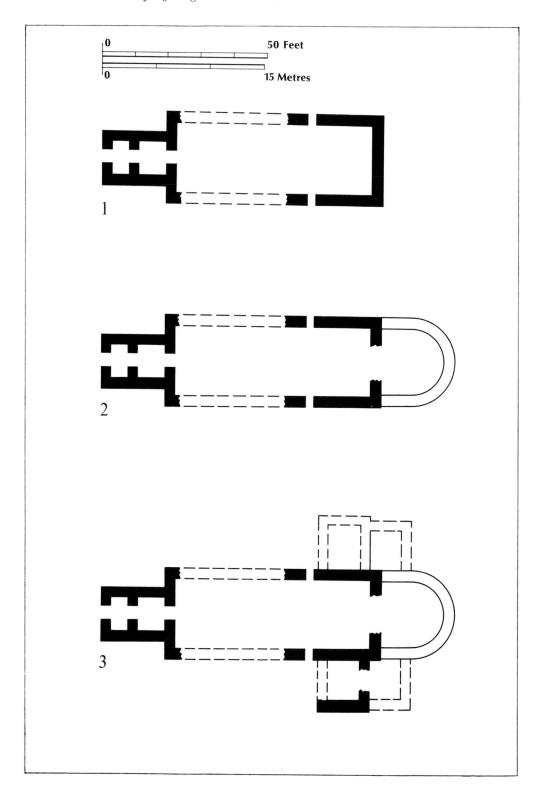

Fig. 5 Deerhurst: development of the pre-Conquest monastic church.   (After Taylor 1977)

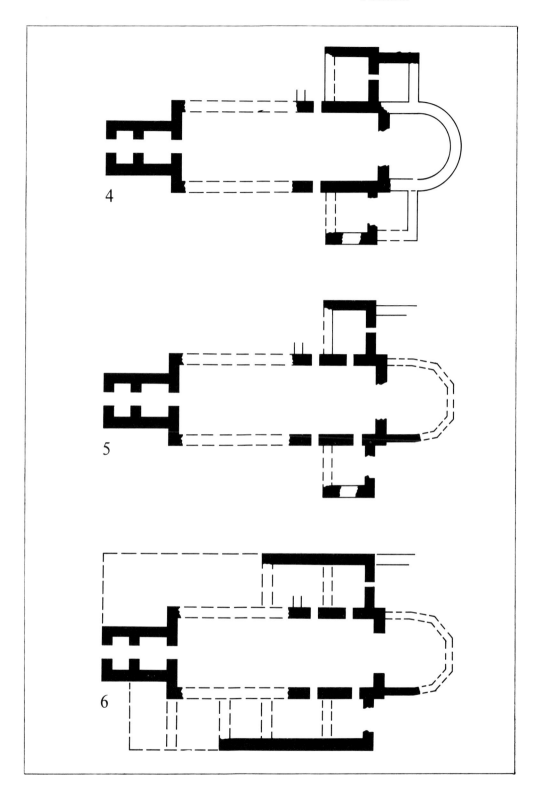

the eighth century (or of an axial extension to the old cathedral?), noted: 'The church is of seemly height, and is supported by solid columns which stand beneath curved arches. Inside the church glitters with fine ceilings and windows. Many *porticus* are grouped round about, and the church has numerous chambers (*solaria*), individually roofed, which contain thirty altars with ornaments of various kinds' (Raine 1879, 394). As usual we are left in doubt as to the exact configuration of the building, but the use of the term *solaria* points to the existence of upper galleries or apartments. Presumably it was these which enabled Alcuin and his colleague Eanbald to cram thirty altars into the church. The church in question was consecrated to the Holy Wisdom (*sophiae sacraverat almae*) in 780. *Porticus*, then, could serve as chapels and contain subsidiary altars.

Where *porticus* flanked the sanctuary it is possible that they also functioned as sacristies: such chambers were necessary to house the objects necessary for worship, for robing and for the safe-keeping of vestments. The *Apostolic Constitutions* (VIII, 13) prescribed that the east end of a church should be provided with adjacent chambers to hold the treasures of the house of the Lord; and where after the mass anything that was left of the consecrated elements could be consumed by the deacons. Paulinus of Nola (d. 431) (Ep. 32) referred to this kind of annex as the *secretarium* (Eisenhofer & Lechner 1961, 114). These requirements would explain the disposition of *porticus* at such early Anglo-Saxon churches as St Pancras, Canterbury, Bradwell, Lyminge and Reculver, where the eastern annexes overlap the junction between nave and chancel and are connected to the sanctuary by a door.

At ground level *porticus* could also be places of burial. Until the Synod of Mainz in 813 it was not permissible to deposit the corpses of abbots, bishops and outstanding laymen within the nave or chancel of the church. (Saints, martyrs and important corporeal relics were apparently exempt from this restriction.) *Porticus*, however, do not seem to have been affected by the prohibition. Burial within them was desirable, therefore, since a grave could be in close proximity to the high altar and to any venerated relics which happened to be beneath or near it. Since space was limited admission was on a highly selective basis.

The fact that *porticus* were regarded as being in some way outside the liturgical fabric of the church (Biddle 1976, 69) may have much to do with the fourth use to which they were sometimes put. Taylor has observed that

> The large openings at Deerhurst on the upper floor contrast sharply with the very small doorways on the ground floor, thus giving a strong impression that they were intended to allow a clear view from the upper floor towards the choir and the apsidal sanctuary. . . . But even more striking is the resemblance which they show to the arrangement of the church which is drawn on fol. 118b of the Benedictional of St Aethelwold, beside the blessing for the dedication of a church. Even after making due allowances for the schematic liberties taken in drawings of this type, the picture seems clearly to indicate the space in front of the altar, with clergy facing the bishop who pronounces the blessing, while a group of lay persons including at least one lady are looking down from a gallery.
>
> (Taylor 1975, 166)

There are analogues for the principle of this kind of arrangement in ninth- and tenth-century churches on the continent, particularly in Germany. Several of these have been discussed in some detail by Taylor in the essay from which the extract above has been taken. The practice of providing vantage points for observing ceremonies in the choir was continued for a time in the Anglo-Norman period. At Christchurch, for example, there is evidence for an intention to erect galleries over the transeptal arms, and it appears that galleries overlooked the crossing in the first Norman churches at Lincoln and Canterbury. Upper storeys of lateral chambers could, therefore, provide accommodation for laity on important occasions without infringing on the priestly area.

It appears that galleries were also common features at the west ends of Anglo-Saxon churches, and this leads us to the second point of liturgical contrast between pre-Conquest ecclesiastical buildings and those of the late Romanesque and Gothic periods. Attention has already been drawn to the fact that liturgical emphasis was often placed upon both ends of the building in Anglo-Saxon schemes, and not merely upon the eastern arm as became conventional in the twelfth and thirteenth centuries. This generalization may be qualified by pointing out that heavy *architectural* stress was frequently laid upon the western parts of Gothic churches, but that this stress was almost invariably achieved by means of external display: towers, recessed portals, or screen fronts bearing tiers of sculpture. The character of the west fronts at Peterborough or Howden, for example, could scarcely be anticipated by the visitor who approached them from within. One might almost say that the outward, material accentuation of the English Gothic west front provided a balance to the inner, spiritual importance of the eastern arm. By contrast, the western portions of a number of significant Anglo-Saxon churches were constructed in response to intrinsic liturgical needs.

Once again, the church of St Mary at Deerhurst provides a good starting point for discussion. In its developed form the western part of the church comprised four stages: a ground storey which acted as an entrance; a first floor chamber with a door and a window towards the nave; a second-floor room with a pair of triangular-headed windows looking into the nave, one of which later served as a door and a west door leading to a balcony; and an upper chamber with provision for access into the roof-space. The first-floor door probably communicated with a timber gallery. Parallels exist in the more elaborate 'west works' of continental churches such as Centula and Corvey. The church of St Riquier at Centula no longer exists, and Mr David Parsons has recently explored some of the problems and pitfalls involved in the recovery of its liturgical layout from documentary sources (Parsons 1977). With Corvey, however, we are on surer ground; much of the west end survives, and there is good evidence to show how the western block was used late in the ninth century: it amounted to a semi-independent church, with its own dedication (St Vitus), altars, and facilities for three choirs (Kreusch 1963, 49–73). The western structure at Deerhurst is on a far smaller scale, but there is a correspondence of principle.

63 Peterborough: west front, c. 1195–1230

At Winchester there was also a correspondence of scale. Excavations carried out on the site of the Old Minster during the 1960s under the direction of Professor Martin Biddle have shown that the pre-Conquest cathedral possessed a western block, constructed during the 970s, which was if anything slightly larger than the west work at Corvey: a rough comparison of the ground areas works out at *c*. 5625 square feet and 4278 square feet, respectively. If the estimate of the excavator is correct (Biddle 1975, 138), then the Winchester west-work was also the taller of the two: over 114 feet as against (originally) *c*. 108 feet. Excavations at Sherborne have shown that there too a substantial western block formed part of the pre-Conquest cathedral (Gibb 1975). In its final state this consisted of a western transept measuring over 75 feet from north to south, which incorporated an earlier axial tower.

How were these western blocks used? Professor Biddle has discussed the functions of the west-work at Winchester and notes that it would have provided an axial entrance to the church, facilities for a raised western choir, and that it occupied the original site of St Swithun's grave. 'The connection between west-works, the tombs of saints, and the cult of relics, well known on the continent (Quirk 1957, 53), seems clearly reflected here . . .' Professor Biddle also draws attention to the relationship between west-works and royalty. At Winchester the west-work was situated close to the royal palace, and formed 'part of a church which for three hundred years had been closely associated with the house of Wessex'. It seems that royal burials had been made in that part of the cemetery which was selected as the site of the west-work, and that 'after its construction some of the most important burials of the late-Saxon period seem to have taken place within it . . .' (Biddle 1975, 138).

How far these functions would hold good for churches of lesser size in other parts of pre-Conquest England it is hard to say. It is possible that the magnitude of the Winchester west-work set the structure in a liturgical as well as an architectural class of its own. But the importance which was evidently accorded to western towers and galleries at surviving churches of lesser status such as Brixworth, Ledsham, Monkwearmouth and Tredington gives strong reason to suppose that dualistic liturgical arrangements featured widely in Anglo-Saxon schemes. The strength of this tradition might also be measured from the fact that in eastern England it lingered on into the twelfth century, finding new expression in the immense western transepts at Bury and Ely, in the west-work at Lincoln, and at Melbourne, Derbyshire, where the church began *c*. 1130 incorporated a gallery of stone at the west end of the nave.

So far we have looked at designs in which the western part of the church had an architectural and liturgical identity quite distinct from the layout of the eastern portion. An alternative approach to dualism in liturgical planning was to make the two ends of a church resemble each other as closely as possible. Churches with western and eastern apses are found as early as the seventh century in parts of North Africa and in Spain – the idea of the western apse was much older and went back to Roman designs – and they appeared in some numbers in Germany during the ninth century. In the early ninth-century monastic church of SS Peter and Paul at St Gall, in Switzerland, for example, the principal altars were placed in apses at opposite ends of the church: St Peter at the west, St Paul at the east. No definite example of a palindromic design of this kind is yet known in England, but it is more than probable that such schemes existed here. This likelihood arises not so much from documentary references (as for example to altars at both ends of the late tenth-century church at Thorney, or to a church at Abingdon which is alleged to have been 'round in both its eastern and western parts'), as from the evidence which has lately emerged from excavations on the site of the ruined priory church of St Oswald at Gloucester. Among other things these investigations have shown that the pre-Conquest church possessed a western apse. Unfortunately it has not been possible to examine the east end of the church, so for the time being the full nature of the layout remains undetermined. Nor has it yet been possible to assign a firm date to the apse, although it appears that the apse was constructed in the tenth century (Heighway 1978). Nevertheless, this discovery is of great significance in confirming that the western apse was within the repertoire of Anglo-Saxon liturgical planners. It is all the more valuable for having been made in archaeological terms rather than in the dubious *post hoc* record of a monastic chronicler, as at Abingdon.

The subject of bi-polar plans takes us finally to Canterbury, where we have the luxury of an eyewitness description of the liturgical layout of the pre-Conquest cathedral. For this we must thank Eadmer, a Canterbury monk who had known the building in his boyhood and who later wrote an account of the cathedral as it had stood in its late Saxon state before it was damaged by fire in 1067 and subsequently demolished to make way for Lanfranc's new church. Eadmer described an eastern *presbytery* raised above a *crypt* and gained by several steps from a *choir* which extended westwards into the *body* of the church and was secluded by a screen. The presbytery contained two altars: one which was placed close to the east wall and contained the remains of St Wilfrid, and another which stood further west and was dedicated in honour of Jesus Christ. The crypt contained an altar in its eastern part, and a corridor which ran westwards to the tomb of Dunstan. Eadmer thought that the crypt resembled the *confessio* in St Peter's at Rome. Dunstan was buried in the choir, apparently between the matutinal altar and the steps leading up to the sanctuary. Beyond the middle part of the church (i.e. further west than east in relation to the total length of the building) two lateral towers rose above (or outside?) the aisles. The south tower served as the main entrance to the church and contained an altar dedicated in honour of Pope Gregory. It also accommodated legal hearings. Its fellow on the north side was built in honour of St Martin, and was also used as a school. The west end of the church was adorned by an *oratory* of Mary, the Mother of God. The entrance to the oratory could not be reached (or seen?) except by steps. In the eastern part of the oratory there was an altar. When this altar was in use the officiating priest faced east, towards the people in the body of the church below. Well behind this altar was the pontifical chair, which was formed of mortared masonry and stood in contact with the west wall.

Although Eadmer sets out the liturgical arrangements of the cathedral in some detail, modern scholars have been unable to agree on the form of the building which he described. This is partly to do with the fact that Eadmer's writings are of minimal assistance in establishing a chronology for the building. Other texts are available to assist in this, but opinions vary as to their relative importance and on matters of interpretation (Parsons 1969; Taylor 1969b; Gem 1970; Gilbert 1970; Taylor 1975). Parsons, for example, considers it likely that extensive remodelling of the church took place in the tenth century. Dr Gem (1970, 200) suggests that the cathedral as it stood in the mid eleventh century 'far from being a building the principal features of which had been established at a date prior to the mid eighth century, must have displayed more notably the modifications which it received during the course of its tenth-century restorations'. Dr Gilbert, on the other hand, is persuaded that the cathedral was largely rebuilt during the pontificate of Archbishop Wulfred (805–832), on a plan which included transepts, and maintains that if this was the case 'it is not likely . . . that it was substantially rebuilt during the tenth century' (Gilbert 1970, 204). Gem, Gilbert and Parsons all agree that the western oratory probably occupied the first floor of some kind of west-work, whereas in his tentative reconstruction of the cathedral Taylor gives reasons for suspecting that the west end of the cathedral was apsidal, enclosing a dais rather than a multi-storey arrangement (Taylor 1969, 111, 117–18; 1975, 157). Like Eadmer, Dr Taylor makes no mention of a western tower or of transepts.

Attention is drawn to this debate in order to illustrate the extent to which it is possible for contemporary views upon the implications of a single text and associated references to diverge. The reconstruction of a vanished building from documentary evidence is an absorbing exercise, yet the problems of analysing, dating and determining the functions of the various parts of standing pre-Conquest churches such as Deerhurst and Brixworth are often great enough. It may be that an attempt to deduce the architectural history of a building that no longer exists and which was described in detail only as it stood on the eve of its demolition is likely to place a strain upon the limited amount of evidence which is available.

Diversity is perhaps the leading characteristic of Anglo-Saxon liturgical planning. The general impression is that the buildings were not, as a rule, particularly large, although it is noticeable that those lesser churches which survive are often tall in proportion to their width. The seventh-century cathedral at Winchester was barely 100 feet long, and no attempt to enlarge it seems to have been made before the second half of the tenth century. Even in its fully-developed state the Old Minster was only *c*. 250 feet from end to end although, as we have seen, the west-work was impressive. Gilbert's search for a yardstick by which to judge the likely dimensions of capital churches in the middle Saxon period took him to York, where lengthy foundations under the eastern arm of the present Minster were once believed to have formed part of the Alma Sophia, consecrated by Archbishop Albert in 780 (Gilbert 1970, 204). But it is now known that these foundations were constructed during the pontificate of

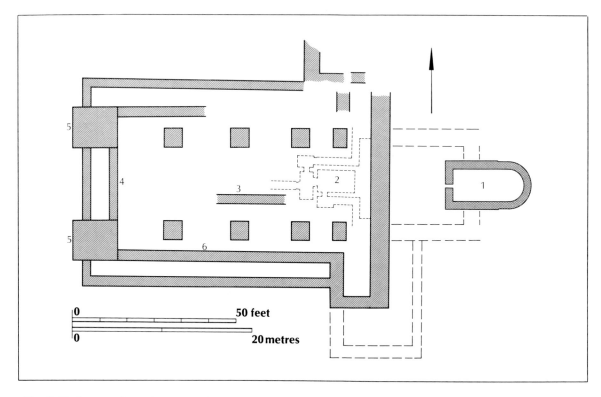

Fig. 6 Hexham: conjectural reconstruction of liturgical layout based on evidence revealed during investigations carried out betweeen 1899 and 1908. Key: (1) eastern church; (2) raised sanctuary with crypt below; (3) ambo or pulpit; (4) area of possible raised western sanctuary; (5) tower; (6) wall or colonnade. (After Bailey 1976)

the Norman Archbishop Thomas (1070–1100) (Hope-Taylor 1971; Phillips 1975). Where noteworthy dimensions did occur, as at Glastonbury and St Augustine's, Canterbury, they were often attained by connecting a number of smaller churches which had been built in close proximity to each other over a period of time. This process of fusion (which is also witnessed at Hexham and Malmesbury), and the process of accretion whereby small churches expanded as a result of the attachment of adjuncts, suggests that many pre-Conquest churches were essentially multi-focal in their liturgical layouts. There are indications that furnishings, fittings and liturgical accessories held a stronger appeal for the users of these intimate buildings than the concept of scale.

The coherent church

The change to a single area of focus, in which the principal liturgical emphasis was placed upon the choir and presbytery, and the various functions which had previously been dispersed in *porticus*, annexes and western complexes were gathered within one coherent design, was already in progress before the Conquest. The Norman invasion led to a rapid acceleration of this process, however, for it stimulated a revolution in monasticism, and hence in churchbuilding, which centred on a rationalized, continental approach to liturgical layout which was to form the basis of all subsequent developments until the Reformation.

Certain items, chiefly the main elements of the plan and elevation, were essential to the coherent state, while others (glass, wall paintings, pavements) might contribute to it. In this sense it was the great Anglo-Norman churches which came closest to the coherent ideal, as in nearly every case the opportunity was taken to build or rebuild according to a single design, in which decoration, iconographic schemes and essential fittings were all conceived as aspects of the whole. After *c.* 1175 the cycle of renewal started over again, and it often took some time for a church to reattain a completed state. Some, such as Westminster and York, were several hundred years in completion, while in many others financial restrictions often led to piecemeal rebuilding or modernization, as at Bridlington, to the remodelling of an existing fabric, as at Great Malvern, or to the abandonment of cherished schemes. From the Early English era onwards there were also renewed pressures towards fragmentation: chantries, projecting or semi-detached Lady Chapels, the proliferation of altars and screenwork in transepts and naves, the great reredos rising between high altar and saint's shrine, and the designation of areas for parochial use. In connection with some of these developments the decorative arts became increasingly particular to single themes or areas appropriate to individual donors or saints. The emergence of the Perpendicular style might possibly be seen as a corrective to this tendency. At least, the masons who invented it, and the patrons who preferred it, laid stress upon unity in the design of tracery, in the constructional details of vaults, in the panelled treatment given to wall-surfaces and piers, and in a general subordination of detail in the interests of overall coherence (Harvey 1961). This interplay or tension between unity and fragmentation can be followed, at several levels, in the review of functions which follows.

The choir – that part of the church where the offices were recited – was now a church within a church. It was screened off from the nave, the transept and the eastern aisles. Moreover it often bore no relation to the architectural divisions of a cruciform church, since in many buildings it projected westwards over the heart of the plan into the eastern bays of the nave.

From the twelfth century onwards the habit grew of housing the entire choir within the eastern arm. It seems likely that the first church to take this step was Canterbury, where it is known that the eastern extension to Lanfranc's cathedral which was begun by Prior Ernulf (1096–1107) contained the choir. However, recent excavations at York have produced evidence which points to the possibility that the cathedral begun there *c.* 1080 was designed with the intention of accommodating the choir east of the crossing. (Even if this was not the case it is still fairly certain that York was the first secular cathedral to move the choir into the eastern arm; the new eastern limb which was added during the pontificate of Archbishop Roger (1154–81) was clearly laid out with this in mind.) But by no means all churches followed suit, and in a number the alternative arrangement was maintained and is in some cases preserved. At Gloucester, St David's and Winchester, for example, the choir occupies all or a part of the crossing, while at Norwich, Peterborough and St Albans the choir juts westwards into the nave. Although these choirs did not correspond with the principal architectural divisions of the plan, their limits were sometimes given subtle accentuation. At Norwich, for instance, the western boundary of the monastic choir was marked by a change in the form of the nave piers, and the site of the sanctuary which contained the nave altar of the Holy Cross is commemorated in similar fashion (Fernie 1977, 384).

Since the choir was an inner church screens played an important part in liturgical arrangements. In monastic churches there were generally two: the rood screen, of timber or stone, which faced the nave; and the pulpitum, usually situated a bay further east and of solid construction, which formed the western boundary of the choir. Rood screens were commonly pierced by lateral doorways, while the pulpitum normally contained a central opening, thereby permitting access into the choir between the return stalls which backed against it. Altars were often placed against the western faces of screens, and some screens were actually designed to house altars: at Southwell, for example, altar spaces were provided within the thickness of the pulpitum which was erected in the 1320s. The central altar placed against the rood screen was of special importance, since it stood beneath the Great Rood which was carried by (or suspended from) a beam spanning the central aisle of the church. A rood beam survives, though displaced, at Little Malvern Priory.

64 Crowland: rood screen, fifteenth century

Many rood screens and pulpita survive, but in no case have both been preserved in combination. In churches which were partially demolished after the Suppression screens often provided a suitable barrier upon which to raise a new outside wall. Rood screens were heightened in this way at Bolton, Blyth and Dunstable, where in each case the nave was retained for parochial use. At Boxgrove it was the eastern limb and transept which were preserved, and the rood screen was carried up to form the west wall of the truncated church. Boxgrove may have kept its pulpitum after the suppression, but it appears that this screen perished during repair work early in the nineteenth century. Ely retained its twelfth-century pulpitum down to 1770, when it was demolished. Drawings of the screen survive and show that it contained three doorways instead of the customary one (St John Hope, 1917). A number of wooden screens of various kinds have survived: at Cartmel, for example, the chancel screen probably dates from the sixteenth century and is reputed to be the work of Flemish craftsmen. A wooden pulpitum remains at Hexham, although it has suffered much interference. The screen now in the north aisle at Crowland is reported to have been transferred from the north transept, where it originally served to seclude the Lady Chapel.

Screens have been particularly vulnerable to damage, often as the result of the superimposition of organ machinery which they were never intended to carry (e.g. at Christchurch), but more completely as victims of liturgical reordering. During the nineteenth century a fashion grew for opening out medieval choirs in the interests of intervisibility between nave and eastern arm. At Hereford, for instance, the ancient choir screen (apparently Norman work with refacing of *c.* 1710) was destroyed during Cottingham's restoration of 1841–52. A Victorian substitute was recently removed. In 1859 the fifteenth-century pulpitum at Chichester was taken out, an action which some claimed precipitated the collapse of the steeple two years later. (Willis did not agree.) The fourteenth-century pulpitum at Chester was moved in 1844–6 by Dean Anson and R. C. Hussey, and later cleared out by Scott during his restoration of 1868–72. Cosin's oak screen of 1662 at Durham was destroyed in 1847; Wren's organ screen at St Paul's perished; Winchester lost Inigo Jones' choir screen, although fragments survive. The list of casualties could be extended to include screens in many of the non-cathedral greater churches. The aim was partly liturgical, a determination to make worship more accessible and public, but aesthetic excuses were also brought forward to counter the protests that were aroused. In many cases the attempt to increase congregational involvement was self-defeating, since the removal of the screen merely served to emphasize the great length of the church and hence to emphasize the sense of distance between congregation and choir. Today this problem is often solved by holding services in the nave, or by inviting the congregation into the choir. Victorian efforts to convert monastic churches and cathedrals into parish churches may have been destructive, but they do underline the very specialized nature of the medieval choir, and in particular the likelihood that the great churches were not primarily designed for the use of lay congregations at all. This is suggested by what we know of the Norman pulpitum at Ely, which must have been a most decisive barrier. Nevertheless, Professor C. N. L. Brooke has recently argued that the real extent of the division between nave and choir has sometimes been exaggerated. Professor Brooke believes that the nave was very much the place of the layfolk, used by them for assembly and worship, and that until the advent of high screens in the fourteenth and fifteenth centuries it would have been possible for laymen to witness most of the offices (Brooke 1977).

Inside the choir tiers of wooden stalls faced inwards towards the central aisle, with a set of return stalls facing east at either side of the pulpitum entrance. The stalls were often set on stone bases, and where these substructures have been examined small objects which were dropped by the monks or canons in choir have sometimes been recovered. To judge from these evocative finds rosary beads seem to have been the commonest losses. In secular cathedrals the capitular dignitaries (dean, chancellor, precentor, treasurer) had their stalls at the four corners of the choir. The abbot, prior or bishop was provided with a special stall or throne, usually on the south side. Few medieval episcopal thrones remain, but the great wooden throne at Exeter may be mentioned as an outstanding survivor. It is one of the products of Bishop Stapledon's largesse, and rises to a height of 57 feet in receding stages. When new it must have been even more remarkable, for there are signs that it was richly painted and gilt.

Choir stalls provided an outlet for inventive talents. The richly-worked sets at Gloucester (*c* 1340–50), Chester (*c*. 1390), and Carlisle (*c*. 1410), for example, are major works of the carver's art. Late in the fifteenth century an important school of carvers emerged at Ripon. Led by Master William Brownfleet these men produced stalls for the collegiate church at Manchester (1505–9), Bridlington (*c*. 1518) and Beverley (1520). Among the many engaging features of medieval stalls, such as elaborate terminals, tabernacle-work, and toy architectural details, one may single out the misericords for special discussion. These are simply tip-up seats, ancestors to

those now found in cinemas and theatres, with a ledge projecting from the underside to give discreet support to the monk or canon during periods of standing in choir. It is estimated that some 3500 misericord seats survive in England and Wales, and nearly 8000 remain in France. Each seat provided only a limited field for embellishment; hence where illustrations on the undersides occur they are usually concise and focused. Subjects of all kinds were represented: fabulous beasts, grotesque heads, biblical scenes and episodes from everyday life – crafts, hunting games, musical instruments, sex, cooking. No subject was taboo, and some seats bear quite eventful pornography. One set of seats at Great Malvern displays scenes which represent the months of the year; this may be compared with the complete set of twelve which narrates the occupations of the months, in sequence, not far away at the parish church of St Mary, Ripple. Misericord carvers shared in the general medieval relish for inverted circumstances: rats hanging a cat (Great Malvern), a cart before a horse (Beverley), and so on. Satire is also evident, and there are numerous instances of foxes and wolves attired as monks or clerics. It is clear that the free range of subjects

65 (far left) *Westminster: misericord*
66 (left) *Beverley: detail of misericord, c. 1520*
67 (below) *Beverley: detail of misericord,*
c. *1520: fox preaching to geese*
68 (right) *Beverley: detail of misericord,*
c. *1520: cat, fiddle and dancing mice*
69 (far right) *Beverley: detail of misericord,*
c. *1520*

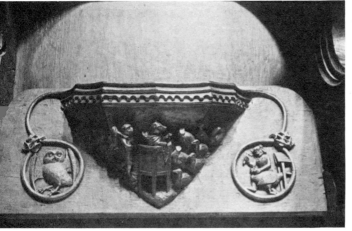

Above, left to right

70 *Wells: foliage capitals and painful problems, c. 1200*
71 *Beverley: imp*
72 *York Minster: chapter-house: pendant with vine leaves, grapes and imp*
73 *York Minster: chapter-house: Virgin and Child*
74 *York Minster: chapter-house: monster with human head*
75 *Rochester: south-west boss of tower*

Below, left to right

76 *Selby: roof boss*
77 *Selby: roof boss*
78 *Canterbury: capital in crypt, c. 1120*
79–82 *Beverley: details of fourteenth-century wall arcade (restored)*

did not disturb the medieval religious, although some of the more explicit scenes were censored by the Victorians, as for example at Chester where five seats were removed and destroyed in the nineteenth century.

Misericords introduce us to a wider issue, that is, the inclusive character of much of the art in medieval churches. The buildings were by no means always accessible to the world at large, but they often reflected it, and in all its aspects. The medieval carver and the churchmen who employed him were neither sentimental nor squeamish. They thus lacked a propensity and an inhibition which together have exerted a strong influence upon the ecclesiastical art of our own age. This can be understood not only from medieval woodcarving, but also from sculptured corbels, bosses, label-stops, capitals and brackets, many of which capture the diversity and savour of life in the Middle Ages with a frankness and humour which, one suspects, would be

unlikely to win the approval of a modern Diocesan Advisory Committee. Walls, piers and roofs of churches depict pain and laughter, love and perversion, violence and tranquillity, heaven and hell, the deformed and the comely, the Christian and the pagan, the malign and the pure, the cosmic and the trivial. The great church was all-embracing, a mirror of life itself, a model of the world.

Eastward of the choir stood the presbytery, which extended to the high altar. The presbytery was raised above the level of the choir from which it was approached up steps. In large churches there was usually a second 'little' or 'matutinal' altar near the foot of these steps, at the east end of the choir. Until the eleventh century the high altar was free-standing. This enabled the priest or bishop to celebrate mass from behind the altar, facing west towards the choir, and allowed access to the altar from all sides. Later on it was often the custom to back the high altar against a reredos, although the practice of circling the altar in order to sprinkle it with holy water was not entirely discontinued; at Christchurch, for example, the fourteenth-century reredos was pierced by two lateral doorways which permitted the priest to complete his circuit around the altar. Altar screens made good hoardings for the display of statuary, of which fine examples or replicas survive at Beverley, St Albans, Sherborne, Southwark and Winchester.

On the south side of the presbytery were the sedilia: seats for the celebrant and those assisting him, together with the piscina where ritual cleansing of vessels could be performed. The lateral enclosures of the presbytery were pierced by doorways (*ostia presbyterii*) communicating with the aisles, through which the monks or canons would leave the choir when participating in processions.

Processions were a key element in medieval ritual. 'In medieval symbolism processions were an antitype of the departure of the Israelites from Egypt and a symbol of the Church's journey to her everlasting home' (Eisenhofer and Lechner 1961, 91). Before high mass on Sundays and important festivals the monks would tour the church and important conventual buildings. The procession was headed by pairs of bearers with crosses, lighted candles, thuribles containing lighted coals and incense, two subdeacons carrying gospel books, and the children with their masters. Moving off to the sound of bells, the procession called at each altar in turn in order to asperse it with holy water. The altars in the transept and eastern arm were usually visited first; the procession would then travel out into the cloister, tour the main conventual buildings, and re-enter the church from the west walk of the cloister. From there the procession would move down the nave, pausing at the altar against the centre of the rood screen (often known as the Jesus altar or altar of the Holy Rood) where the collect would be sung by the abbot or cantor. Bells were rung as the two ranks filed through the lateral doorways of the rood screen and rejoined to enter the choir through the pulpitum entrance. When the bells stopped, the mass began. Processional habits naturally varied from church to church, according to the layout of the building, the disposition of its altars and the importance of the occasion. In some churches the processional route and stations were picked out by marks or tiles

151

83 Abbey Dore: presbytery, c. 1200–10

84 Abbey Dore: ambulatory, with stubs of partitions for chapels on eastern side

in the pavement. The importance of processions in relation to the planning of major churches can hardly be over-emphasized. The developing configurations of east ends in the twelfth and thirteenth centuries were closely connected with the requirements of processional circulation, while the long naves of wealthy twelfth-century Benedictine churches seem to have been intended as avenues to enhance the spectacle and solemnity of the return to the choir. At St Albans the nave ran to ten bays, at Bury twelve, at Ely thirteen, and at Norwich fourteen. In canons' churches, by contrast, the naves were often shorter, and possessed either no aisles at all, as originally at Ripon, York and possibly Llandaff, or a single aisle, usually to the north, as at Bolton, Brinkburn and Hexham.

In addition to the principal altars in the presbytery, the choir and the nave, other, subsidiary altars with individual dedications occupied available spaces in the church. In Anglo-Norman churches of the late eleventh and early twelfth centuries the lateral apses of the transept furnished part of this accommodation. Quite often these apses were of two storeys, as at Christchurch, Pershore, Tewkesbury, and probably York. Usually they occurred singly, one at each side of the crossing, as at Romsey, but in a few cases they were built in pairs, either of graduated projection, as at Binham and St Albans, or of approximately equal length, as in the eastern transepts at Canterbury and Lincoln. By the mid twelfth century apsidal forms were largely abandoned in England in favour of square or rectangular chapels. The Cistercian order led the way in this respect with their rectilinear plan forms and by partitioning the eastern sides of their transepts and ambulatories. At Abbey Dore, for example, the eastern side of the procession path behind the high altar was subdivided into a row of chapels. The great eastern transept at Durham (the Chapel of Nine Altars), a thirteenth-century design of Cistercian extraction, was used, as its name suggests, in much the same way. Space for other altars could be found against the piers of the nave, in the nave aisles, in the transept (especially if it was aisled), and even, as at Gloucester, in the galleries above the aisles of the eastern arm. At Chichester in the thirteenth century extra aisles to the north and south of the nave provided further accommodation.

The cult of the Virgin took a strong hold in England from the end of the twelfth century, and by the end of the Middle Ages there were few large churches which lacked a chapel dedicated in her honour. The usual site for the Lady Chapel was east of the presbytery, either inside the gable end, as at Old St Paul's and York, or jutting out beyond it, as at Chichester, Exeter, Hereford, Llandaff and Tewkesbury. In certain cases, however, the Lady Chapel was placed in or beside a transept, as at Arundel, Bristol, Crowland, Oxford and Rochester. Occasionally the Lady Chapel was situated off to one side, virtually as a semi-independent church, as at Ely, Ramsey and Peterborough. Lady Chapels were generally rectangular in plan, but polygonally-ended designs were favoured at Lichfield, Chester St John and Wells, and cruciform plans are sometimes encountered, as at Gloucester and, originally, at Great Malvern.

Lady Chapels tended to fragment the coherent single-concept church. In a sense they harked back to the pre-Conquest notion of an additive design. Parochial requirements led to further pressures in this direction. Mention has already been made of the fact that the majority of the greater churches were not built to serve the needs of lay congregations. Certain orders, notably the Cistercians, excluded the laity altogether (with the exception of the *conversi* or lay-brothers who were within the membership of the community), but the Benedictines and Augustinians were more outgoing, and quite commonly made portions of their churches available for lay worshippers. Nave aisles were favourite places for parish altars. At Blyth and Dorchester, for example, south aisles were added for parochial use, while at Romsey the north aisle and transept were made over for parochial purposes. At Christchurch and Pershore parochial altars stood in the nave. The parishioners at Wymondham also had the use of the nave, and in the fifteenth century they adapted it to suit their needs by widening and raising the aisles (thus blocking the triforium), adding new roofs and constructing an axial western tower. At Leominster the twelfth-century south aisle of the priory church was replaced by a parochial nave late in the 1230s; this nave was itself enlarged by the addition of another aisle about eighty years later. Gerald of Wales stated that in the twelfth century the parish altar of St Mary Magdalene was situated at the west end of the cathedral at Lincoln. Possibly a section or storey of the west-work was designated as the parish church.

Conflict could arise in churches which were shared between religious and parishioners. At Dunstable, for instance, it is reported that in the fourteenth century the parishioners unilaterally decided to extend their territory from the north nave aisle, where they already had an altar, into the central alley of the nave. They went so far as to stake their claim by building a wall in the nave and setting up a new altar (Vallance 1947, 21–2). This particular clash ended in a compromise; the parishioners and their wall were allowed to remain, but the canons were to have priority over the parish when the nave was needed for processions or services. A parish church dedicated to St Oswald occupied the south aisle of the nave of the Benedictine abbey at Chester. In the 1360s the monks began to rebuild the nave, and displaced the parishioners who moved into the nearby guild chapel of St Nicholas (Burne 1961, 91–2; 136–9).

One way to avoid such problems was to construct a separate parish church or chapel somewhere in the vicinity of the cathedral or abbey. This was done at Rochester, for example, where there was a citizens' church dedicated to St Nicholas on the north side of the cathedral, and at Sherborne, where a large aisled church stood in tandem with the abbey. At Beverley a parochial chapel dedicated to St Martin was built near the south-west corner of the Minster in the fourteenth century, and before the end of the twelfth century there was a church dedicated to St Mary outside the east end of the cathedral at York. A church dedicated to St Andrew stands in the same position at Pershore. At Lincoln there were two churches within the cathedral close, St Mary Magdalen (which was moved out of the cathedral) and

St Margaret, both within the jurisdiction of the Dean and Chapter (Owen 1971, 45); St Margaret's, at least, was probably in existence before the Conquest. There are other cases in which the relationship between a major church and dependent or associated parochial building can be traced back before the Conquest. St Margaret's, Westminster, for example, had an Anglo-Saxon ancestor, although the present church does not occupy the original site. Excavations recently carried out on the site of the demolished church of St Mary Major, Exeter, just west of the cathedral, revealed traces of a substantial Anglo-Saxon building. The pre-Conquest church was at least 131 feet long, with an eastern crypt and what may have been a free-standing tower to the north. A case has been made out to the effect that this was the church which Bishop Leofric (1046–72) took over and used as a cathedral when the see was transferred from Crediton in 1050 (Bidwell 1978, 43). The sixteenth-century church of St Michael-le-Belfrey, situated close to the south-west tower of York Minster and suggestively aligned midway between the axes of the cathedral and the old Roman fortress, is alleged to have had an Anglo-Saxon predecessor.

St Michael-le-Belfrey stood adjacent to the cemetery of York Minster, and this leads us to consider the functions of great churches as places of burial. The subject may be considered on two levels: first, the practical requirements and characteristics of the church as a place of interment; and secondly, the existence of the church as a place where prayers and masses could be offered for the benefit of the souls of those who were or had been associated with it. This latter function formed a large part of the *raison d'être* of the greater churches, and to a considerable extent accounts for the inflow of cash into fabric funds from donors who were looking for an intercessionary return on their investment.

In some instances the cemeteries appear to have preceded their churches. At Deerhurst, for example, graves were disturbed by the builders of the first stone church (Rahtz 1976), while the cemetery associated with the Anglo-Saxon church at Exeter, mentioned above, was preceded by several phases of burial, including a group of skeletons which radio-carbon determinations have dated to the fifth century (Bidwell 1978, 43).

Burial fees were an important source of income to cathedrals and some monasteries, and churches which acquired a territorial monopoly on burial such as Winchester (Biddle 1976, 69; Kjølby-Biddle 1975), yielded up their rights to local parochial churches only with reluctance. As for the church buildings, we have already seen that the *porticus* of Anglo-Saxon cathedrals and monasteries were favourite sites for the graves of leading individuals. The practice of burial within the body of the church was introduced gradually from the ninth century, although where laity were concerned it was not until the twelfth century that all restrictions were lifted. Much can be perceived from tombs about changing attitudes to life and death. In the medieval period the designs move from the simple dignity of Norman slabs towards increasing complexity and display. Some of the most remarkable monuments date from the Decorated period: the Percy tomb at Beverley (*c*. 1336–40), and the serene stellate riches in the walls of the eastern aisles at Bristol. In the fifteenth century tombs begin to suggest a tension between Man's sense of power on the one hand, and an acute consciousness of his frailty on the other: the tomb structures grew ever more elaborate, while the effigies were frequently carved with gruesome realism as emaciated cadavers. Tomb structures and canopies provided opportunities for architectural experiments. The idea of the fan-vault, for example, seems to have been tried out first as a non-structural device over the tomb of Sir Hugh Despencer (d. 1349) at Tewkesbury. The first hints of Renaissance taste are to be detected in monuments, such as those of Henry VII at Westminster, Thomas Fitzalan (d. 1524) at Arundel, Margaret, Countess of Salisbury (d. 1541) at Christchurch, and Paul Bush, Bishop of Bristol (1543–53).

The subject of burial leads us to chantry chapels. Literally speaking a chantry is an intercessionary mass, but during the thirteenth century it became increasingly usual for those with the necessary means to cater for the repose of their souls not merely by purchasing masses but also by providing resources sufficient for the construction and permanent staffing of a chapel in which such masses could be said. Sites were found for these chapels on an *ad hoc* basis, usually tucked between piers or

85 Arundel: Fitzalan Chapel, c. 1524   *86 Arundel: Fitzalan Chapel*

87 (right) Worcester: interior of Prince Arthur's chantry chapel, 1502–4

buttresses, but occasionally occupying entire aisle bays, as in the cases of the chantries of Bishops Alcock and West at Ely, fitted up between *c*. 1490–1500 and 1523–36, respectively. Locations close to important altars or relics were preferred and were frequently specified in wills. Chantries were founded in growing numbers during the fifteenth and sixteenth centuries, and it has been estimated that there were over 2000 chapels in existence at the time of the Suppression (Cook 1947). Many were remarkable: stone cages carved with a refinement which had never been achieved before or since. Some were built on generous scale. The chapel of Abbot Ramryge (d. 1521) at St Albans, for instance, occupies a complete bay and rises to two storeys. Not all were of stone. A few were of metal, while at Hexham the chantry chapel of Prior Leschman (*c*. 1490) is an example of a composite breed, of stone and timber.

The endowment of chantries froze much wealth. Restrictions were imposed from as early as 1279, when the Statute of Mortmain required, among other things, that proposals for the endowment of chantries should be subject to official scrutiny in order to ensure that they would not divert revenue from the king. In the sixteenth century measures of suppression were passed in 1529, 1545 and 1547. Many chapels were subsequently destroyed, and few of those which avoided outright destruction

88 *Derby Cathedral: entrance to family vault, c. 1605*
89 *York Minster: surface of a tenth-/eleventh-century graveyard, with monuments* in situ. *The graves were encountered during repairs beneath the south transept in 1968–9*

escaped damage, since chantry chapels were natural and easily-accessible targets for iconoclasts. The reign of Edward VI and the early years of Elizabeth were periods of particularly ruthless activity. Even today, however, deprived of their colour, without their lights, lacking their fittings, shorn of much of their statuary, the voices of their priests silenced, the survivors continue to impress.

The suppression of chantries did not put an end to burial inside large churches. Aristocratic families continued to bury their dead inside private vaults down to the nineteenth century. Sometimes the exact whereabouts of these chambers has been forgotten but they are sometimes rediscovered in the course of excavations. Others have simply been sealed up. A typical example of the kind of vault with which some major churches are honeycombed has lately been examined at Derby Cathedral, where Elizabeth, Countess of Shrewsbury (Bess of Hardwick) prepared a resting place for herself in advance of her death in 1607.

Chantries and monumental tombs represented only a tiny fraction of the total population of burials in a medieval church. Men and women of middling rank whose status or means were insufficient to provide them with an individual tomb might nevertheless acquire gravespace, perhaps with a marker slab let into the floor. Most of these slabs have now gone, victims of repaving in the eighteenth and nineteenth centuries, and few of those that remain can be trusted to correspond with the grave of the person commemorated below. Medieval graves are notorious for their confusion and for the extent to which they interrupted one another. The only grave which

90 *Little Malvern: 'weeper' on tomb chest, late fourteenth century*
91 *Painted plaster cover of tomb of Walter de Gray, Archbishop of York (1215–55)*
92 *(below) Archbishop Walter de Gray: notice mortuary chalice, crozier, episcopal ring, vestments and tooling on interior of sarcophagus*

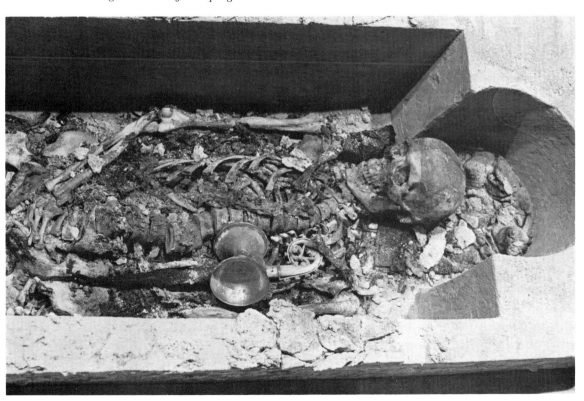

mattered to a sexton was the one he was excavating. As William Davenant put it:

> Lie close in the church and in the churchyard.
> In every grave make room, make room!

A heavy monument, or better still a chantry chapel, conferred the additional advantage of protecting the occupant against disturbance.

It was inevitable that churches would encroach on their cemeteries in the course of enlargement. When embarrassingly large numbers of skeletons were displaced by excavations for new foundations the skulls and long-bones were often collected up and dumped into charnel pits or stacked in bone houses. Charnel houses were sometimes specially constructed, as at Beverley, Malmesbury, Norwich and Worcester, but quite often some existing area within the building was taken over for the purpose of storing disturbed bones. When John Aubrey visited Hereford Cathedral in 1650 he found the undercroft below the thirteenth-century Lady Chapel to be 'the greatest charnel house for bones that ever I saw in England'. Medieval builders usually had scant respect for graves which lay in the path of their work, but there were occasions when churchyards were deliberately buried rather than destroyed before the start of new operations. At York in the eleventh century, for example, the ground surface of part of a pre-Conquest cemetery was deliberately covered over as a preliminary to the construction of the transept of the Norman cathedral. In consequence a remarkable series of Anglo-Scandinavian graveyard monuments was preserved intact and *in situ* beneath the Minster (Hope-Taylor 1971).

Cults

Relics were avidly collected by monasteries and cathedrals throughout the Middle Ages. In the eleventh century rival parties of monks fought with one another for the possession of relics in disputed ownership. Accounts of elaborately-organized body-snatching expeditions are not uncommon in monastic chronicles. From the twelfth century onwards supply increased to meet demand, and as pilgrimages through Europe and into the Middle East became more frequent, so the cross fragments, phials of blood, bones, hair, teeth and other disgusting items multiplied at the hands of returning travellers. In the fourteenth and fifteenth centuries anomalies were being noted by discriminating travellers, however, and Geoffrey Chaucer was under no illusions when he wrote of the Pardoner:

> In his mail he had a pilwebere
> Which as he saide was oure Lady's veil;
> He said he had a gobbet of the sail
> Thatte St Peter had whan that he went
> Upon the sea, till Jesu Christ him hent.
> He had a cross of laton full of stones;
> And in a glass he hadde pigges bones.

The collection of relics described by John Ap Rice at Bury in 1535 was probably typical of many:

> Amongst the reliques we found moche vanitie and superstition, as the coles that Saint Laurence was tosted withall, the paring of S. Edmunds naylles, S. Thomas of Canterbury pennekny and his bootes, and divers skulles for the hedache; peces of the holy crosse able to make a hole crosse of; other reliques for rayne and certain other superstitiouse usages, for avoyding of wedes growing in corne, with suche other.
>
> (Wright 1843, 85)

Relic cults operated on several levels. First, there was (and is) the belief that saints are close to God and so may intercede on behalf of those who honour them. Secondly, the corporeal remains of saints, and objects associated with them, were thought to be sources of spiritual energy which could work miracles of healing upon those who managed to touch or approach them. Famous relics did not merely heal. They might also exercise political or military influence. According to the *Historia de Sancto Cuthberto* (Arnold 1882) Guthfrith, a ninth-century Danish King of Northumbria, was helped to the throne by the intervention of the saint (d. 687). Guthfrith, unlike some of his compatriots, was a Christian. He died in 895 and was buried in the cathedral at York (Harrison 1960, 238). His connection with St Cuthbert's clergy is of interest, for as Professor Sawyer has pointed out:

> Religious communities were granted estates and privileges for spiritual reasons; in return their members were expected to intercede on behalf of benefactors. The effectiveness of such intercessions was greatly increased by the power of those saints whose remains were the main treasure and *raison d'être* of such communities . . .
>
> (Sawyer 1978a)

In England and Wales before the Conquest, and for some time afterwards, the most popular cults centred on individuals who had played key parts in British ecclesiastical history. A gazetteer of relics and their locations known as the *List of the Saints' Resting Places* (Birch 1892, 87–94) sheds light on Anglo-Saxon preferences. The *List* as we now have it was probably compiled during the first half of the eleventh century, but the author had access to a great deal of earlier material and incorporated some information which reflected the distribution of relics in the ninth century. It is best regarded as a Northumbrian composition, with Midland addenda and some Southern rewriting. Eighty-six saints and martyrs were mentioned by name, shared among fifty-four religious establishments. SS Alban and Columba were listed first. Then came the Northumbrian Saints: St Cuthbert (at Uban ford: i.e. Norham, one of the ninth-century staging points between the abandoned monastery at Lindisfarne and Chester-le-Street); St Oswald; St John of Beverley (Beverley); St Egbert, St Wilfrid and St Wihtburh, all at Ripon. St Oswald was evidently in pieces since although his head was with St Cuthbert at Norham, one of his arms was at Bamburgh and the rest of his body was at the priory with a western apse which had been founded in his honour at Gloucester in 909. Such fragmentation was common and often led to fraud. The *List* is of added interest for the confirmation it provides of the speed with which the cult of St Dunstan had developed at Canterbury. Dunstan (d. 988) was the only saint mentioned by name at Christ Church, although it was noted that there were 'many other saints with him' (Birch 1892, 92).

The post-Conquest era supplied such important bishop-saints as St Hugh of Avalon (Lincoln), St Thomas Cantilupe (Hereford) and of course St Thomas Becket (Canterbury). In about 1500 a foreign visitor reported that:

> . . . the magnificence of the tomb of St Thomas the Martyr, Archbishop of Canterbury, is that which surpasses all belief. This, notwithstanding its great size, is entirely covered with gold; but the gold is scarcely visible from the variety of precious stones with which it is studded . . . everything is left far behind by a ruby, not larger than a man's thumbnail, which is set to the right of the altar. The church is rather dark, and particularly so where the shrine is placed, and when we went to see it the sun was nearly gone down, and the weather was cloudy; yet I saw that ruby as well as if I had it in my hand . . .
>
> (Sneyd 1847, 30–1)

Forty-three years later the shrine was seized and its constituent materials confiscated. The ruby 'was caused by King Henry VIII . . . to be set in a ring, which he wore upon his thumb' (Sneyd 1847, 84).

York, by contrast, never became the centre for a really popular cult. Early in the twelfth century Archbishop Thomas II (1108–14) toyed with a plan for seizing the remains of St Eata from Hexham, but he decided against it when the saint appeared in person and warned him off in a dream. Later in the century York did acquire the body of William Fitzherbert, an archbishop who died in suspicious circumstances in 1154. William was canonized in 1227, but despite strenuous efforts to advertise the shrine his cult never seems to have generated much enthusiasm (Wilson 1977, 9). Canonization was not always essential; the wretched Edward II, murdered in 1327, was acquired by the Abbot of Gloucester and made a fortune for the abbey. The ingredients of success with relics were miracles beside the shrine and shrewd promotion. Confessors, virgins, martyrs and bodies which failed to decompose or secreted fragrant liquid were held in particular esteem.

Small items were normally kept in special containers known as reliquaries which were placed on or in altars. Complete saints presented a greater challenge. At first it was customary to bury the bodies of saints and martyrs under altars, but very soon an alternative habit developed of bringing the remains of important individuals to the surface. St Martin (d. 397), for example, was transferred from his grave to a new shrine at pavement level in the church at Tours during the fifth century. Bede relates how in 698 the body of St Cuthbert (d. 687) was lifted into a receptacle beside the high altar at Lindisfarne. In the ninth-century poem *De Abbatibus* there is an account of the elevation of the body of an Irish priest named Ultan, who in life had enjoyed a reputation as one who 'could ornament books with fair marking' (Campbell 1967, 21, lines 227–30). Excavations in York Minster in 1968 uncovered the coffin in which St William was buried in 1154: this was a reused Roman sarcophagus which had been let into the floor of the nave, its upper part projecting above the pavement.

Important relics could influence the shape of the churches in which they were kept. Security and accessibility were twin needs which had to be reconciled, particularly if a cult became popular. In Anglo-Saxon churches crypts were sometimes used

93 Hexham: crypt, c. 675

to house and display relics. A crypt had advantages: it was a strong room which offered a measure of protection to the relics it contained; relics could be located below the sanctuary and hence in close proximity to the main altar(s); and there was a psychological benefit in displaying relics in intimate, even claustrophobic surroundings. The general principles of the design of early crypts have been discussed in detail by Taylor (1968, 17–52). Systems of narrow, disorientating corridors were used at Hexham and Ripon (both of the seventh century). At Brixworth and Wing ring crypts have survived, and another has been excavated at Cirencester. In a ring crypt 'the pilgrims were usually led right round the relic chamber in a ring shaped corridor which they entered at one side of the church and left at the other. From a position half way round the corridor they obtained a view of the relics by looking back along the axis of the church through a chamber of passage called a *confessio* to the relic which lay beyond' (Taylor 1968, 18). Eadmer stated that there was a crypt with a *confessio* beneath the sanctuary in the pre-Conquest cathedral at Canterbury, although the exact layout of this chamber and the extent of Eadmer's objectivity are matters of dispute (Gem 1970; Gilbert 1970). In a third type of arrangement the crypt consisted of a chamber projecting beyond the east end of the church. Crypts of this kind are numerous in Germany, where they are known as *aussenkrypta*, and examples have recently been excavated in England at Winchester and, apparently, Exeter.

Crypts continued to function as display areas for relics in some Anglo-Norman churches, but whereas Anglo-Saxon crypts tended to be very specialized, those of the Anglo-Norman period were more versatile. The crypts at Canterbury, Winchester, Gloucester and Worcester amount to complete under-churches, an idea which was taken to its ultimate conclusion at Christchurch Cathedral, Dublin. These spacious crypts provided room for extra altars, chapels and congregational functions. Several are on record as having been used for chapter meetings. Three crypts were embodied in the twelfth-century church at Christchurch: one beneath the eastern limb and one apiece under the arms of the transept. The lateral crypts are probably best regarded as basement chapels, mirroring the first-floor chapels above. At Lastingham the eleventh-century crypt below the presbytery seems to have been designed to maximize falling ground at the east of the church.

The practice of using a crypt to house corporeal relics went back to the Gregorian remodelling of Old St Peter's *c*. 600 (Toynbee and Perkins 1956) and ultimately, via such early crypt schemes as that at S. Apollinare, Ravenna, to the veneration of martyr graves in the catacombs of Rome. But despite this tradition the crypt was never regarded as a compulsory feature in Anglo-Saxon churches. In England the custom of exhibiting relics in crypts died out almost entirely during the twelfth and thirteenth centuries. Instead relics were transferred to a position which many had already occupied for several centuries: a shrine behind the high altar. Some cults centred on a shrine in a nave (as at York) or transept (as at Hereford), but the eastern arm was the usual site. The change was prompted in part by a desire to display relics in a more sumptuous shrine and spacious surroundings, but also to cater for swelling numbers of pilgrims. If a church was extended eastwards an entire bay could be set aside for the feretory, east of the sanctuary, without disturbing the high altar. This disposition permitted one-way circulation for pilgrims around the choir, brought relics into close proximity to the high altar, and made room for a larger shrine. The reredos acted as a partition between presbytery and feretory. In some churches, such as York, the sense of enclosure was heightened further by the provision of additional screens. Just as the body of the saint was a temple occupied by the Holy Spirit, so the church provided an inner chamber wherein the saint could dwell (Brooke 1977).

Very few medieval shrines have survived, and only that of St Edward the Confessor at Westminster preserved the characteristic ensemble of base, canopy and associated altar. However, the fourteenth-century shrine of St Werburgh at Chester was rebuilt in the nineteenth century and is still to be seen, while fragments of others survive at Dorchester (recently reassembled), Ely, Hereford, Oxford, St Albans and Salisbury (Coldstream 1976).

At the Reformation shrines were systematically destroyed or dismantled, cult objects were confiscated, and the precious metals and gems of reliquaries were absorbed without effort by the Exchequer. Bishop Barlow, on tour in West Wales in 1528, wrote to Thomas Cromwell:

> ... I admonished the canons of Sainte Davids according to the kynges injunctions in no wyse to set forth fayned reliques for to allure people to supersticion, nether to advance the vayne observacion of unnecessary holy dayes abrogated by the kynges supreme authoritye, on sainte Davids daye the people wilfully solemnysinge the feest, certean reliques were set forth which I caused to be sequestered and taken awaye, detayninge them in my custody untill I maye be advertised of your lordships pleasour. The parcels of the reliques are these: two heedes of sylver plate enclosinge two rotten skulles studded with putrified clowtes; Item, two arme bones, and a worme eaten boke covered with sylver plate.
>
> (Wright 1843, 184)

Not infrequently these visits by Cromwell's agents disclosed more than relics. When John Bartelot went to the establishment of the Crutched Friars, London, in 1525, he found the Prior 'at that tyme beyng in bedde with his hoore, both nakyd, about xj. of the clok in the for none, upon a Fryday', while Richard Southwell's search of Walsingham Abbey in 1536 revealed a 'secrete prevye place' which contained 'instrewments, pottes, belowes, flyes . . . of strange colers . . . poysies, and other thinges' which were implements of alchemy (Wright 1843, 60; 138).

Surfaces and sounds

A great church was a liturgical theatre, a place of assembly, and it was often the centre of a cult. It was also meant to teach. Pope Gregory's suggestion that wall paintings should be regarded as 'books of the people' was heeded, and just as space within the building was allocated for liturgical purposes, so the surfaces of walls, spandrels, vaults, splays and piers were used as fields for didactic illustrations. It is not always appreciated that great churches were commonly plastered and decorated both inside and out; nor is it easy to summon up the lustre of a medieval church interior in the mind's eye. The imagination is faced with a double difficulty in this: not only does it have to reinstate vanished paintings on large expanses of blank masonry, but it also has to contend with the fact that most of the greater churches have been robbed of their medieval window glass. We have been deprived of the light by which the paintings were seen. Outside, buildings with walls of rubble construction (and sometimes of ashlar) were usually given an external coat of plaster or

94 *York Minster: plaster painted in imitation of masonry at exterior of north transept,* c. *1095*

95 *Boxgrove: choir vault,* c. *1210; painted decoration,* c. *1550*

96 *Boxgrove: detail of painted vault*

Hexham: north transept, first half of thirteenth century

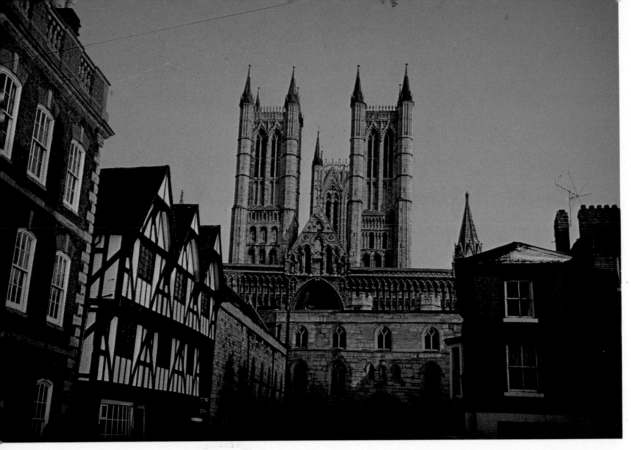

Lincoln: west front

Tewkesbury, from the south-east

Above Mosaic of Anglo-Saxon
window-glass recovered by
excavation of a single building at
the monastery of Jarrow

Above right
Durham: detail of the
Anglo-Saxon stole from St
Cuthbert's coffin

Right
Malmesbury: six seated apostles
and angel within lunette on east
wall of south porch, *c*. 1160–70

Dorchester: painted
reredos with
Crucifixion, St Mary
and St John.
Fourteenth century

Pershore, from the
south-west

limewash. This acted both as a protective envelope and as a surface upon which counterfeit masonry joints could be painted in order to simulate the neat appearance of regular walling.

Internal walls were either plastered or covered with limewash or size. The pigments – such as cinoper (iron oxide), charcoal, malachite, cinnabar, white lead – were mixed with limewater or skim milk and applied with brushes of hog or squirrel hair (Caiger-Smith 1962, 118–28; Thompson 1936). The techniques of painting on a dry wall (as against the method of fresco, in which the paint was applied while the plaster was still wet) were described by 'Theophilus' in his *De Diversis Artibus*, probably composed in the first half of the twelfth century:

> When figures or representations of other things are portrayed on a dry wall, first of all sprinkle it with water and continue until it is completely wet. All colours which are to be used on it are mixed with lime and applied to this wet surface so that, as they dry with the wall, they adhere to it. As a ground, under azure blue and viridian, a colour known as dark grey is laid, mixed of black and chalk-white. On this colour when it is dry, a thin glaze of azure blue, mixed with the yolk of an egg which has been diluted with a lot of water, is spread, and on top of this again a thicker glaze to enhance its beauty.
>
> (Dodwell 1961, 13)

Anglo-Norman churches, with their burly piers, small windows and large areas of plain wall-surface offered ample scope for the artist to develop iconographic programmes which were put before him by the religious. In a church which was conceived and built to a single design, as many of the Anglo-Norman churches were, it was possible to organize the paintings as aspects of the structure, often in tiers or formal sequences.

During the thirteenth and fourteenth centuries the role of the painter changed. Windows invaded walls, while the increasing complexity of piers, mouldings and vaults and the growing importance of architectural sculpture set further limitations. Instead of being called upon to design integrated schemes of illustration, the artist was now confined to smaller zones: spandrels, vault cells, window splays. Unity and harmony of design, previously matters with which the painter had been very much concerned, were now firmly within the province of the mason and his new associate, the glazier.

By far the largest number of extant English wall paintings are to be seen in parish churches and it is uncertain to what extent the themes they portray would have been characteristic of the murals which existed in abbeys and cathedrals. Certainly most parish churches were unable to afford the more expensive pigments and hence were restricted to a basic range of colours and effects. Few parishes would have been able to indulge in such fancies as the reflecting stars, executed in talc and tin-leaf, on the vault of the Chapel of Our Lady Undercroft at Canterbury (Tristram 1955, 148–9). Many of the themes were recurrent: the Nativity and Passion of Christ, the Wheel of Life (Leominster) and of Fortune (Rochester), the Weighing of Souls, the Living and the Dead, episodes from saints' lives (Ely; St Anselm's Chapel, Canterbury;

Durham Galilee), the Apocalypse (Westminster Abbey), Christ in Majesty (St Gabriel's Chapel, Canterbury; Winchester), the Trinity (Tewkesbury), the Deadly Sins (Arundel), the Virgin and Child (Chichester), confrontations with devils (Melbourne). What seems clear is that medieval wall paintings were not thought of as superficial decoration, like religious wall-paper, but as integral aspects of the

97 St Albans: crucifixion painted on west face of nave pier, c. 1275 (cf. Pl. 36)

function and appearance of the church; instructive, warning, exhortative, numinous and, yes, entertaining. Paintings of the Romanesque period tend to be formal and hieratic; those of the Gothic era more naturalistic, with a greater feeling for line. At St Albans there is a series of five crucifixion scenes on the piers of the nave. These murals occur on the western faces of the piers, and probably served originally as back-drops for nave altars. Painted between *c*. 1215 and 1275 the scenes progress from a stylized towards a realistic portrayal of Christ's agony (Roberts 1971).

Use of colour was not restricted to set-piece illustrations. Arches, window-heads and arcades were frequently picked out with geometrical motifs, while spare surfaces were painted in imitation of masonry or stencilled with repeating patterns. The custom of lining-out was pure convention. At York, for instance, artificial joints are to be seen running right over a capital at the former entrance to the southern apse of the eleventh-century transept in total disregard of the capital's form and purpose. Tombs were regularly painted and gilt, as were screens, thrones and shrines. External sculpture, too, was visited by the brush: at Exeter and Wells it has been shown that the carved figures on the west fronts were vividly coloured.

Music played an important part in medieval liturgy. The changing idioms of medieval performance are now matters for academic discussion and experimental recreation, but there are tangible reminders of medieval musicianship both on and under the surfaces of our great churches. Pottery acoustic jars have been found in the choir at Fountains Abbey, and resonance-channels have been uncovered by excavation in the fourteenth-century church of the Whitefriars at Coventry (*Medieval Archaeology* 1962–3, 317). These devices seem to have been intended to enhance the timbre of vocal music through sympathetic resonance at certain frequencies. The principle was recounted by Vitruvius, and derived ultimately from the Greeks, who used resonance-amplifiers in their theatres. Nothing definite is known about medieval ideas on acoustics, and the purpose of acoustic jars in churches is not explained. However, the experience of modern singers shows that plainchant, sung unaccompanied in a building with a swampy acoustic, tends to drop in pitch during performance. The provision of an instrumental note at the beginning of each section does not assist in maintaining pitch once singing has begun, whereas a resonator could provide a permanent pitch 'datum' for the singers which would always keep them in tune. It must be admitted, however, that this explanation could hardly be extended to cover the acoustic pots which are encountered from time to time in the walls of parish churches and the references to them which occur in the accounts of their churchwardens.

The Greeks and Romans were also organ builders. The knowledge that they accumulated seems to have been lost in the West in the fifth century, but it was recovered, like so much else, from Arabic sources (Sumner 1952). The Arabs in particular seem to have been responsible for developing the pneumatic organ, which came to supersede the less manageable instruments of the hydraulic type. (A hydraulus is depicted in the ninth-century Utrecht Psalter.) Organs must have been in use in some Anglo-Saxon churches by the end of the seventh century, since Aldhelm, who died in 709, mentioned decorative schemes on organ cases. Tenth-century churchmen seem to have taken a keen interest in organs. Dunstan, Archbishop of Canterbury (960–88) is known to have been an active musician and organ-builder. We have a suspiciously rhetorical account of an instrument which was built by Elphege, Bishop of Winchester (935–51). Elphege commissioned an organ for the Old Minster which possessed forty notes and sliders, each with ten pipes. It was said that the instrument required three musicians to play it and no less

than seventy men to operate the blowers. Now that the layout of the Old Minster has been recovered by excavation one wonders where Elphege's monster was located.

The organ seems to have been used in the Mass from at least as early as the twelfth century. By the fourteenth century there were three varieties of instrument in regular use: large, fixed organs, which often occupied tribunes or pulpita (at Crowland there was a 'great organ' over the entrance in the time of Abbot Lytlyngton, 1437–69); smaller 'positive' organs, also stationary but sometimes placed adjacent to the main instrument to allow for dynamic contrasts and to accompany solo singers; and the tiny 'portative' organs which could be moved from one part of the church to another or carried in procession. Keyboards do not seem to have been used much before the end of the thirteenth century; prior to this pitches were selected by operating sliders. The first reed stops were introduced about a century later (Sumner 1952).

Selections of medieval instruments are often depicted in churches: in stained glass, as at Great Malvern (clarion, dulcimer, lute, harp, portative organ, tabor, shawm), and in masonry, as in the twelfth-century crypt at Canterbury, and along the wall of the north nave aisle at Beverley. Whether these 'secular' instruments were ever used in connection with sacred music before the Reformation is extremely doubtful, but it is worth remembering that between the fourteenth and seventeenth centuries England nourished a musical tradition which was second to none, producing such organist-composers as John Dunstable (d. 1455); Henry Abyngdon (c. 1420–97), for a time Precentor at Wells; Robert Fayrfax (d. 1521), probably organist at St Albans; John Taverner (c. 1495–1545), born in Boston, Lincolnshire, and subsequently Master of the Children at Wolsey's Cardinal College (later Christ Church), Oxford;

171

98 (left) *Great Malvern: detail of window in north transept; angel playing dulcimer*
99 (above) *Canterbury: capital in crypt, c. 1120*

100–101 Beverley: medieval instruments

Christopher Tye (*c*. 1497–1573), organist at Ely; and William Byrd (*c*. 1542–1623), who was reared in Lincoln and spent part of his career as organist at the cathedral. First-hand information about these men, their colleagues and their instruments is scarce. The professional musician was on a par with other craftsmen. He was looked upon as an *artifex* – 'maker' – and although his work might be admired it was treated very much as a commodity. The idea of the artist as a man apart, the heroic individual, belongs to the nineteenth century. Accordingly biographical information is often sparse, and we know about as little of such composers as Dunstable and Taverner as we do of master-masons of the calibre of Ivo de Raghton and Thomas Witney. But we hear occasional snatches, as in this account which referred to Dr Tye as

> . . . a peevish and humoursome man, especially in his latter dayes, and sometimes playing on ye Organ in ye chap. of qu. Elizab. wh. contained much musick, but little delight to the ear, she would send ye verger to tell him yt played out of Tune, whereupon he sent word yt her ears were out of Tune.
>
> (MS of Anthony Wood, cited in Scholes 1956, 1062)

Liturgical chant had its origins in the worship of Judaism. Chant was an integral part of liturgy, and from the earliest days of the Anglo-Saxon Church the idea prevailed of a body of singers, *schola cantorum*, combined with the clergy. So close was this association that the term 'choir' came to denote not only the singers but also that part of the church in which they were located.

172

Until the tenth century liturgical music was monodic, but thereafter experiments in harmony began, first by duplicating the chant at a fifth or fourth below the principal line (*organum*), and later, following experiments in methods of notation by men such as Guido d'Arezzo (*c*. 995–1050) and Franco of Cologne, through increasingly ambitious polyphonic compositions. The essence of plainchant has been summed up by Professor Mellers:

> The monks' intention, in singing their chant, must have been very close to the intention of the Indian vina player: by dedication to the Word – his Christianized raga – the plainchanter aimed to liberate the spirit, allowing the melodies to flow, unaccompanied, mainly by step and by pentatonic minor thirds, overriding metrical time and the pull of harmonic tension. He sought freedom from the self through the revelation of the divine; and the nasal quality of his vocal production, reinforced by the church's vaulted echoes, would have had unmistakable Eastern affiliations.
>
> (Mellers 1968, 9–10)

Mellers continues:

> There is a close analogy between the structure of a Machaut motet and that of a Gothic cathedral. The main structure of the cathedral is a feat of mathematical engineering, to which the individual craftsmen add their contribution. Similarly, the medieval motet is built on the rock of the plainsong cantus firmus, the other parts being added separately, each as an independent entity, beautiful in itself, if more beautiful in relationship to the whole . . .
>
> (Mellers 1968, 15–16)

Functions secular and spiritual

Medieval churches were put to many secular and non-liturgical uses. These included defence, schools, fairs, trading, law-courts, political council meetings, sanctuary, storage. However, with the exceptions of justice and education there is little evidence to show that great churches were regularly designed to accommodate these functions. On the contrary, bishops sometimes went out of their way to discourage them. During the 1230s Robert Grosseteste, Bishop of Lincoln (1235–53), wrote several letters to diocesan and cathedral clergy in which he deplored the fact that parish churches and churchyards were being used as places for games and commerce. On another occasion he frowned upon the use of the cathedral for the New Year Feast of Fools (Luard 1861, 71, 74, 118, 161). Schools and judicial proceedings were frequently housed in porches or annexes, as in the case of the lateral towers at pre-Conquest Canterbury, described by Eadmer, or the porch-school at Howden. A porch, even more than a nave, was situated on the frontier between the world of Man and the domain of God: a circumstance which would not have been lost on those who used porches for concluding solemn agreements, transactions and weddings.

Symbolism pervaded all facets of church design: orientation, plan, elevation, proportion, iconography, wall painting, lighting, floor-levels. Indeed, it has been claimed that 'To those who designed the cathedrals, as to their contemporaries who worshipped in them, this symbolic aspect or function of sacred architecture over-shadowed all others' (Simson 1956, xvii).

Symbolism operated at several levels. First, and most obvious, was the cruciform plan and aspiring elevation. Secondly, there is the matter of investment in the fabric. This would have been even more striking before the Reformation than it is now, partly on account of the colour, furnishings, silks, precious metals, gemstones and glass with which the churches were enriched, and partly because of the much sharper contrast which then existed between the height and bulk of a great church and the scale of other buildings in its vicinity. Lincoln Cathedral, for example, already dominant upon its hill, possessed a spire which was 524 feet high. It could be seen from the Wash. The spire of Old St Paul's rose *c.* 520 feet, and those at Salisbury and Norwich stand to 404 feet and 320 feet respectively. We have seen that great churches were rarely built out of routine income. Strenuous efforts had to be made to raise funds for their construction. Then, as now, there were complaints about extravagance and useless ostentation, first from the Cistercians and later from the

102 Wells: west front, c. 1230–60

friars. Indeed, the whole debate is prefigured in the Gospels: one recalls the accusation of waste levelled by the disciples at the woman who brought the 'alabaster box of spikenard very precious' in order to anoint Christ on the eve of his arrest. Cathedrals and abbeys represented all that could be provided in terms of skill and technical excellence. They were the outcome of a quest for the superlative and celebrations of God-given talent and ability.

Thirdly, there is the suggestion that symbolism is latent in the dimensions and proportions of medieval churches. This has been touched upon in the preceding chapter, but it is perhaps worth repeating the opinion that symbolism in the dimensioning of churches is best viewed as a function of applied science, not as a manifestation of metaphysical scheming on the part of master-masons. This is not to deny that there could be *appreciation* of the buildings in metaphysical terms; ratios and proportions which enjoyed great prestige formed part of the basis of the medieval master-builder's design technique and hence were naturally and inevitably inherent in the buildings he produced. Nor is it necessary to suppose that projects never occurred in which mathematical invention exceeded the needs of technical convenience. A persuasive case has been made for the deliberate implication of symbolic dimensions in the late eleventh-century church at Cluny, a building of which a chronicler noted that 'many things in it are discerned to be wrought in a mystic sense' (Conant 1963, 11). For Chartres Mr John James has shown how two-dimensional systems, based on the Roman foot of 296 mm and the *Ped Manualis* of 354 mm, respectively, were affiliated in the design of the great western rose window. In part of his detailed analysis of these superimposed geometries Mr James has observed:

> . . . the two foot units which flow over one another as they separately determine their own parts of the rose, are summarized at the outside where the four-leaf lights use the Roman foot and the eight-leaf lights use the Ped Manualis. Without continuing to belabour each detail, every minor element and every moulding reflects one or other of the basic measures. In careful geometry everything is made a part of everything else; nothing stands alone. Thus it was with God's Universe, thus it should be in man's efforts in praise of Him.

> (James 1973, 9)

If geometry was implicit in a building then iconographical programmes were explicit, the two addressed, perhaps, to God and Man respectively. Theological themes could be displayed and interrelated in windows, on walls and with sculpture. Sculpture did not simply serve to embellish a church; it formed an important part of the apparatus of Scriptural exegesis, as in the frieze which runs across the western facade at Lincoln (Zarnecki 1970), or at Wells where William Worcestre noted in 1480 that the tiers of sculpture on the west front represented the Old and the New Law (Harvey 1969, 288–91).

Protestant iconoclasm in the sixteenth and seventeenth centuries reduced the greater part of this legacy of medieval art to a collection of headless saints and vacant image-housings. Erosion and the restorer's zeal have claimed much of what survived. Today it is natural to regret the excesses of those who flung stones through medieval windows, hacked off the limbs of statues, stripped or obliterated wall paintings and dumped carved woodwork on bonfires. But it is not difficult to understand them. Ours is a view comparable to that of an antique-shop owner visited by vandals, whereas the action of the iconoclasts, aimed as they were at an elaborate tissue of medieval superstition and religious mythology, were at least logical. As Paul Tillich has observed: 'Holiness provokes idolatry'.

It is clear from medieval commentaries that large churches could themselves be invested with symbolic programmes. In his *De gemma animae*, written perhaps in the 1120s, Honorius of Autun passed in review over the different parts of a church – orientation, plan, foundations, crypts, pavement, tiles, windows, roof– and assigned a symbolic significance to each (Mortet 1929, 14–19). Something along the same lines was attempted about a century later in England; again, the church fabric was a source of inspiration to the poet, although in this case it would be a mistake, I suggest, to regard the passage as evidence of any kind of formal symbolic programme inherent in the builders' designs. Writing of the new cathedral then taking shape at Lincoln *c*. 1225 the author of the *Metrical Life of St Hugh* discussed the significance of the various elements and materials of the building. A brief extract will serve:

> The foundation is the body, the wall the man, the roof the spirit; a threefold division of the church. The body belongs to the earth, man to the clouds, the spirit to the stars.
>
> (Dimock 1860, 32–7; trans. Harvey 1972, 236–9)

Such imagery arises from a personal response.

103 Selby: detail of wall arcade in north aisle of presbytery

7

The Building Church

Only the hand that erases can write the true thing.
Meister Eckhart

OOKING ACROSS THE four-and-a-half centuries from the Norman invasion to
the Dissolution it is clear that certain periods were characterized by a greater
architectural energy than others. Something of this ebb and flow is evident
from studies which evaluate the achievements of medieval patrons and artists in
stylistic or artistic terms. Surprisingly, however, there have been few attempts to
give quantitative dimensions to medieval churchbuilding. In what numbers were
great churches being built or rebuilt at different times? When were the periods of
greatest and least activity? What were the factors which could stimulate or retard
architectural activity? Today the building industry is regarded as a sensitive indi-
cator of the state of the national economy; can the same be said of the Middle Ages?
These are the issues which form the theme of this chapter.

It must be said at once that the materials for the survey are incomplete, and until
the advent of the Normans they are altogether inadequate. Ghosts of trends are
perceptible before the Conquest – a revival of architecture in the second half of the
tenth century, perhaps a period of 'comparative stagnation' in the first half of the
eleventh (Gem 1975) – but in general references to churchbuilding in Anglo-Saxon
documents are so sporadic as to be worthless for purposes of systematic analysis.
Until more Anglo-Saxon cathedral and monastic churches have been investigated
by modern archaeological methods, and the results published, the pattern of pre-
Conquest churchbuilding must remain obscure.

After the Conquest much more evidence becomes available, but not all important
enterprises are now either witnessed in the standing fabric or mentioned in written
sources. This is particularly true of some churches which were extensively rebuilt
after *c*. 1250. Little is known about the cathedral at Lichfield before the thirteenth
century, for example. The extent of the Norman contribution at Beverley has never
been ascertained. What was the significance of the Lady Chapel begun at Westminster *c*. 1220 in relation to the architectural history of the abbey? (Brown *et al*. 1963,
132). The 'right goodly new church' which was started at Bath in 1501 led to the
virtual obliteration of the building it replaced.

The historical documentation of medieval monastic houses is extensive. Chronicles, charters, registers, letter-books, account rolls, inventories, minutes of visitations and the records of central government may all inform about various aspects of building operations. It remains the case, however, that the extant records of very few English and Welsh monasteries have been subjected to full scrutiny. Most obedientiary rolls remain unpublished, for example, and it has been suggested that reliance upon selective printed extracts has sometimes led to spurious precision in the dating of surviving monastic buildings (Dobson 1976, 12). Moreover, the material which occurs in greatest abundance derives in the main from a small and in certain respects unrepresentative group of houses, notably the eight monastic cathedrals. The *Valor Ecclesiasticus* of 1535 records that some eighty per cent of religious houses were then valued at less than £300. The physical remains of these smaller establishments have mostly vanished, and only a handful have left their archives by way of compensation.

While the losses are irredeemable it should nevertheless be possible to take a sample of those buildings which remain, and by comparing their individual developments to produce figures for building activity which are illustrative of the mass. The seventy-five churches listed in the Gazetteer form a convenient if rather arbitrary group for a preliminary assessment of this kind. Inevitably there are a number of important absentees, now either in ruins (such as Bury St Edmunds, St Augustine's Canterbury, Glastonbury) or flattened (Evesham, Winchcombe). On the other hand the sample contains all the medieval cathedrals apart from St Mary's, Coventry, together with a cross-section of Benedictine, Augustinian and collegiate establishments. (Particulars of the building histories of ten Cistercian churches have been included in order to correct the bias towards houses of black monks and canons.)

It is necessary first of all to define what is meant by 'building activity'. For the purposes of this survey only major campaigns of building (such as towers, naves, transepts, eastern limbs) have been counted. Smaller works like chantries, windows and shrines have been ignored, even where they represent great outlay. Conventual buildings, with the exception of chapter-houses, have also been excluded. Thus simplified, the figures of campaigns of building have been graphed. On Fig. 7 Graph I records the amount of *new work* which was started at the eighty-five churches under consideration in each decade from 1070 to 1530; Graph II shows totals of projects which were *in progress* during the same period at a select group of forty of the most

104 Canterbury

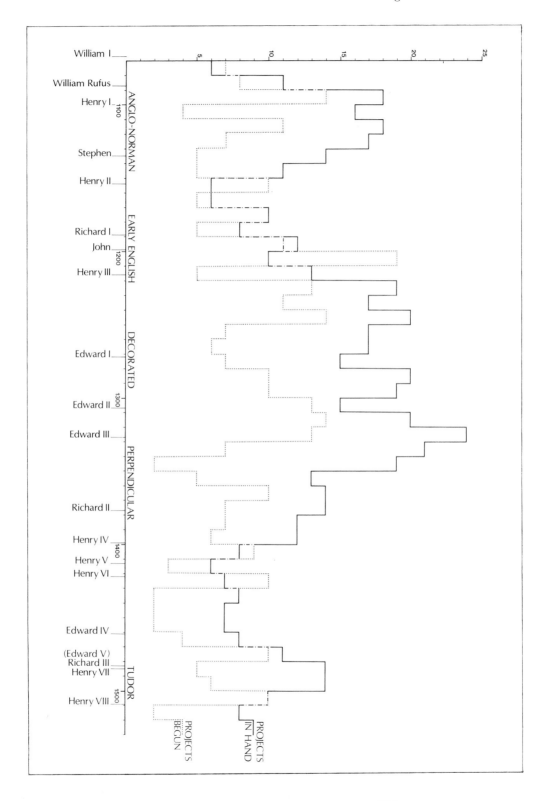

Fig. 7 Graph I (dotted line) represents numbers of major building projects begun *at cathedrals and abbeys, by decade (sample: 85 buildings). Graph II (solid line) represents numbers of major building campaigns* in progress *in each decade (sample: 40 buildings)*

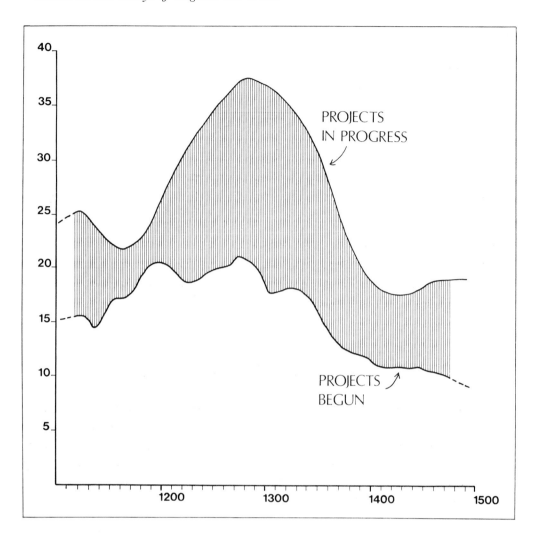

Fig. 8 Graph III (lower curve) represents the average trend of major building projects begun *at cathedrals and abbeys, by decade (sample: 85 buildings). Graph IV (upper curve) represents the average trend of major building campaigns* in progress *in each decade (sample: 40 buildings)*

important and well-preserved churches. On Fig. 8 Graphs III and IV show the *average trends* of Graphs I and II, respectively. Although the information on which the graphs are based is incomplete it is believed that they give a fair indication of the relative numbers of campaigns involved.

Three points deserve mention in connection with the interpretation of the graphs. First, the line graphs should not be viewed as a direct expression of levels of investment. No attempt has been made to quantify expenditure on each scheme. Information about monastic outlay on construction work is available in a number of cases (e.g. for Ely, Exeter, Westminster and Winchester) but these sources are generally intermittent and seldom provide enough data for a continuous review of spending over a long period. Moreover, such factors as the proximity and ownership of quarries, access to transport facilities or timely donations of building materials are not always susceptible to direct economic measurement. Secondly, concealed within the figures for Graph II (on Fig. 7) are certain schemes which for one reason or another took an excessively long time to complete. The nave of Westminster Abbey and various works at Chester are cases in point. To some extent, therefore, this graph is paradoxical, since it reflects a combination of positive and negative factors. Thirdly, it is likely that the totals of new schemes and works in progress during the twelfth century and the first half of the thirteenth are understated. The reason for this has already been mentioned, namely the tendency for each new campaign to subtract from or cloak an earlier fabric. These qualifications aside, it is considered that the figures provide a useful frame within which to study the fluctuations of ecclesiastical building in the Middle Ages, and to discuss some of the stimuli which could have been involved.

Patterns

Between 1070 and 1530 there were approximately 360 major campaigns of construction at the eighty-five churches under review. This averages out at *c*. 4.2 campaigns per church, although some buildings, like Abbey Dore and Brinkburn, were scarcely altered after the thirteenth century, while for much of the time the appearance of others, such as Chester and York, was in a permanent state of flux. The operations were far from uniform in distribution, but a distinct pattern does emerge when they are all viewed in perspective (Graphs III and IV on Fig. 8). This pattern may be described as consisting of three phases of growth, each greater than the last, followed by a long, subdued coda.

Most of the leading technical and artistic innovations of English medieval church architecture were made within the period spanned by the phases of growth: to be precise, between *c*. 1090–1100, when the rib-vault was invented at Durham, and *c*. 1300, when the lierne vault appeared at Bristol and Pershore. In the structural field only the fan vault and some developments in tower design were to follow, while many of the characteristic motifs of the Perpendicular style were in view before the end of the reign of Edward I (Harvey 1961, 152). By this time all else in matters of plan, masoncraft, design technique and statical knowledge had been settled. Each of the three phases of growth will now be considered in turn.

The Norman revolution

The Norman reorganization of the English Church late in the eleventh century was accompanied by an outburst of churchbuilding of extraordinary intensity and

105 Westminster: nave, c. 1259–69, 1376–1498

106 Durham: nave, c. 1100–30

vigour. Between 1070 and 1100 about thirty cathedrals and important monastic churches were begun in England. Over half of them were started in the decade 1090–1100, and a number were either complete (e.g. Lincoln, York, Canterbury) or sufficiently advanced for use (e.g. Winchester, Durham, Ely, St Albans) by the first years of Henry I's reign.

107 Pershore: lierne vault of eastern arm, c. 1295

This achievement, momentous by any standards, is all the more remarkable for the fact that an urgent programme of castle building was in progress at the same time. Nor is there very much evidence of thrift in what was done. Such economies as may have been gained by the use of impressed labour, rubble walling, prefabrication and simplified detail were often outweighed by the sheer scale upon which the

Normans chose to build. Admittedly some of the grandest schemes, like Ely, London St Paul's and Winchester, took decades to finish, but in most cases their basic dimensions were in view from the start. Norman expertise in organization and logistics, acquired in course of the more or less continuous warfare to which they devoted a large part of their energies, must have contributed to this success but by itself does not explain it.

At first sight conditions in late eleventh-century England were not ideal for purposes of ecclesiastical building. Outbreaks of disorder continued for many years after the invasion. In 1069 English resistance in the north and parts of the midlands was countered by Norman reprisals of exceptional ferocity. There was unrest in the fenlands in 1070, and a crisis in 1075 when Earls Waltheof and Ralf, survivors of Edward's court, combined with Roger, Earl of Hereford, in revolt against William. There was an abortive attempt to synchronize this rising with a Danish invasion, and the rebellion was suppressed. A Danish invasion scare in 1085 was followed by further devastations, and ten years later there was more trouble when a consortium of barons challenged William Rufus.

Such events unsettled, and in places crippled the ecclesiastical economy. Conditions in the north were particulaly tense: the archbishop had to move around his province with an armed escort; in 1080 Walcher, Bishop of Durham, perished in a riot at Gateshead; and in 1087 work on a new Benedictine monastery at Lastingham was brought to a standstill because of lawlessness in the neighbourhood. Elsewhere royal extortion, punitive action by the military and the depredations of new estate owners took their toll. Early in the 1070s the monks of Ely were complaining that they had suffered losses of land and jurisdiction. St Albans' estates fell in value by nearly one-quarter after the Conquest (Welldon Finn 1971, 105), although they were up again by the time of the Domesday Survey in 1086. Not all manors recovered so promptly. Estates of York, Westminster and London, for example, remained in a depressed state for several decades. When William Rufus was taken seriously ill in 1093 the *Anglo-Saxon Chronicle* reported that he took a sudden interest in religion. 'To many monasteries he made grants of land, which he subsequently withdrew when he recovered . . .' (Garmonsway 1972, 227).

This is a bleak picture. However, there were several factors which worked to the advantage of the Norman churchbuilders. Firstly, England in the eleventh century was a wealthy nation (Sawyer 1965). Something of the extent of this wealth may be glimpsed in records of the large sums of protection money which were paid out to avoid Scandinavian aggression during the reign of Ethelred. According to the *Anglo-Saxon Chronicle* £10,000 was paid out in 991, £16,000 in 994, £24,000 in 1002, £36,000 in 1007, £3,000 from East Kent in 1009, £48,000 in 1012, £21,000 in 1014 and £72,000 in 1018. How large these sums were in relation to the size of the currency as a whole is not clear, but it would seem that the losses were made good (perhaps, as Sawyer has suggested, with the profits of a flourishing wool trade), and there can be little doubt that it was the scale of English resources which formed one of the strongest inducements to William to attempt the invasion. Hence despite the damage which was deliberately inflicted on the economy it was still possible to build on a large scale. England even subsidized architecture abroad: several church projects were undertaken in Normandy after the Conquest, with the assistance of income diverted from English monasteries (Musset 1966).

Secondly, we have seen in an earlier chapter that there were weaknesses in the Old English Church which offered scope for extensive and largely unopposed reform. The new and refounded Benedictine and secular cathedral establishments which were set up during the concluding decades of the eleventh century formed part of the political apparatus which the Conqueror and his immediate successors used to clamp their authority on the new acquisition. Norman policy demanded the relocation of a number of major churches. The removal of sees from the countryside into towns such as Chester, Lincoln and Norwich meant that in several cases a fresh start could be made. The proliferation of Benedictine and, in the twelfth century, Augustinian and Cistercian houses often permitted the selection of unencumbered sites.

The technique of using churches to assist in the process of political consolidation can be seen in south Wales, where ten emergent towns were provided with Benedictine priories shortly after the Conquest. Most of these houses were dependent on monasteries in Normandy or England. Dr L.A.S. Butler has pointed out to me that this ensured a supply of clergy from outside the locality, and it meant that the responsibility of supervision was placed upon a wealthy mother house. The tithes and offerings of burgesses supported an Anglo-Norman church and not a Welsh one. At this time Wales possessed no urban centres of the kind which had developed in England; hence bishops' sees could not be transferred to them. Instead military earthworks were erected at Bangor and St David's, while the sees of Llandaff and St Asaph were strategically attached to existing castle towns nearby.

When there was no change of site it appears that the Normans had few scruples about knocking down existing churches. There were a few – perhaps more than we think – such as Beverley, Wimborne and Sherborne where existing work was retained. One or two others seem to have been mothballed for a while, either for reasons of poverty (Ripon, perhaps Hexham), or because it was felt that the church was no longer of sufficient importance to merit immediate attention (possibly Wells and Dorchester). Elsewhere the Normans preferred to destroy and build anew.

The characteristics of Anglo-Saxon church design might be summed up in three words: retention, addition and connection. There seems to have been a strong sentimental attachment to buildings with a long history of sanctity. Enormous sums of money were spent on the internal enrichment of pre-Conquest cathedrals and abbeys, but if enlargement became necessary it was usual to extend a revered structure by the addition of adjuncts, or to provide a supplementary building nearby, rather than to erase what was already there and start afresh. It was said that Wulfstan, Bishop of Worcester (1062–95), the only member of the Old English episcopate to escape the Norman purge, shed tears at the prospect of having to

108 Wymondham: nave, c. 1107–30

demolish an ancient church within his close in order to make way for a new cathedral. When the Conqueror went north to deal with unrest in 1069 his men made the metropolitan cathedral at York 'an object of scorn'. The limited architectural achievements of the Anglo-Saxons presented no psychological barrier to Norman builders.

The first churches erected in England after the Conquest bore a close resemblance to Norman models. Other churches begun slightly later, such as Eye (1075), St Mary's York (1088), Blyth (1089) and Binham (1090), were also of continental-Norman extraction.

Almost immediately, however, Norman architecture in England became Anglo-Norman. Ingredients of a compound style were present before the Conquest, notably a marked tendency towards prolongation, evident at Westminster (*c.* 1045–50 to

1065) but absent in Normandy, and a feeling for variety in planning. The eastern arms of churches begun at Lincoln in 1072, Worcester (1084) and Christchurch (1099) were of three bays, in contrast with the two-bay units which were customary in Normandy, while those at St Albans (1077), Winchester (1079), York (*c.* 1080) and Ely (*c.* 1082) were four bays long. At London St Paul's, Ely, Norwich, Bury and St Albans the naves were lengthened far in excess of standard Norman dimensions. Despite this emphasis on linear effect there was no general increase in the distances *across* great churches. Spans were kept within the limits preferred by continental-Norman masons, i.e. *c.* 27–33 feet. This is an important clue to the technical character of the early Anglo-Norman building boom: additional scale was achieved by 'stretching' conventional layouts rather than by radical development.

Most of the known layouts can be divided into two categories, which differed chiefly in the planning of the eastern arm. In the first of these the presbytery, which almost always terminated in an apse, was flanked by aisles which led to lateral chapels. In the second, the aisles were passed round the central apse to form a semi-circular ambulatory, sometimes with subsidiary chapels projecting from the outer curve. An occasional variation on the triapsidal theme involved the insertion of additional apses between the transeptal chapels and the presbytery aisles. This arrangement, which gave seven apses in graduated formation, was adopted at St Albans, Binham and St Mary's York.

The liturgical advantages of the triapsidal and ambulatory plans must have been evenly matched, since the two achieved equal popularity in the late eleventh century and appeared side by side in the same town (as at Canterbury) or district (Winchester and Christchurch). Only in the west midlands did the ambulatory plan find general though not exclusive favour, being selected at Worcester, Pershore, Gloucester and Tewkesbury, and subsequently at St Mary's cathedral priory, Coventry. Gloucester and Tewkesbury shared an uncommon arrangement in elevation whereby the galleried second stage, present in the eastern arm, was omitted west of

the crossing, the nave piers rising higher than usual to compensate and the tribune storey being diminished (as at Gloucester) or suppressed altogether (Tewkesbury). At Tewkesbury, Gloucester and maybe Exeter the ambulatory was formed by canting the ends of the aisles inwards and connecting them with a short section running north–south. A feeling seems to have existed that the west end of a church was the most suitable place for experimentation: western transepts, screen fronts, twin towers, axial towers and deeply-recessed portals were among the distinctive features which were used, in various permutations, to conclude a design.

189

109 (left) *Rochester nave, c. 1115–30*
110 (above) *Tewkesbury: nave, first half of twelfth century; vault, c. 1330*

Some of the most original ideas emerged in the depressed and devastated north. The cathedral begun at York in about 1080 differed from other known major Anglo-Norman churches of the period in that it possessed no aisles. As a result the clear span was huge, about 45 feet, and the transept incorporated a central crossing, with tower above, of unprecedented area: over 2000 square feet. York presented a new concept so far as the dimensioning of English churches was concerned. Its span rivalled the new Cluny, San Ambrogio Milan, Santiago de Compostela and Speyer, all begun around 1080.

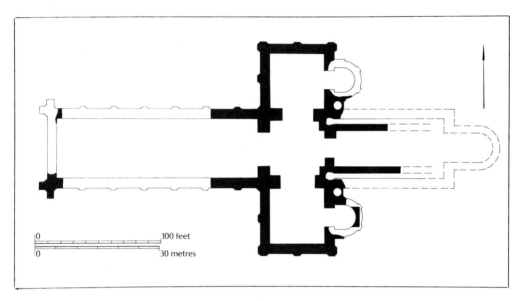

Fig. 9 York Minster: plan of the Anglo-Norman cathedral, begun c. 1080. Areas shaded with solid black represent walls found. The church was unusual in that it possessed no aisles. The exact configuration of the east end is uncertain, although portions of the substructure have been found and recorded. (After Phillips 1975)

The eastern arm at York was particularly unusual. Externally the main width of the nave was preserved, but within the presbytery was narrowed down to a span of 27 feet (i.e. a normal width for an Anglo-Norman church of this status). This was achieved not by incorporating aisles but by inscribing what virtually amounted to a second building within the outer shell, somewhat along the lines of the double hull of a thermos flask (Philips 1975). The gaps between the inner and outer walls functioned as corridors. The exact configuration of the east end is unclear and may only be surmised from the substructure. However, it looks as if the lateral corridors were connected by a transverse passage which ran between the east end of the presbytery and the entrance to the apse. This reconstruction is conjectural,* but if it is correct then we are presented with a design in which the eastern chapel was visually and liturgically divorced from the presbytery: an arrangement which foreshadows the Early English concept of a semi-independent Lady Chapel. The eastern arm was

* It is strongly suggested by the great eastern foundation, which was 21 feet broad and contained timber reinforcement distributed in a way which implies a double wall (see Peers in *Antiq J* 11, 1931).

111 Selby

also long (over 100 feet, minus the apse), and the eastern position of the pulpitum suggests that the choir was housed within it. Here was another innovation, for at this time it was customary for the choir to occupy the crossing. In layout, therefore, York was radical.

Durham, in contrast, was more conventional in planning but adventurous in construction. Whereas the master at York seems to have been content with a timber roof throughout (unless the double walls of the eastern arm imply a barrel vault), the architect at Durham envisaged, perhaps invented, a system of ribbed vaults.

Norman builders regularly vaulted aisles, chapels and crypts, but previous attempts to cover main spans with stone seem to have been few. The presbytery of Ste-Trinité, Caen, begun *c*. 1062, was successfully overspread with a groin-vault, so too was the eleventh-century church at Nivelles. However, vaults of this kind were hazardous for large spans because the creases of the vaults were susceptible to dangerously high levels of stress. Apart from this weakness there were erectional difficulties, while the application of a groin-vault to a rectangular bay necessitated either the striking of curves from different levels or unsightly stilting.

At Durham all these disadvantages were removed at a stroke by building diagonal arches across the bays, thereby reinforcing the creases, and by filling the intervening panels with rubble masonry. The task of centring was simplified, while the problem of levels was sorted out by making the diagonal arches pointed: this permitted a curve to be struck from a convenient level without introducing distortion at the crown. In the nave the thrust delivered by the ribs was passed out to the aisle buttresses by a system of half-arches inside the tribune. Although the cathedral was not consecrated until 1133 it has been suggested that the essentials of the vaulting method were worked out in the 1090s.

Durham and York were conceived as unitary schemes. They deserve attention because between them they anticipated much of what was to follow: the pointed arch, the flying buttress, the concept of the all-stone church, the eastern choir and semi-independent eastern chapel. These acorns took over a century to germinate, but they were being planted, in England, before the end of the eleventh century.

The vigour of Anglo-Norman Romanesque, its capacity for innovation under adverse conditions and, above all, the scale on which it was practised raise questions about the professional organization of the men who were responsible. During the single decade 1090–1100 work was in progress or begun on at least thirty-two cathedrals, abbey and priory sites. If major castles and important churches which have not survived are added the figure nears fifty. The authoritarian climate may have assisted by ensuring a steady supply of unskilled labour, but even after allowing for some cross-feeding of personnel between projects we are still dealing with very

112 Durham: flying buttresses concealed in nave tribune

113 Ely: Prior's Door, c. 1140

114 Ely: detail of Prior's Door

large numbers. An established building industry meets its own manpower needs by recruiting young men for training in the crafts it requires. The Anglo-Saxons would have had no difficulty in producing skilled carpenters and artists, but it seems unlikely that the Anglo-Norman building industry could have become self-sufficient in master-masons much before 1100, unless there was a larger body of experienced native masons working in the Edwardian period than it has been fashionable to suspect.

Early English

The twelfth century was no quiet time for builders, but much of what went on was as a result of commitments made during the reigns of Rufus and Henry I. There were naves to finish, towers to add and various adjustments to make. Not all that was contemplated was completed. At Tewkesbury, for instance, preparations were made for a pair of western towers to flank the cavernous western portal, but the scheme was cancelled. The lower level of activity in the 1130s and 1140s could have been due to the disruption of monastic affairs during the disorders of Stephen's reign, but a more likely explanation is reflected by the graphs of projects in progress (II and IV) which show that many of the greatest churches begun between *c*. 1080 and 1120 were still in

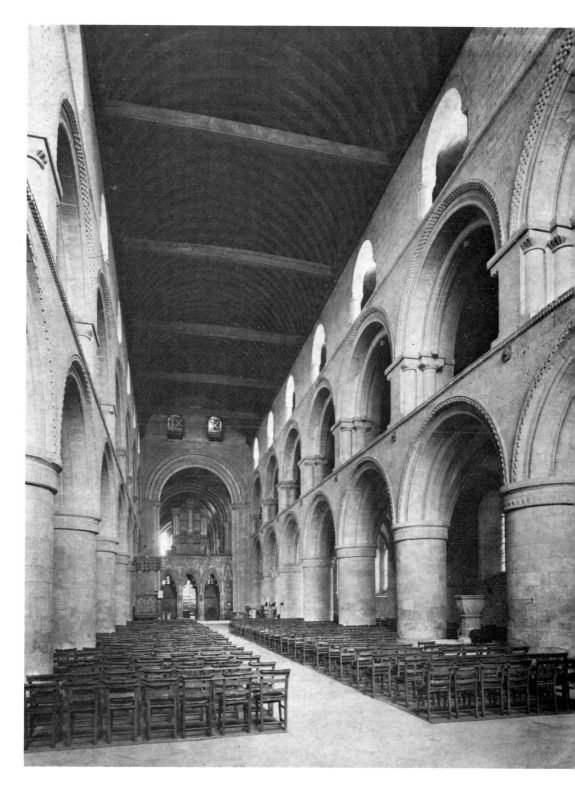

115 Southwell: nave

process of continuation until the middle years of the century and hence were not yet ripe for renewal. This 'knock on' effect is also found during the Early English and Decorated periods, and is further to be noted in connection with the large numbers of Cistercian and Augustinian houses which were being founded during the second quarter of the twelfth century (Graph V on Fig. 10). A period of consolidation often intervened between the formal establishment of a new monastic house and the start of work on its first permanent church.

During the second half of the century the pace of new building began to accelerate. This was the time when the first integrated designs of Gothic configuration were

116 Romsey: south arm of transept and apse, c. 1150

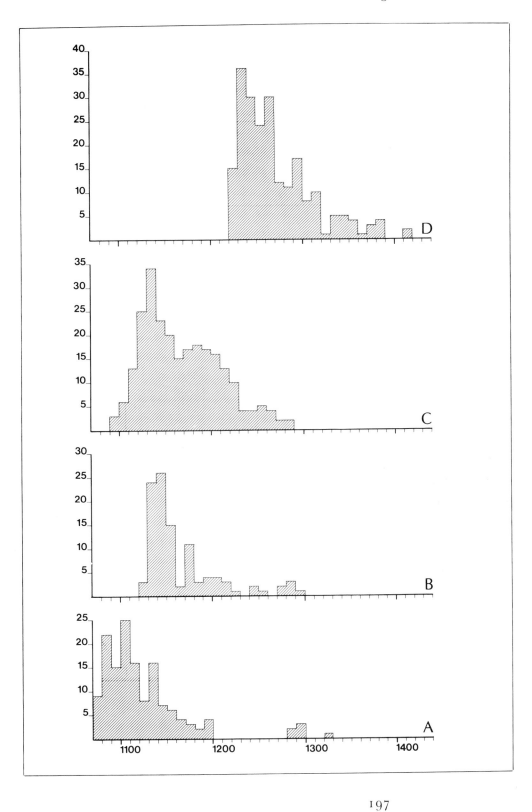

Fig. 10 Foundations of monastic houses after the Conquest: (a) Benedictine; (b) Augustinian; (c) Cistercian; (d) Friars. (Source: Knowles & Hadcock 1971)

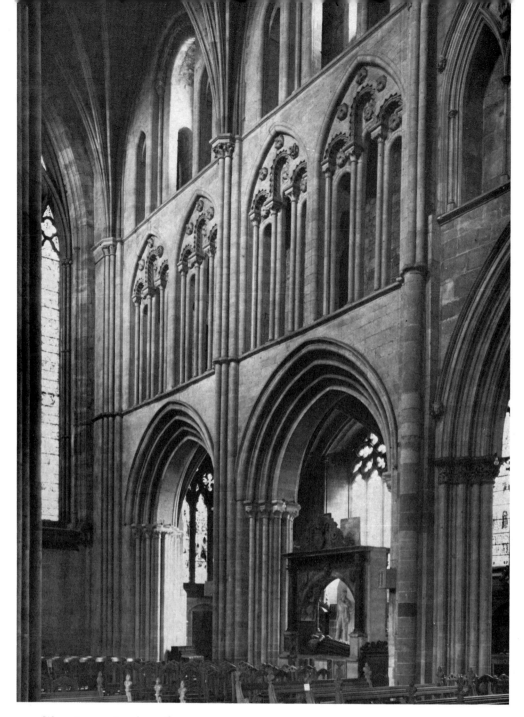

117 Worcester: western bays of nave, c. 1175

making their appearance in England: at Wells, Canterbury, Ripon and Worcester, all around *c*. 1175. Between *c*. 1175 and 1250 about seventy-five *fresh* campaigns were organized at the greater churches in our sample. Record numbers of projects were initiated during the first half of the reign of King John. The Interdict imposed by Innocent III in 1208 and the disturbances of the following decade seem to have had a

118 Ripon: western bay of nave, c. 1190–1200

discouraging effect on new work, but by 1219 England had been reduced to order and during the next thirty years activity was kept at a high level. Taken as a whole the thirteenth century was a period of singular architectural growth.

Circumstances differed from those which had attended the building boom of a century earlier. Patrons could now call upon, and choose between, larger numbers of skilled masons. The best quarry sites had been singled out. Standards of accuracy in cutting and setting stone were never higher than in the first half of the thirteenth century. Prospects for diversity and innovation were good.

The campaigns of the Early English period were mostly works of *re*building. There were, it is true, churches such as Abbey Dore, Lanercost, Old Malton and Nun

119 Old Malton: west front, c. 1200–10

Monkton where a late start had been made, but in most cases the sites of the greater churches were already fixed. This meant that decisions on modernization had to take account of existing fabrics. Salisbury was the only cathedral to be transferred to a virgin site (1220), although the new cathedral at Wells was probably set out alongside its predecessor rather than upon it. Consequently the operations of Early English builders were usually either works of extension, to the east (as at Chichester in 1187), west (Durham *c*. 1170), or even both (St Albans), or they involved the progressive demolition of a Norman church in a manner which permitted continuity of worship, as at Lincoln.

Liturgically it was the eastern arm which was of greatest importance, so it was here that rebuilding usually began: at Beverley (*c*. 1220), Boxgrove (*c*. 1200), Brecon, Chester (1194), Ely (1239), Hereford (*c*. 1190), Hexham, Lichfield (*c*. 1195), Llandaff (1193), Lincoln (1192), Pershore (*c*. 1210), Rochester (*c*. 1200), St David's (*c*. 1220), Southwark (*c*. 1212), Southwell (1234), Wimborne, Winchester (1202) and Worcester (1224). Apart from Lincoln and Pershore all these developments

120 Boxgrove: central crossing, c. 1180; choir, c. 1200–25

were rectangular in basis, ending either in a flush east front or opening onto a projecting chapel of lesser width and (usually) height. At churches where the cycle of renewal had begun before *c*. 1175, as at York where a new choir had been built during the pontificate of Archbishop Roger de Pont-l'Evêque (1154–81), attention shifted to the transept.

Several factors may be singled out in connection with this surge of activity. First, the twelfth century saw the birth of a new architectural style. Gothic was at once an aesthetic and a technical revolution. Although the structural essentials of the new style had been invented and tested by masons working in the Romanesque tradition, Gothic was not so much a development from Romanesque as a cancellation of it. Gothic offered space where previously there had been restriction, refinement in place

121 Boxgrove: choir

203

122 (left) *New Shoreham: eastern arm, c. 1190–1220*
123 (above) *New Shoreham: boss of south choir aisle vault*

of bulk, light instead of dark. It was entirely appropriate that Gothic builders should have concentrated on methods of illuminating the churches they designed. Their innovations paralleled developments in intellectual life, brought about by contacts with Islam and the assimilation of Greek and Arab learning which were transforming natural philosophy and scientific thought. The patrons of the later twelfth

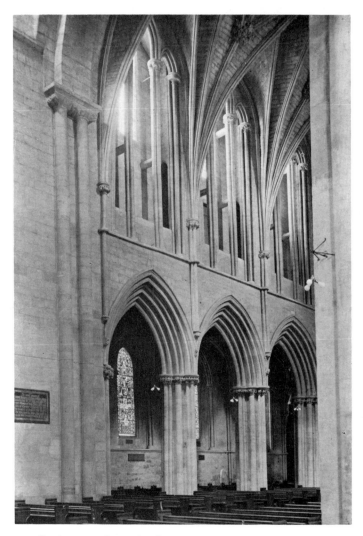

124 Pershore: north arcade of eastern arm, c. 1220–

century were aware that they were living in a new age. The churches they commissioned formed a tangible expression of that consciousness. It was as if those who built in the new style breathed 'air from another planet'.

To some extent the political and cultural prestige of the Benedictine houses declined during the twelfth century, while the cathedrals gained in influence. The

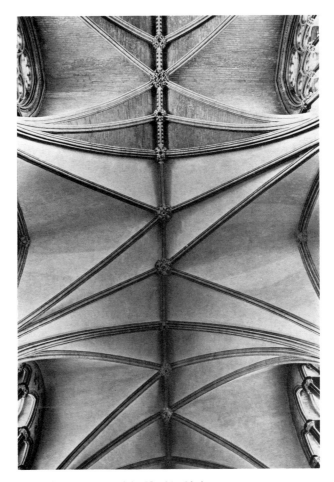

125 Lincoln: vault of St Hugh's Choir, c. 1210

mechanism for this displacement had been created by the Normans at the same time as they were setting up their spectacular Benedictine abbeys, for it was they who transformed the English cathedral into an urban phenomenon.

> ... we may in the twelfth century consider the chapter and bishop together as an intellectual centre, rich, powerful, often well educated, and always established in an urban community rather than in the rural isolation of most of the monasteries. The cathedral library, the cathedral school, the cathedral archives, the *gesta* of its bishops, the writings of its canons, the bishop's jurisdiction, the bishop's patronage of learning, play a large part in this age, intermediate between the monastery on the one hand and the princely courts on the other.
>
> (Haskins 1971, 48)

With the exception of Canterbury no English cathedral acquired an intellectual *cachet* comparable to that, say, of Laon or Chartres. But there were several, such as Lincoln and St Paul's, which grew into centres of more than local significance.

Courtier-bishops, exactly intermediate 'between the monastery . . . and the princely courts', presided at the monastic cathedrals of Winchester, Worcester and Durham. It is no coincidence, therefore, to find that the development of Gothic in thirteenth-century England was in no small measure the affair of cathedral and collegiate establishments. Great churches which remain wholly or nearly Norman are typically monastic.

Secondly, there were changes in the economic climate which were favourable to new building. Early in the twelfth century England's stock of bullion had come close to exhaustion, and as late as the reign of Henry II the output of currency was still low. But from about 1180 until 1280 'the volume of the English currency was rising like a rocket . . . figures indicate an astonishing fifteen or twenty-fold increase in the quantities of coinage leaving the mint' (Metcalf 1977, 6–7).

The English economy, abruptly swollen with silver in exchange for wool exports, also underwent internal change. The first half of the twelfth century had been a period of material consolidation for the greater churches, when their manors were commonly leased out for steady returns. This system of 'farming' was basically static, but since the estates of cathedrals and abbeys were still in process of enlargement ecclesiastical incomes continued to increase. In the years around 1200 came a shift of policy. Landlords now began to assert direct control over their estates through their own 'reeves, bailiffs and other officials – agents of their lord who accounted in detail for every issue and every expense and who were liable to the last farthing for the balance between income and expenditure' (Miller 1971, 10). The unfolding of this policy is witnessed in records of the affairs of the Benedictine abbey of Ramsey, where a new interest in agricultural profits 'invigorated and developed a whole system of administrative direction and control during the thirteenth century' (Raftis 1957, 120).

Meanwhile established towns grew larger and new towns often prospered (Platt 1976, 25). Profits of trade brought about by a multiplication of fairs and markets in their turn encouraged the maintenance and improvement of communications. Monastic officials at Durham travelled as far afield as Boston, in Lincolnshire, in order to undertake transactions on behalf of their cathedral priory (Fraser 1969, 46).

All these developments facilitated ecclesiastical building. Better communications, especially bridges, were an aid to the transport of materials. Urban growth led to a diversification of specialized crafts. There came into existence a class of educated administrator competent to handle the increasingly intricate secretarial and administrative requirements of big building programmes. Records kept at Westminster in the 1240s and 1250s reveal the presence of groups of clerks and accountants whose task it was to co-ordinate the supply and delivery of materials and to regulate the composition of the workforce in response to the changing needs of the work in hand (Colvin 1971). Most important of all, ecclesiastical incomes rose, garnered by direct, efficient management. At Salisbury the value of the cathedral's assets rose by 168 per cent in the course of the thirteenth century.

126 Chester: chapter-house vestibule, c. 1240

The climax

The third and final outburst of building was the greatest of all. It started around 1250 and was sustained with mounting vigour until the early years of the fourteenth century. Coming as it did on the heels of an era of outstanding architectural creativity, this was a climax superimposed upon a climax.

Artistic invention was an important stimulus. The adoption of bar tracery at Binham and Netley in the 1240s, and at Westminster in the 1250s, rendered all existing buildings obsolescent. No longer were windows merely pierced through walls; they were now as never before artistic ventures in their own right, and could be enlarged to the point where a great church became a crystal palace. Architectural sculpture moved on from its cool Early English elegance towards increasing elaboration. A trend towards naturalism in the carving of foliage reached a moment of maximum resolution just before 1300, and then began to slip out of focus.

In other respects these operations can be seen as an expression of factors which we

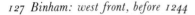

127 Binham: west front, before 1244

128 (right) *Westminster: transept, c. 1246–59*

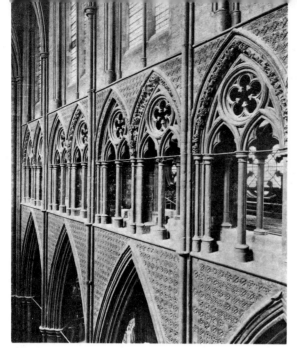

129 *Westminster: triforium of north transept arm*

130 *Carlisle: east window,* c. *1320*

131 *York Minster: part of great west window,* c. *1330–8*

132 *York Minster: detail of west window*

211

133 Lincoln: 'Bishop's Eye' window in south transept arm, c. 1335

134 Southwell: chapter-house, detail of stall canopy

135 Southwell: chapter-house, detail of entrance, c. 1295

136 Selby: screen backing against reredos, c. 1320

137 *Bridlington: south arcade of nave,*
c. *1260–1300*

138 *Howden: nave,* c. *1280–1310*

have already noted earlier in the century: a rising population, intensified entre-preneurial activity, diligent management and expanding markets, all now under-pinned for a time by the firm government of Edward I. Practical needs played a part. The monastic population 'reached its highest aggregate total *c*. 1300' (Knowles and Hadcock 1971, 47) and it had to be housed. Additional altar-space had to be created for the devotions of the religious. Means also had to be found to cater for the needs of parishioners, themselves increasing in numbers, where they were accustomed to share the nave or transept of a great church. Lastly, this was a period which saw the installation of large, expensive shrines, like those to St Werburgh at Chester and St Chad at Lichfield, both *c*. 1310, which required spacious eastern extensions to provide them with worthy surroundings.

One of the most remarkable things about the Decorated era is the extent to which secular and military building went on alongside ecclesiastical works. The heyday of urban wall-building fell within the period *c*. 1250–1330, when borough after borough provided or refurbished its defences (Turner 1971, 13–16). Edward I's campaigns of 'pacification' in Wales involved the construction or rebuilding of major castles at Beaumaris, Conway, Builth, Flint, Hope, Aberystwyth and Rhuddlan, together with important works at twelve other castles and numerous subsidiary bases (Brown *et al*. 1963, 294). These operations sucked in labour from far and wide. When Aberystwyth castle was started in 1277 120 masons were summoned from as far afield as Somerset and Dorset (1963, 299). In the same year a workforce of nearly 1850 men was assembled at Flint, and work began on the site of Edward's ill-fated abbey at Vale Royal.

Workmen had to be paid. Dr A. J. Taylor has estimated that over one-and-a-half million silver pennies were issued in less than six months during 1295 for the wages of builders at Beaumaris Castle alone (1961, 123). Cathedrals and abbeys were not erected with such urgency as castles, and as a rule ecclesiastical workforces were much smaller. Even so, churchbuilders had to be paid in hard cash, and without it a project would come to a standstill. Down to *c.* 1150 great churches were fairly elementary in detail and design; hence the ratio of skilled craftsmen to unskilled labourers would be low, and the wage-bill modest. Thereafter, as architectural detail and sculpture became increasingly complicated, and additional categories of craftsman (glazier, marbler, plumber, etc.) multiplied, larger resources of ready money would be needed. Thirteenth-century England was 'awash with silver' (Metcalf 1977, 6), and the average trend of projects in progress seems to be very much in line with the money supply. A comparison of this kind is much too crude to allow any definite correlation, but there are signs that it would be a subject worth detailed investigation.

There is a darker side to the picture of affluence and glittering new buildings. Conditions which were favourable to kings and ecclesiastical landlords were not necessarily to the advantage of all humbler folk. Before the end of the twelfth century there are signs that the population was growing. This expansion continued throughout the thirteenth century and created a

> . . . pressure of population on rural resources, which, to judge by the upward movement of rents and corn prices, were not increasing quickly enough to give them a livelihood, had forced many farm labourers to look elsewhere for employment. Unfortunately for them the population crisis was accompanied by an intensification of feudal tyranny: customary rights were abridged, customary obligations redoubled. Villeinage therefore immobilized an important class of tenants and made it very difficult for heirs in villeinage to move. But younger sons, and members of other classes, were not similarly impeded by feudal covenants, and had every inducement to evade their trammels. The records are full of their journeyings. Mostly they gravitated to the towns where life was so complex that they might hope for sufficient work to maintain themselves and their families.
>
> (Bridbury 1975, 54)

Dr Bridbury's observations have been quoted at length because they accord very closely with the circumstances attending large-scale building works in the same period. At Westminster, for example, accounts which were kept for the rebuilding of the abbey in 1253 provide an unusually detailed picture of the composition of the labour force and the allocation of resources over thirty-two consecutive weeks. For just under half this period unskilled workers formed over fifty per cent of the labour force, but accounted on average for less than thirty-two per cent of the wage-bill. Bridbury suggests that the migrants 'were forced into jobs to which entry was free, and in which employment was fluctuating and uncertain' (1975, 55). The accounts from Westminster, at least, tend to confirm this.

139 Ely: choir triforium, c. 1322–36

Table 1 Relative proportions of payments for building work at Westminster Abbey from 28 April to 6 December 1253. All figures have been rounded off. The column showing expenditure on materials includes sums for task-work and carriage. Figures for the week 9–15 June are not available, but the weeks have been numbered consecutively. (Source: Colvin 1971, 249–85.)

Week	Total workforce	Craftsmen (% total)	Labourers (% total)	Total wage-bill (c. £)	Craftsmen (% total)	Labourers (% total)	Materials (c. £)	Total expenditure (c. £)	Wages (% total)	Materials (% total)
1	305	50.8	49.2	21	69	31	28	49	42.9	57.1
2	338	47.9	52.1	25	60	40	28	53	47.2	52.8
3	364	45.1	54.9	31	58	42	32	63	49.2	50.8
4	384	44.5	55.5	32	56.3	43.7	21	53	60.4	39.6
5	384	44.5	55.5	31	61.3	38.7	28	59	52.5	47.5
6	390	45.4	54.6	33	57.6	42.4	53	86	38.4	61.6
7	391	43.7	56.3	34	58.8	41.2	28	62	54.8	45.2
8	433	49.2	50.8	32	62.5	37.5	38	70	45.7	54.3
9	426	48.4	51.6	31	61.3	38.7	23	54	57.4	42.6
10	408	47.3	52.7	33	63.6	36.4	25	58	56.9	43.1
11	396	45.7	54.3	35	60	40	27	62	56.5	43.5
12	327	57.2	42.8	29	75.9	24.1	28	57	50.9	49.1
13	321	58.6	41.4	26	73.1	26.9	42	68	38.2	61.8
14	333	59.5	40.5	28	71.4	28.6	71	99	28.2	71.8
15	318	56.6	43.4	28	67.9	32.1	9	36	77.8	22.2
16	318	56.6	43.4	27	70.4	29.6	25	52	51.9	48.1
17	232	60.8	39.2	19	73.7	26.3	7	26	73.1	26.9
18	232	60.8	39.2	21	71.4	28.6	15	36	58.3	41.7
19	216	57.9	42.1	20	75	25	5	25	80	20
20	250	56.8	43.2	24	70.8	29.2	85	109	22	78
21	267	55	45	25	68	32	11	36	69.4	30.6
22	310	50	50	24	66.7	33.3	24	48	50	50
23	292	46.9	53.1	28	64.3	35.7	41	69	40.6	59.4
24	318	50.3	49.7	23	69.6	30.4	33	56	41.1	58.9
25	314	50	50	29	65.5	34.5	11	40	72.5	27.5
26	296	52.7	47.3	28	67.9	32.1	14	42	66.7	33.3
27	270	48.1	51.9	26	69.2	30.8	13	39	66.7	33.3
28	100	70	30	10	80	20	6	16	62.5	37.5
29	106	67	33	12	83.3	16.7	10	22	54.5	45.5
30	109	66.1	33.9	11	81.8	18.2	6	17	64.7	35.5
31	109	66.1	33.9	11	81.8	18.2	5	16	68.8	31.2

Table 2 Breakdown of workforce at Westminster Abbey for the week 30 June to 6 July 1253. (Source: Colvin 1971, 7.)

White cutters	56
Marblers	49
Layers	28
Carpenters	23
Polishers	15
Smiths	17
Glaziers	14
Plumbers	4
Labourers	220
Total	426

The thirteenth century provided the optimum economic and social conditions for large-scale enterprises of rebuilding. These conditions lasted into the early decades of the fourteenth century, by which time the costs of war with Scotland and France, followed by a series of crop failures and an accelerating outflow of English sterling currency, saw an end to the era of unabated architectural growth. Skilled masons were never particularly numerous in the medieval period. Between 1301 and 1320 only eight masons were admitted as Freemen of York, for example (Knoop and Jones 1932, 348, with other cases), while in the bustling city of Bristol in the sixteenth century only three apprentices were indentured to masons during the decade 1532–42 (Hollis 1949). Cathedral building was nevertheless a labour-intensive process. The existence of a large reservoir of unskilled or semi-skilled labour, available for exploitation on a casual basis, was thus a definite asset for those who undertook it.

Fig. 11 Builders' wage rates in southern England, calculated in pence per day. (Sources: Phelps-Brown & Hopkins 1955; Colvin 1971)

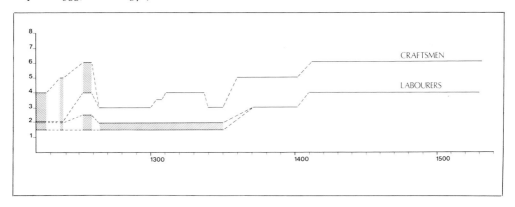

140 *Tewkesbury: nave vault, c. 1330*

141 *Tewkesbury: presbytery vault, c. 1340, bosses and badges later*

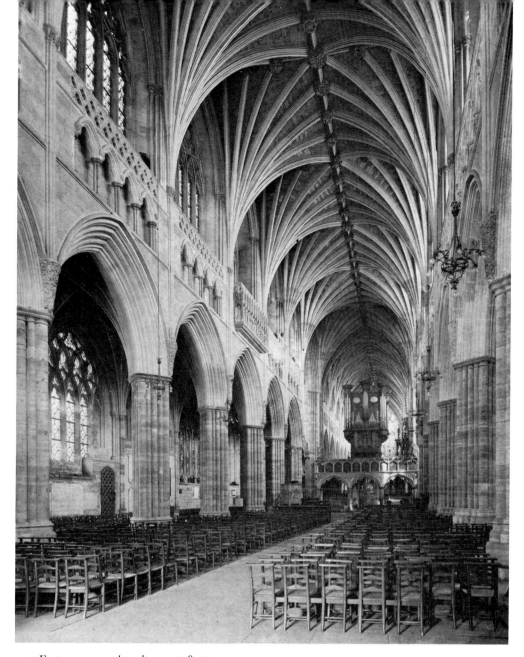

142 Exeter: nave and vault, c. 1328–70

Decline

Probably every other parish church in England was rebuilt or in some way modified between *c*. 1350 and 1500, but we have no Perpendicular cathedral (Harvey 1974, 170) and few Perpendicular monastic churches. Only Great Malvern and Sherborne were visited by the idiom from end to end, and both involved revision of an existing fabric rather than the fresh start which was made for the Tudor church at Bath. When Bath Abbey was rebuilt early in the sixteenth century, however, the entire church was less than half the length of its Norman ancestor.

143 Sherborne: nave, remodelled c. 1460–90

The century and a half between the accession of Edward III and the battle of Bosworth Field is a period of contradictions. It has been described as an age of recession and as an age of economic growth. Fine new parish churches were built while others were left to fall down. Three hundred houses stood vacant in Gloucester in 1487 while Salisbury prospered. For the student of the building Church the period is equally perplexing. New work did not stop, but numerically operations were nowhere near the levels that had been sustained during the thirteenth century. The decline in numbers of new schemes set in long before the Black Death; indeed, a downturn in the average trend is visible before the end of the reign of Edward I. A concomitant of the architectural boom of the thirteenth and early fourteenth century was an increase in the resources necessary for routine maintenance and repairs. Not all churches were in a position to meet these requirements. At Pershore, for instance, various obligations of hospitality and building outstripped income. In 1327 the monks had still not made good all the damage which had been sustained in a fire in the 1290s, and eighteen years later Pope Boniface acknowledged that the house was seriously in debt.

Another factor arose from competition presented by the friars. Friaries were an urban phenomenon. During the thirteenth century they multiplied rapidly, often several to a town. As they became established much of the ready money which had previously accrued to the greater churches by way of burial fees was diverted to the friars. In the second quarter of the fourteenth century, when contemporary writers noted a lack of money (Prestwich 1977, 50), such shifts could be critical for churches which were already on the verge of insolvency. Offerings at cathedral and monastic shrines still formed an important source of revenue, and churches which possessed them now redoubled their efforts to attract pilgrims. Writing at the end of the fourteenth century, Abbot Walter Frocester of Gloucester recalled the 'multitude of persons flowing thither from various cities, towns and villages' to visit the tomb of Edward II in the 1320s and 1330s. During the time of Abbot John Wygmor the aisle of St Andrew was completed 'right from the foundation to the end' on the proceeds. Frocester mused that if all the cash received had gone into the fabric fund it would

144 Gloucester

145 Gloucester: choir vault carried west over crossing, c. 1350–60

have enabled a complete rebuilding of the abbey, so great were the offerings: 'cloths of gold and silk and other precious objects sold for low prices. Better ones, as well as those which were worn out' (Myers 1969, 779).

By the fourteenth century the acquisition of land by monastic houses had virtually ceased. At some, such as Chester, the main expansion of assets had reached an end by *c.* 1200 (Burne 1962, 49). Elsewhere, as at Bolton, growth continued until early in the fourteenth century (Kershaw 1973, 128). The Great Famine of 1315–17 has often been singled out as a turning point in the history of medieval land colonization, but the economic damage it wrought may well have been intensified by other factors. Dr Maddicott has argued that

> If the population was checked during this period, and if the area under cultivation shrank, it was not solely because a countryside full of land-starved smallholders had become especially vulnerable to the impact of poor harvests and grain shortages, but rather because death, seigneurial exploitation and the King's taxes all worked together to place the peasant's resources in a new and more precarious position.
>
> (Maddicott 1975, 75)

The ecclesiastical landlords were among the first to feel the pinch. Manorial accounts at Ely reveal a sharp drop in agrarian profits in the second quarter of the fourteenth century, and this recession has been linked with the turning away from demesne farming which occurred during the same period (Miller 1951, 105). Crowland underwent a financial crisis around the middle years of the fourteenth century, exacerbated by unfriendly neighbours who diverted watercourses and rustled livestock. At Durham gross income in 1308 amounted to £4526. In 1335 it was down to £1752, in 1340–1 to £1931, and in 1348–9, the year of the Black Death, £1212. Such losses, serious enough in cash terms, were even more damaging in real terms.

The Black Death was selective in its effects upon the monastic population. Forty-seven monks died at St Albans, for example, whereas only four perished at Christ Church, Canterbury. At Romsey there were ninety nuns in 1333; in 1478 there were but eighteen, and the total never rose above twenty-five until the Dissolution (Liveing 1906, 121). In contrast Norwich cathedral priory's inmates seem to have come through the plague unscathed.

The spectacular mortality caused by the Black Death has sometimes distracted attention from the insidious effects of subsequent epidemics. Further pandemics occurred in 1361 and 1369, while at Canterbury plagues attacked the cathedral priory almost every decade during the fifteenth century, accounting for at least sixteen per cent of all deaths. 'Of the fourteen years in which plague was recorded at Christ Church only four coincided with outbreaks which have hitherto been deemed national' (Hatcher 1977, 17).

The declining population of the fourteenth and fifteenth centuries affected churchbuilding in two ways. First, it relieved pressure on land and reinforced the trend towards a leasehold economy which was already in progress before the Black

Death. As costs of demesne cultivation rose one by one the monasteries abandoned the technique of direct management and returned to a *rentier* system. Conditions now tilted in favour of the tenant farmer, who might expect to enjoy a larger acreage on better land at a lower rent. At Crowland a villein owning ten virgates is mentioned in 1394 (Page 1934, 152). In the same decade Crowland was experiencing difficulty in 'securing tenants for vacant holdings to fill manorial offices' (1934, 152). At Bolton manors were being farmed out *c*. 1380–1430: a period of falling demesne profits (Kershaw 1973, 181). Some churches, like Winchester, took steps to counteract the effects of bleaker times by more efficient management. Others fell into confusion. Boxgrove was in financial distress *c*. 1410. The affairs of Bolton were in poor shape in the mid fifteenth century. At Ripon the church was so dilapidated *c*. 1450 that for a time the canons were obliged to hold their services elsewhere.

Here, however, we must notice that a simple correlation between poor economic performance and diminished architectural activity cannot be assumed automatically. Under Abbots Thomas (1392–1417) and Lytlington (1427–70) considerable building work was undertaken at Crowland, though largely financed through gifts rather than income. Between *c*. 1400 and 1435 work proceeded at Canterbury on the chapter-house, pulpitum, south-west tower, south transept vault and cloisters, although the income of the house fell by nearly half during the period.

This ability to keep building was often connected with the second consequence of the economic changes of the age. In the thirteenth century monastic administration was normally decentralized. Different aspects of domestic management were placed in the hands of officials known as obedientiaries. Building, as we have seen, was generally the responsibility of the sacrist, who administered arrangements for finance and supply. Near the end of the fourteenth century a tendency towards centralization appears. In 1391 the new prior of Christ Church, Canterbury, Thomas Chillenden, resolved 'to retain his control over the finances of the monastery . . . he fused the more important functions of the central office with his own and assumed the role of prior-treasurer' (Smith 1943, 191). Chillenden took personal responsibility for the rebuilding of the nave, and it appears that his intervention led to a marked acceleration of progress. Likewise at Bristol in 1511 Abbot Newland was described as 'master of the work', and Abbot Islip of Westminster (1500–32) assumed the functions of sacrist (Knowles 1959). If the problems of a shrinking income could sometimes be surmounted by forceful leadership, the prospects for success obviously depended on the drive and calibre of individual abbots and priors. Not all houses were fortunate in this respect, and some, such as Selby and Chester, experienced periodic descents into lawlessness and dissolute living. A picture of prevailing laxity has sometimes been painted of monasteries in the fifteenth century, but while it is true that records of visitations provide many glimpses of unbecoming conduct we cannot be sure that such conditions were general. In about 1390 the Prior of Cartmel was taken to task because of his visits to taverns and the dilapidated state of his priory. At Dorchester *c*. 1441 the canons went hunting and fishing after

146 Canterbury: nave, c. 1380–1405

dinner, and it was said that one of the canons kept a goshawk which had been purchased at the expense of the abbey. We do not know if these incidents were typical, but it does appear that some of the resources which had previously been assigned to churchbuilding were now channelled into the making of more comfortable quarters for the religious.

In England as a whole the post-plague era was by no means the period of universal decay that has often been depicted. Dr Bridbury has argued the opposite: that the later Middle Ages provide 'an astonishing record of resurgent vitality and enterprise'. Other interpretations have been put forward (e.g. Dobson 1977), but it is true that much vitality lay with the leaseholders, the small capitalists and the guilds. One

would expect, therefore, that the greatest architectural display would occur in the churches with which these men were affiliated. And that is where we find it: in the great Perpendicular enterprises of Boston, Yarmouth, Hull, Lavenham and Cullompton, and in the civic splendours of St Mary Redcliffe, Bristol, Cirencester and St Michael, Coventry. Far from being a period of architectural decline the later Middle Ages saw redoubled building activity, but at a neighbourhood level. Where parishioners shared great churches they might improve them. The parishioners at Wymondham made extensive alterations to the monastic nave in the fifteenth century, and added a noble western tower. In 1403 the Bishop of Winchester granted a faculty for the extension of the parochial north aisle at Romsey. In 1464–7 a certain Thomas Shotter bequeathed 6s 8d for the 'fabric of the new aisle', and left 20s to the Brotherhood of St George which used it (Liveing 1906, 183). In towns, where guilds and fraternities flourished, contributions might be made to church fabrics. The craftsmen's guilds at Brecon fitted out a series of fine chapels in the priory, and the crypt of Old St Paul's became the regular meeting place of an affluent fraternity.

The late medieval bishops of Welsh dioceses were keen builders. Bishop Skeffington (1508–33) organized a team of masons to rebuild the nave of Bangor. Bishop Standish of St Asaph (1518–35) bequeathed £40 'for paving the choir', and Bishop Morgan of St David's (1496–1504) contributed to his church. Miles Salley, Bishop of Llandaff (1500–16), left his mitre and staff to be sold for works at the cathedral (Williams 1962, 452–3).

A notable feature of these last enterprises was a preoccupation on the part of patrons with towers. This is interesting, because of all the elements which went to make up a great church a tower was the most liturgically useless, if also the most impressive. The central tower had been a leading feature of the greater church, and sometimes a source of anxiety to its users, since the eleventh century. Now towers were built as if literally to crown the achievements of former days. They went up at Howden (c. 1400), York (1408–74, with interruptions), Gloucester (from 1450), Great Malvern (c. 1450), Norwich (spire, 1450s), Durham (1465–90) and Chester (from 1493). At Canterbury in about 1493 Cardinal Morton commissioned his architect John Wastell to double the height of the central tower, perhaps in order to celebrate the arrival of his cardinal's cap (Tatton-Brown 1978, 7). Quite a few towers were added or heightened in the sixteenth century: at Bangor (–1532), St David's (1509–22), Southwark (c. 1520), Derby (1510–32) and Fountains. At Bolton work on a new west tower was halted by the Dissolution. The unfinished tower still stands, as if the workmen have only knocked off and will return.

Conclusion

In about 1497 a Venetian visitor to England reported that the countryside seemed 'very thinly inhabited'. He commented on the 'great fertility of the soils' and noted

147 (left) *Wymondham*

148 Gloucester: central tower, c. *1450–60*

the rain 'which falls almost every day during June, July and August'. He was particularly impressed by ecclesiastical wealth:

> . . . for there is not a parish church in the kingdom so mean as not to possess crucifixes, candlesticks, censers, patens and cups of silver; nor is there a convent of mendicant friars

228

149 *Great Malvern: central tower, c. 1450–60*

so poor as not to have all these same articles of silver, besides many other ornaments worthy of a cathedral in the same metal. Your Magnificence may therefore imagine what the decorations of those enormously rich Benedictine, Carthusian and Cistercian monasteries must be. These are, indeed, more like baronial palaces than religious

150 Great Malvern: tower vault

houses . . . I have been informed that amongst other things, many of these monasteries possess unicorns' horns, of extraordinary size. I have also been told that they have some splendid tombs of English saints, such as St Oswald, St Edmund and St Edward, all kings and martyrs.

(Sneyd 1847, 29)

But this was a static wealth, not the dynamic wealth of the profits of land. The ornaments, precious metals and jewels were often gifts or bequests from aristocrats and royal patrons. Whereas 250 years before gifts had often taken the form of cash, lands or materials, and could lead to a new nave or eastern arm, in these closing years resources were channelled more into works particular to individual donors: highly-wrought chapels, stalls, windows, screens, intricate vaults. This emphasis on precision detail was in contrast with the more expansive, labour-intensive programmes of the thirteenth and early fourteenth centuries, when upwards of thirty great churches could be in process of renewal in a single decade, with capacity to spare.

The ending is best told in the words of some of those who witnessed it. Some abbots and priors protested, many went quietly, not a few offered bribes. In 1537 the Abbot of Crowland wrote to Thomas Cromwell, and sent him

. . . this berar parte of owr fenne fyshe, ryght mekely besechyng yow lordship favorablye to accepte the same fyshe, and to be gud and favorable lorde unto me and my pore house . . .

(Wright 1843, 152)

230

Some of the religious appear to have been relieved by the dismantling of the monastic system. Richard Beerely, a monk of Pershore, apologized to Cromwell for his 'lowly scrybullyng' and stated that

> . . . at thys tyme ys gruggyng yn my conchons that the relygyon wyche we do obser and keype ys no rull of sentt Benett, nor yt no commandyment of God . . .

Beerely related how

> Monckes drynk an bowll after collacyon tell ten or xii of the clock, and cum to mattens as dronck as myss, and sume at cardes, sume at dyss . . .

151 York Minster: west front

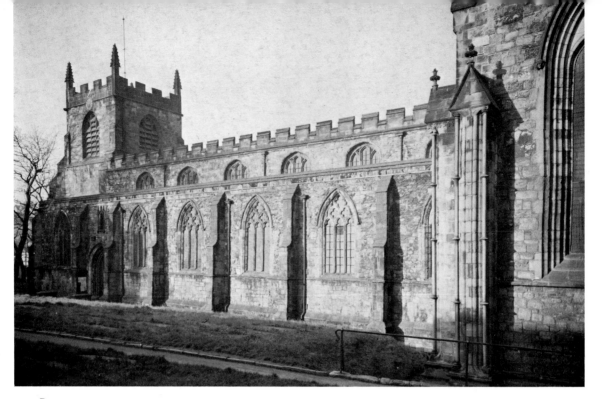

152 *Bangor*

153 *Ely: vault of Bishop West's Chapel, c. 1530*

232

154 (right) *Westminster: Henry VII's Chapel, 1503–19*

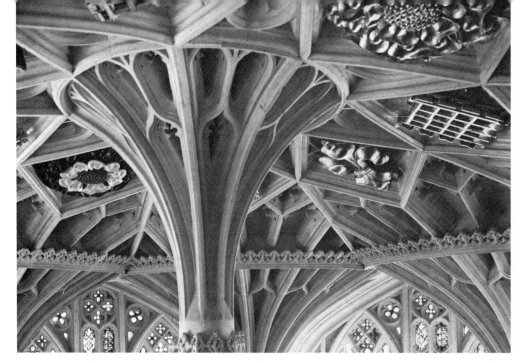

155 *Westminster: Henry VII's Chapel, detail of pendant vault*

The misdemeanours of abbots and priors made good propaganda, and incidents of the kind which occurred at Langdon, Kent, on 23 October 1535 were eagerly reported. Cromwell's agent, Dr Layton, informed his master:

> Wheras immediatly discendyng from my horse, I sent Bartlett, your servant, with alle my servantes, to circumcept the abbay, and surely to kepe alle bake dorres . . . I my self went alone to the abbottes logeyng jonyng upon the feldes and wode, evyn lyke a cony clapper fulle of startyng hoilles, a goode space knokkyng at thabbottes dore, *nec vox nec sensus apparuit*, saveyng thabbottes litle doge that, within his dore faste lokked, bayede and barkede. I fownde a short polax standyng behynde the dore, and with yt I dasshede thabbottes dore in peisses . . . and set one of my men to kepe that dore, and aboute howse I go with that polax in my hande, *ne forte*, for thabbot is a daingerouse desperate knave and a hardy. But for a conclusion, his hore, *alias* his gentle womman, bestyrrede hir stumpis towardes her startyng hoilles, and ther Bartlett wachyng the purset towke the tendre damoisel, and affter I hade examynede hir, to Dover ther to the maire to sett hir in sum cage or prison for viij. dais, and I browgt holy father abbot to Canterbury, and here in Christeschurche I will leve hym in prison.

(1843, 75–6)

Richard Bellasys, one of Cromwell's Commissioners in the north in 1537, was more brisk. After reporting that he had 'taken down all the leads of Jarvaxe [Jervaulx], and maid it in pecys of half foders, wyche leade amowntythe to the nombre of eghten skore and fyve foders, wythe thryttye and ffowre foders and a half that were there byfore', he announced:

> And as for Byrdlington, I have doyn nothing there as yet, but sparythe it to Marche next, bycause the days now are so short; and from suche tyme as I begyn, I trust shortlye to dyspache it . . .

234

157 (right) *Deerhurst: Anglo-Saxon monastery to parish church*

156 Little Malvern: priory to parish church

From Lewes Priory we receive a remarkable picture of the demolition of a great church:

> . . . the laste I wrote unto your lordshyp was the xxth daye of thys present monith (March) . . . by the whych I advertised your lordshyp of the lengthe and greatenes of thys churche, and how we had begon to pull the hole down to the ground. . . . Now we are pluckyng down an hygher vaute, borne up by fower thicke and grose pillars. . . . Thys shall downe for our second worke . . . we browght from London xvij. persons, 3 carpentars, 2 smythes, 2 plummars, and on that kepith the fornace. Every of these attendith to hys own office: x. of them hewed the walls abowte, amonge the whych ther were 3 carpentars: thiese made proctes to undersette wher the other cutte away, thother brake and cutte the waules. Thiese ar men exercised moch better then the men that we fynd here in the contrey. . . . A Tuesday they began to cast the ledde . . .

(1843, 180–1)

158 Lincoln

In a few cases requests for the preservation of churches succeeded. One such plea was made by Thomas Lawarr in 1536 in respect of

> . . . a power howse called Boxgrave . . . wherof I am ffounder, and there lyethe many of my aunsytorys, and also my wyffys mother; and for bycawse hyt is of my ffoundacyon, and that my paryshe churche is under the roofe of the churche of the said monastery, and have made a power chappel to be buried yn . . .
>
> (1843, 119)

Boxgrove was reborn as a parish church, along with some other survivors which have formed the subject of this book.

The Gazetteer

ACH ENTRY CONTAINS facts about the origins of the foundation, a synopsis of
the post-Conquest building history, the date of Dissolution (where applic-
able), a set of references, and a sketch plan reproduced at a scale of roughly 1
inch to 100 feet.

Details about the origins and pre-Conquest histories of the great churches should
be used with caution. The first mention of a church is not necessarily to be equated
with the moment at which the church was established. Our knowledge of subsequent
events, such as refoundations or changes of status, depends upon the extent to which
relevant and trustworthy information has survived. Hence the schemes of dates
which are offered here are likely to present an oversimplified picture.

Exact or approximate dates for building work are given where they are known or
can be surmised with reasonable confidence. Often, however, a campaign is assigned
to the nearest quarter of a century (e.g. C13i), or, where appropriate, to a central
date indicated on stylistic grounds. This is to avoid the impression of false precision
which is sometimes created when building dates are determined according to the
terms of office of abbots or prelates who were associated with the work. Building
programmes were rarely so tidy in their timing. Nor did they always coincide with
the careers of the master-masons who were responsible for the controlling designs.
Only major construction operations are covered.

The references are provided for the guidance of those who would like to look into
the history of a church or churches in greater detail. They are introductory rather
than comprehensive, therefore, but an attempt has been made to mention most of the
main architectural studies, to draw attention to some of the valuable accounts by
eighteenth- and nineteenth-century writers, and to include a selection of works
which deal with specific aspects or features of churches (glass, screens, roofs, bosses,
etc.).

Very few general volumes are listed in the Gazetteer, but further particulars about
the cathedrals are to be found in J. H. Harvey's *Cathedrals of England and Wales* (1974),
in which the contributions of individual architects and craftsmen are discussed and
listed. See also the same author's *Gothic England* (2nd ed., 1948) which contains a

237

classified bibliography, and the select bibliography in his *English Cathedrals: A Reader's Guide* (1951). Francis Bond's *Gothic Architecture in England* (1905) is a mine of information on most matters connected with the greater churches. For pre-Conquest buildings consult H. M. and J. Taylor, *Anglo-Saxon Architecture*, volumes I and II (1965), and H. M. Taylor's volume III (1978). Sir Alfred Clapham's *English Romanesque Architecture After the Conquest* (1934, reprinted 1969) remains unsurpassed as a general introduction to churches of the Anglo-Norman period, although it has now been overtaken on certain matters of detail by the results of recent archaeological investigations. Many of the churches mentioned here, including some of the important non-cathedral buildings such as Beverley, Christchurch, Malmesbury, Tewkesbury and Wimborne, were given their own volumes in *Bell's Cathedral Series*. More recently all the churches have been visited, described and discussed by Sir Nikolaus Pevsner and his assistants in *The Buildings of England* (volumes published by county, 1951–76). For information on monastic history consult M. D. Knowles and R. N. Hadcock, *Medieval Religious Houses: England and Wales* (1971), and M. D. Knowles, *The Monastic Order in England* (1940), *The Religious Orders in England I* (1948), II (1955) and III (1959).

ABBEY DORE

Holy Trinity and St Mary
Fd 1147: Cistercian Monks. D. 1536.
MAIN BUILDING DATES: *c.* 1180– : western bay of presbytery and transept; C13i: eastern bays of presbytery and ambulatory; 1632–4: restoration, S tower, blocking of nave arch, crossing screen; 1904: restoration.

REFERENCES: RCHM *Hereford* I, 1–9 (Modified plan Vol. III opp. 226); R. Paul: 'The Church and Monastery of Abbey Dore', *Trans Bristol Gloucestershire Archaeol Soc* XXVII, 117–26; C17 restoration: T. Blashill in *Trans Woolhope Natur Fld Club* (1901), 184–8; see also *J Archaeol Ass* XLI (1885), 363–71; E. Sledmere: *Abbey Dore, Herefordshire: its building and restoration* (1914). History: D. H. Williams in *Monmouthshire Antiq* 2 (1966), pt 2, 65–104. Screen: Vallance (1947), 89.

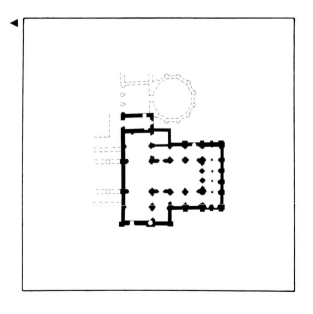

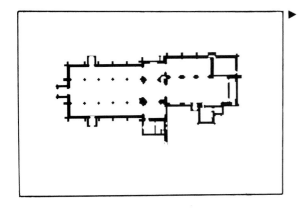

BANGOR
St Deiniol
See: C6
Refd 1092: secular canons.

MAIN BUILDING DATES: (*c*. 1120–39: Norman church);*c*. 1200– : presbytery; C14i–ii: nave aisles; *c*. 1496–1534: modifications; 1506–34: nave arcades and W tower; 1866–75: transept and restoration (Scott).

REFERENCES: RCAHM *Caernarvonshire* II (1960), 1–9. H. Hughes: 'The Architectural History of . . .' *Archaeol Cambrensis* (1901), 179–204, (1902), 261–76, (1904), 17–32. C. A. R. Radford: 'Bangor Cathedral in the Twelfth and Thirteenth Centuries: Recent Discoveries', *Archaeol Cambrensis* (1949), 256–61. See also*Archaeol Cambrensis* (1850), 188–93. Tiles: S. W. Williams in *Archaeol Cambrensis* (1895), 107–11. M. L. Clarke: *Bangor Cathedral* (1975).

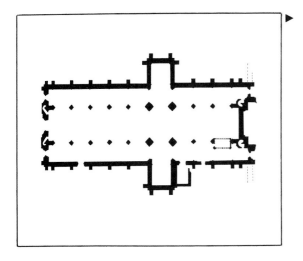

ARUNDEL
St Nicholas
–1177: secular canons. 1177–1380: Benedictine Monks. Refd 1387: collegiate. D. 1544.

MAIN BUILDING DATES: 1380–97: eastern arm, transept, nave, W porch; C15: Lady Chapel; 1860: chantry chapel; 1873: dividing wall.

REFERENCES: E. Freeman: 'The case of the collegiate church of Arundel', *Archaeol J* 38 (1881), 244–70. *Archaeol J* 92 (1935), 403; *Sussex Archaeol Collect* 107 (1969). Wall painting: *J Brit Archaeol Ass* VI (1851), 440. Chantries: Cook (1947), 179–81. Screen: Vallance (1947), 130–3. History: VCH *Sussex* II, 108–9. See also *Archaeol J* 116 (1959), 246–8.

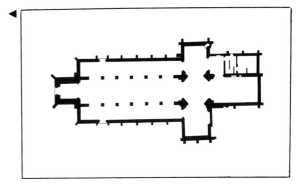

BATH
SS Peter and Paul
See: 1090 (from Wells); 1192 (with Glastonbury); 1218 (Bath and Wells). Fd*c*. 676: nuns. Refd 963–4: 'Benedictine' Monks. D. 1539.

MAIN BUILDING DATES: (*c*. 1090–1166: Norman church);*c*. 1496–1539: presbytery, transept, nave and W front; 1514– : Prior Bird's chantry;–*c*. 1600: vaulting; 1860–73: restoration and nave vault; 1895–1901: repairs to W front.

REFERENCES: J. Britton: *History and Antiquities of Bath Abbey Church* (1825). J. T. Irvine: 'Description of the remains of the Norman cathedral of . . . exposed during the repairs made between 1863 and 1872', *J Brit Archaeol Ass* XLVI (1890), 85–94. See also *Proc Somerset Archaeol Natur Hist Soc* 60, pt 1, 33–6; pt 2, 1; pt 2; *Archaeol J* 87 (1930), 412–16. Chantry: Cook (1947), 146. History: VCH *Somerset* II, 69–81.

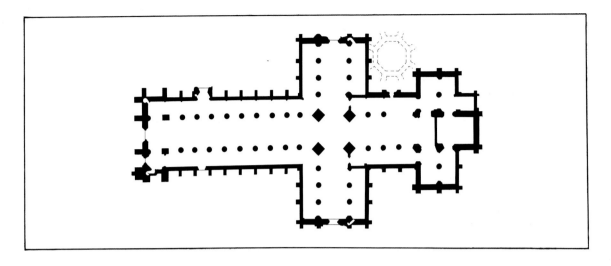

BEVERLEY

St John

Fd *c*. 690: secular canons.

MAIN BUILDING DATES: *c*. 1220– : eastern arm, transept, first bay of central nave aisle (first two bays at triforium level); *c*. 1310– : nave; *c*. 1340– : reredos; *c*. 1390– : W end of nave, N porch and W towers; 1416: E window; 1716–40: restorations; 1825: reconstruction of reredos; 1866–78: restorations (Scott).

REFERENCES: G. Oliver: *History and Antiquities of Beverley* (1829). 'Memorials of Beverley Minster: the Chapter Act Book', *Surtees Soc* 108 (1903). J. Bilson: 'On the discovery of some Remains of the Chapter House of . . .' *Archaeologia* 54 (1895), 425–32. J. Bilson: 'Norman work in the Nave Triforium of . . .' *The Antiquary* 27 (1893), 18–23.

R. Whiteing: 'Beverley Minster', *J. Brit Archaeol Ass* 29 (1923), 135–8. R. Whiteing: *Georgian Restorations at . . . 1712–1740* (n.d.). J. Bilson: 'Beverley Minster, some stray notes', *Yorkshire Archaeol J* 24 (1916–17), 221–35. W. Stephenson: 'On the Discovery of a Well in . . .' *Yorkshire Archaeol J* 5 (1879), 126–33. P. Venables: 'St John of Beverley, his miracles and his minster', *Assoc Architect Socs Rep and Pap* XVII, 229–35. R. C. Hope: 'Notes on musical instruments on labels of arches in the nave of . . .' *Trans East Riding Antiq Soc* III (1895), 63–6. B. Allsop: 'A Note on the Arcading and Sculpture in the South Aisle of . . .' *Architectural History* 2 (1959), 8–18. See also Bilson in *Architectural Review* III (1897), 199; and *Durham Northumberland Archaeol Soc Trans* 1896. Screens: Vallance (1947), 133–5. History: VCH *Yorks* III, 353–9.

BINHAM

St Mary the Virgin

Fd *c*. 1091: Benedictine Monks. D. 1539.

MAIN BUILDING DATES: *C*. 1091– : Norman church; C12i–ii: nave; C12iii–iv: completion of nave; *c*. 1240: W front; 1812: alterations and removal of N aisle.

REFERENCES: *The Antiquary* III (1881), 73. *Archaeol J* 80 (1923), 334. F. H. Fairweather in *Supplement to Blomefield's Norfolk*, ed. C. Ingleby (1929), 324–7. Screen: Vallance (1947), 91. History: VCH *Norfolk* II, 343–6. L Marr: *Binham Priory* (n.d.).

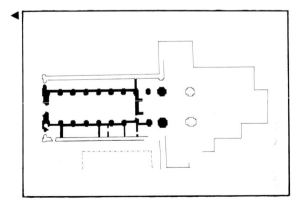

BLYTH
St Mary the Virgin
Fd 1088: Benedictine Monks. D. 1536.
MAIN BUILDING DATES: *c.* 1090– : nave and N aisle;
c. 1290– : S (parish) aisle; *c.* 1400: W tower; C15i:
chancel screen; 1933: N vestry.

REFERENCES: J. Raine: *History and Antiquities of Blyth*
(1860). P. Venables: 'The Benedictine priory of
the Blessed Virgin Mary, Blyth, Notts.' *Ass
Architect Socs Rep and Pap* XV, 141–67. C. C.
Hodges: *Blyth Priory* (1881). J. Bilson: 'Notes
on . . .' *Yorkshire Archaeol J* 20 (1909), 447–54. F. H.
Fairweather: 'Some additions to the plan of the
Benedictine Priory Church of St Mary, Blyth,
Notts.' *Antiq J* 6 (1926), 36–42. Screens: Vallance
(1947), 91–3. See also *J Brit Archaeol Ass* 39 (1933),
39–43; *Yorks Archaeol J* 21 (1910), 168–75. History:
VCH *Notts* II, 83–8.

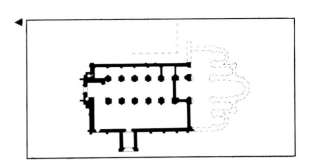

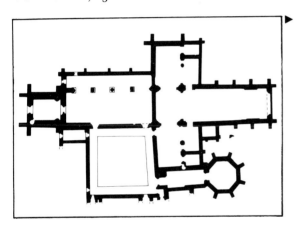

BOLTON
Blessed Virgin Mary
Fd 1154: Augustinian Canons. D. 1540.
MAIN BUILDING DATES: (C12iii–iv: eastern arm,
crossing); *c.* 1190–1240: nave, N nave aisle, W
front; C14i: N aisle windows, rebuilding of transept; 1520– : W tower (unfinished).

REFERENCES: *The Antiquary* I (1880), 194. A.
Hamilton Thompson: *Bolton Priory* (1928). G.
Rowe: 'Bolton Abbey', *Assoc Archit Socs Rep and Pap*
XVI, 57–62. *Archaeol J* 125 (1968), 331–3. Screen:
Vallance (1947), 93. History: VCH *Yorks* III,
195–9. See also: Kershaw (1973).

BOXGROVE
St Mary
–1066: secular canons. Refd 1105: Benedictine
Monks. D. 1536.
MAIN BUILDING DATES: C12i: transept and two
eastern bays of nave; C12iii–iv: crossing and central tower; C13i: presbytery; C14: sacristy; C16i:
chantry chapel; central tower rebuilt after Dissolution; 1813: repairs; 1944– : damage and repairs.

REFERENCES: VCH *Sussex* II, 52–60; IV, 141 ff. W.
St John Hope: 'Boxgrove church and monastery',
Sussex Archaeol Collect 43 (1901), 158–65. *Archaeol J*
92 (1935), 415–16. See also: *Sussex Archaeol Collect*
59, 18; *The Builder's J*, April 1904. Screen: Vallance
(1947), 21, 93. Chantry: Cook (1947), 145.

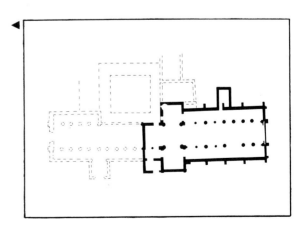

BRECON
St John the Evangelist
See: 1922
Fd *c*. 1110: Benedictine Monks. D. 1538.
MAIN BUILDING DATES: C13i–ii chancel, transept, tower, portion of N chapel of S transept arm; C14i–ii: nave; C14iii: chapel of N transept arm; 1862 and 1874: restorations (Scott); 1913: restoration.

REFERENCES: *Archaeol Cambrensis* (1925), 470–6; (1951), 171–2. Screen: Vallance (1947), 94. D. Walker: *Links with the Past* (1976).

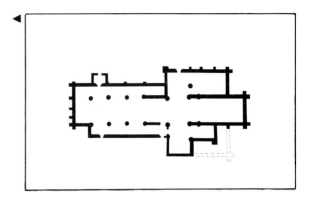

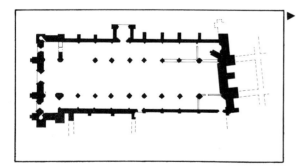

BRIDLINGTON
St Mary the Virgin
Fd *c*. 1115: Augustinian Canons. D. 1537.
MAIN BUILDING DATES: C13i: lower stage of NW tower; C13ii–iii: nave, aisles, N porch, NW tower; C15: W front, SW tower, three western bays of S nave arcade; C16: blocking of W side of crossing; 1870s: restoration and upper stages of W towers (Scott).

REFERENCES: VCH *Yorks E Riding* III, 199–205. *Ass Architect Socs Rep and Pap* III (1854), 40. J. Bilson: 'Bridlington Priory Church', *Yorkshire Archaeol J* 22 (1913), 238–9. See also *Yorkshire Archaeol J* 21 (1910), 168–75. Stalls: J. S. Purvis in *Yorkshire Archaeol J* 29 (1929), 157–201. M. Pricket: *The Priory Church of Bridlington* (1831). J. Caley: 'Copy of a survey of the priory of . . . in Yorkshire, taken about the 32nd year of Henry VIII', *Archaeologia* XIX (1821), 270–5.

BRINKBURN
SS Peter and Paul
Fd −1135: Augustinian Canons. D. 1536.
MAIN BUILDING DATES: *c.* 1190− : eastern arm, transept, tower, nave; C13i–ii: W front; 1858: reroofing and restoration, SW angle of nave rebuilt (Austin).

REFERENCES: *A History of Northumberland* VII, 478–92. R. J. Johnson: in *Trans Durham and Northumberland Archaeol Soc* (1862–68), 103. *Archaeol J* 133 (1976), 140–5.

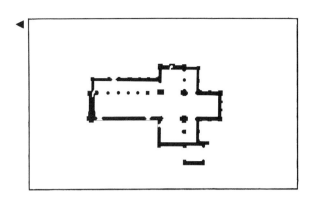

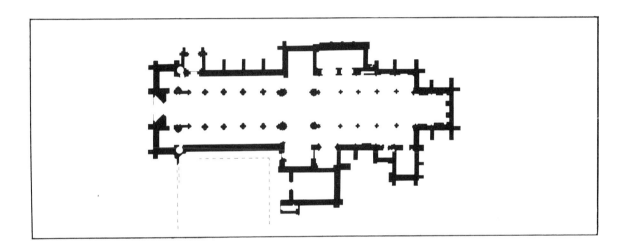

BRISTOL
St Augustine (now Holy Trinity)
See: 1542–1836; 1836–97 with Gloucester; 1897–
Fd 1140: Augustinian Canons. D. 1538.
MAIN BUILDING DATES: C12iii: chapter-house; C13i–ii: Elder Lady Chapel; C14i–ii: eastern arm; C15ii–iii: transept and tower; 1868–88: nave and western towers (Street); 1888− : restoration.

REFERENCES: Browne Willis: *Mitred Abbeys* (1718), 225–9. R. W. Paul: 'The plan of the church and monastery of St Augustine . . .'*Archaeologia* 63 (1912), 231–50. H. Bock: 'Bristol Cathedral and its place in European Architecture', *Bristol Cathedral 800th Anniversary Booklet* (1965). N. Pevsner: 'Bristol, Troyes and Gloucester', *Architectural Review* 113 (Feb. 1953). Tiles: R. Warren in *Proc Clifton Antiq Club* 5 (1904), 122–7. Stalls: Mary P. Perry in *Archaeol J* 78 (1921), 233–50. Norman remains: C. Lyneham in *Proc Clifton Antiq Club* 6 (1905), 59–61. Choir screen: R. H. Warren in *Proc Clifton Antiq Club* 6 (1905), 6–10; *Trans Bristol Gloucestershire Archaeol Soc* 27 (1904), 127–30. Harrowing of Hell relief: M. Q. Smith in *Trans Bristol Gloucestershire Archaeol Soc* 94 (1977), 101–6. Heraldry: I. Ware in *Trans Bristol Gloucestershire Archaeol Soc* 25 (1902), 102–32. Work of Abbot Knowle: *Proc Clifton Antiq Club* 5 (1904), 132–62. Architectural history: *Trans Bristol Gloucestershire Archaeol Soc* 20 (1897), 55–75. History: VCH *Glos* II, 75–9.

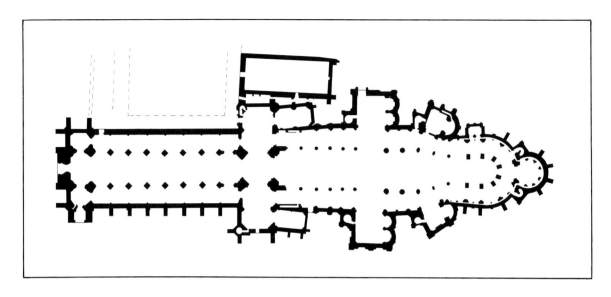

CANTERBURY

Christ Church

See: *c*. 600

Fd *c*. 600: secular canons. Refd 1070: Benedictine Monks. D. 1539.

MAIN BUILDING DATES: (1070–7: first Norman church; fragments of transept and eastern arm); *c*. 1096– : extension of eastern arm and crypt; 1175–84: choir, Trinity Chapel, Corona; C14i: chapter-house (part); *c*. 1380–1405: nave and remodelling of south transept arm; C15i: completion of chapter-house; C15i–ii: SW tower; *c*. 1450: remodelling of N transept arm, Lady Chapel; C15iv–C16i: central tower; 1834–40: NW tower; 1904–12: restoration; 1974– : restoration.

REFERENCES: J. Armitage Robinson: 'The Early Community at Christ Church, Canterbury', *J Theological Stud* 27 (1926), 225–40. D. Parsons: 'The Pre-Conquest Cathedral at . . .' *Archaeol Cantiana* 84 (1969), 175–84. H. M. Taylor: 'The Anglo-Saxon Cathedral Church at . . .' *Archaeol J* 126 (1969), 101–30. E. C. Gilbert: 'The Date of the late Saxon Cathedral at . . .' *Archaeol J* 127 (1970), 202–10. R. D. H. Gem: 'The Anglo-Saxon Cathedral Church at . . . : a further contribution', *Archaeol J* 127 (1970), 196–201. R. Willis: *The Architectural History of . . .* (1845). E. C. Gilbert: 'The First Norman Cathedral at . . .', *Archaeol Can-* *tiana* 87 (1973), 25–50; see also T. Tatton-Brown in *Bulletin* of the CBA Churches Committee 9 (1978). Norman crypt: E. P. L. Brock in *J Brit Archaeol Ass* (1895), 242–50. J. Dart: *The History and Antiquities of . . .* (1726). W. Woomoth: *A History and Description of Canterbury Cathedral* (1816). C. E. Woodruff & W. Danks: *Memorials of . . .* (1912). W. D. Caroe: 'Canterbury . . . Choir during the Commonwealth and after', *Archaeologia* 62 (1911), 353–66. A. Oswald: '. . . the Nave and its Designer', *Burlington Mag* 75 (1939), 221–8. R. A. L. Smith: *Canterbury Cathedral Priory: a study in monastic administration* (1943). C. E. Woodruff: 'The Financial Aspect of the Cult of St Thomas of Canterbury', *Archaeol Cantiana* 44 (1932), 13–32. W. Urry: 'Cardinal Morton and the Angel Steeple', *Friends of Canterbury . . . 38th Annual Report* (1965). C. A. Hewett & T. Tatton-Brown: 'New Structural Evidence regarding Bell Harry Tower and the South-East Spire at Canterbury', *Archaeol Cantiana* 92 (1976), 129–36. M. H. Caviness: *The Early Stained Glass of Canterbury Cathedral circa 1175–1220* (1977). See also: *Archaeologia* X (1792), 37–49; *Ass Architect Socs Rep and Pap* XIV, 128–49. Wall paintings: *Archaeologia* 52 (1890), 389; *Archaeol J* 35 (1878), 282–8; Tristram I and II; *Archaeologia* 63 (1912), 51–6. Roof bosses: *Archaeologia* 84 (1934), 41–61. Screens: Vallance (1947), 35. Chantry chapels: Cook (1947), 72 ff. History: VCH *Kent*, II, 113–21.

CARLISLE
Holy Trinity
See: 1133
−1092: secular canons. Refd 1123: Augustinian
Canons. D. 1540.

MAIN BUILDING DATES: C11iv–C12i: Norman
church; C13iii–C14: upper stage of eastern arm;
C15i: tower, N arm of transept, stalls; *c*. 1450–60:
pulpitum; 1646: removal of five western bays of
nave; 1853–70: restoration (Christian).

REFERENCES: R. W. Billings: *Carlisle Cathedral*
(1840). Browne Willis: *Mitred Abbeys* (1718), 229–
34. C. J. Ferguson in *The Builder* (May 1893); *J Roy
Inst Brit Architects* 38 (1902) viii, 102–4. Sculptured
capitals in choir: *Cumberland Westmorland Antiq
Archaeol Soc* II, 280. Glass: F. C. Eeles in *Trans
Cumberland Westmorland Antiq Archaeol Soc n ser* 26
(1926), 312–17. Screens: Vallance (1947), 36.
Chantry chapel: Cook (1947), 80.

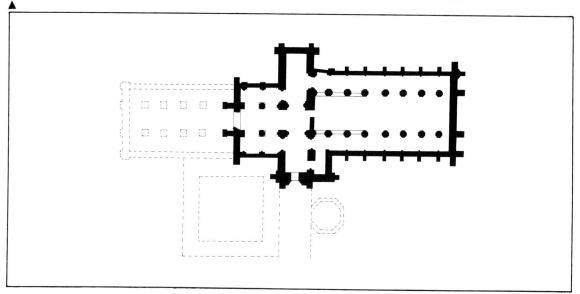

CARTMEL
St Mary the Virgin
Fd 1189–94: Augustinian Canons. D. 1536.

MAIN BUILDING DATES: *c*. 1190–1220: eastern arm
and transept; C13i–ii: part of N choir aisle; *c*.
1395–1420: nave; C15: tower; C16i: choir screen.

REFERENCES: J. C. Dickinson: 'The Architectural
Development of . . .' *Trans Cumberland Westmorland
Archaeol Soc n ser* 45 (1946), 49–66. VCH *Lancs* II,
143–8; VIII, 254–65. *Archaeol J* 127 (1970), 270–1.
J. L. Petit: 'Cartmel priory church . . .' *Archaeol J*
XXVIII, 81–91. H. F. Rigge: 'Harrington tomb in
Cartmel church', *Cumberland Westmorland Antiq
Archaeol Soc* V, 109. W. O. Roper: 'Cartmel
Church', *Trans Cumberland Westmorland Archaeol Soc*
XIII (1895), 293–8. See also *The Builder* (Oct.
1899).

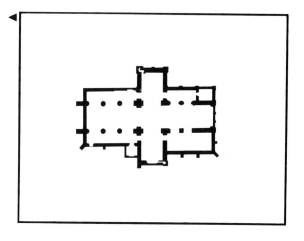

CHESTER
St John Baptist
See: 1072/5–1102
Fd/Refd ?906: secular canons. D. *c.* 1547.

MAIN BUILDING DATES: C12i–ii: W bay of presbytery, crossing, transept (frags), four eastern bays of nave arcade and N aisle; C12iv: nave triforium;

C13iii: nave clerestory; 1574– : NW tower (fell 1881); 1859–66: S nave aisle; 1882: N porch.

REFERENCES: J. H. Parker: 'The collegiate church of . . .' *Chester N Wales Architect Archaeol Hist Soc* II, 329–46. H. Raikes: 'The church of . . .' *Chester N Wales etc*. I, 135–44. Description: *The Antiquary* VII (1883), 225. Fall of tower: *The Antiquary* III (1881), 282. See also *Archaeol J* 94 (1937), 307–8.

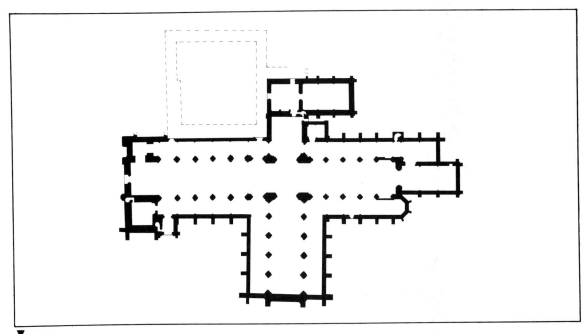

CHESTER
St Werburgh
See: 1541
–875: SS Peter and Paul, ?nuns. Refd after 907: secular canons. Refd 1092: Benedictine Monks. D. 1540.

MAIN BUILDING DATES: C11iv–C12i: N transept arm and traces of presbytery; *c.* 1240: chapterhouse vestibule; *c.* 1250– : chapter-house; *c.* 1260–90: Lady Chapel (restored 1872); *c.* 1285–1315: choir; C14i: crossing and first bay of nave; *c.* 1350– : S transept arm up to triforium; *c.* 1360: S nave aisle; *c.* 1390: stalls; *c.* 1485–1537: N nave arcade, clerestory, upper stage of central tower, W front, upper stage of S transept arm; 1868–72: restoration (Scott).

REFERENCES: Browne Willis: *Mitred Abbeys* (1718), 249–53. T. Rickman: 'On the architectural history of Chester Cathedral', *Chester N Wales Architect Archaeol Hist Soc* II (1864), 277–88. J. H. Parker: *The Medieval Architecture of Chester* (1858). R. V. H. Burne: *Chester Cathedral* (SPCK 1958). R. V. H. Burne: *The Monks of Chester* (SPCK 1962). F. Bennett: *Chester Cathedral* (1925). Norman remains: *Chester N Wales etc*. I, 60–7. E. K. McConnell:'The Abbey of St Werburgh, Chester, in theThirteenth Century', *Trans Hist Soc Lancashire Cheshire* (1904), 42. Architectural history: G. Scott in *Chester N Wales etc*. III, 159–82. Jacobean work: E. Barber in *Chester N Wales etc. n ser* 12 (1906), 5–21. S transept arm and cloisters; stalls, misereres and woodwork of choir; discovery of Ralph Higden's tomb: E. Barber in *Chester N Wales etc. n ser* 9 (1904), 5–19; 99–114; 115–28. Misericords: see also *Chester N Wales etc*. (1894), 46–57. See also A. Ashpitel in *J. Brit Archaeol Ass* V (1850), 177–86; *The Builder* (March 1893); *Archaeol J* 5, 17–20.

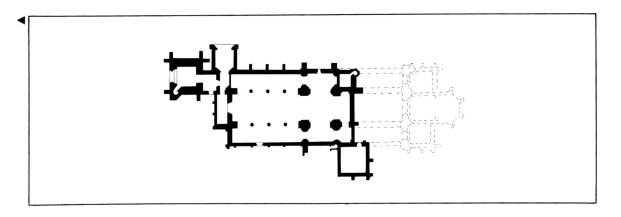

CHICHESTER
Holy Trinity
See: 1075
Fd/Refd 1075: secular canons.
MAIN BUILDING DATES: C11iv–C12i: presbytery; C12i–ii: nave; 1186–99: retrochoir; C13i: upper stage of SW tower; C13iv: eastward extension of Lady Chapel; C15i: campanile; 1861–6: central tower; 1899–1902: NW tower.

REFERENCES: Hay: *History of Chichester* (1804). R. Willis: 'The Architectural History of . . .' (1861; repr. 1972). Freeman: 'Some of the characteristic features of . . .' *Sussex Archaeol Collect* I, 142–8. J. Cavis Brown: 'Plan of Chichester Cathedral in the year 1635', *Sussex Archaeol Collect* I, 184. W. D.

Peckham: 'Some notes on . . .' *Sussex Archaeol Collect* 111 (1973), 20–6. E. S. Prior: 'Chichester Masoncraft', *Proc Harrow Architect Club* (1904). Restorations: O. H. Leeney in *Sussex Archaeol Collect* 86 (1947), 155–63; tower (fell 1636), 185–6. Norman apse: *Medieval Archaeol* 1967, 282; 1969, 250. G. Hills: 'Chichester Cathedral', *J Brit Archaeol Ass* XX (1864), 155–60. See also *Archaeol J* 92 (1935), 390. G. Zarnecki: 'The Chichester Reliefs', *Archaeol J* 110 (1953), 106–19. Wall paintings: VCH *Sussex* III, 149–50; Tristram II, 524; *Sussex Archaeol Collect* 43 (1900), 229; 52 (1909), 1. W. R. Stephens: *Memorials of the south Saxon see and Cathedral Church of Chichester* (1876). History: VCH *Sussex* II, 47–51; architecture: III, 105–46.

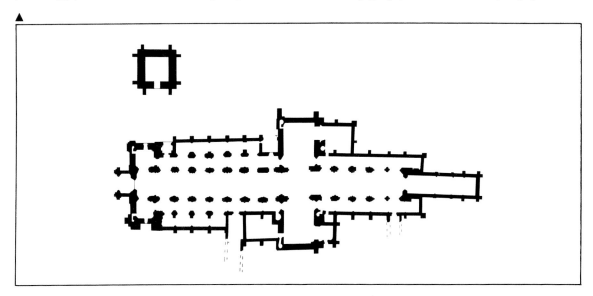

CHRISTCHURCH

Christ Church

–1150: secular canons. Refd 1150: Augustinian Canons. D. 1539.

MAIN BUILDING DATES: *c.* 1090–1120: crypts, transept, transept apses, nave; *c.* 1195–1225: nave clerestory; C13i: nave aisles altered, N porch, N transeptal chapels; C14iii–iv: Lady Chapel, retrochoir, pulpitum; C15: W tower and front; C15ii–C16i: choir; C16: chantry chapels in choir aisles; 1819: stucco nave vault.

REFERENCES: C. R. Peers in VCH *Hants* V, 101. B. Ferrey: *Christ Church, Hants* (1834). G. J. Combs in *J Roy Inst Brit Architects 3 ser* 15 (1908), 557–81. See also: *Archaeol J* 123 (1966), 204–5. Rood screen: *Archaeol J* 5 (1848), 142–5. Screen enclosing Draper Chapel: Vallance (1947), 99. Chantry chapels: Cook (1947), 147 ff. Masons' designs on plaster in room above north transept chapel: *Gentleman's Mag ser 3,* (1860), 277; 9 (1861), 635.

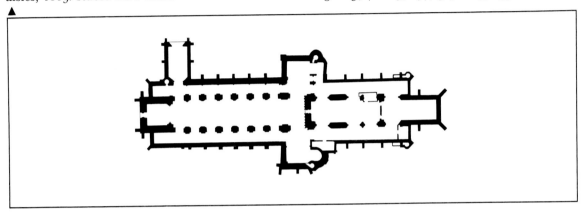

CROWLAND

St Mary the Virgin, St Bartholomew and St Guthlac

Fd 716–57. Refd 946–55.

971: Benedictine Monks. D. 1539.

MAIN BUILDING DATES: (1091– : Norman church; 1114–90: rebuilding; *c.* 1200–36: alterations; *c.* 1260: remodelling of W end of nave); *c.* 1400: N nave aisle; *c.* 1430–70: NW tower; 1720: collapse of nave roof; 1860: repairs.

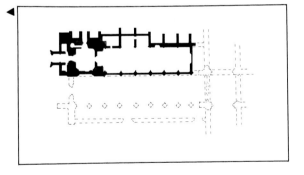

REFERENCES: E. Moore: *Fen and Marshland Churches*, 62. E. Moore: 'On Croyland abbey', *Assoc Architect Socs Rep and Pap* III, 272–83; VI, 20–7. A. S. Canham: 'The Archaeology of Crowland', *J Brit Archaeol Ass* XLVII (1891), 280–300. See also *The Builder* (Sept 1894). W. F. Bolton: 'The Croyland Quatrefoil and Polychronicon', *J Warburg Courtauld Inst* 21, 295. Screens: Vallance (1947), 99. History: VCH *Lincs* II, 105.

DORCHESTER

SS Peter, Paul and Birinius
See: 634–1072
–1140: secular canons. Refd 1140: Augustinian
Canons. D. 1536.

MAIN BUILDING DATES: C12iii: fragments of presbytery and transept; C13i–ii: presbytery N aisle; *c.*
1300: presbytery arcades and S aisle; *c.* 1320: S
nave arcade and aisle; *c.* 1350: E end; *c.* 1605: W
tower and reduction of transept.

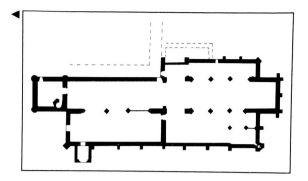

REFERENCES: J. H. Parker: *Dorchester Church* (1845).
W. C. Macfarlane: 'Dorchester Abbey Church',
Newbury Fld Club III, 5–9. E. Freeman: 'On the
architecture of . . .' *Archaeol J* 9 (1852), 158–69,
262–80, 329–35. N. C. S. Poyntz: 'The Abbey
Church of Dorchester', *J Brit Archaeol Ass*
XLVII(1891), 222–4. See also *Archaeol J* 67 (1910)
334–5. Glass: E. S. Bouchier: *Notes on the stained
glass of the Oxford district* (1918). Screen: Vallance
(1947), 101. See also *The Antiquary* VI, 70. History:
VCH *Oxon* II, 87–90; VII, 56–61.

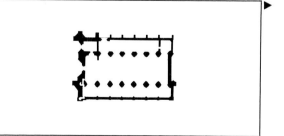

DUNSTABLE

St Peter
Fd 1131–2 (or before 1125?): Augustinian Canons.
D. 1540.

MAIN BUILDING DATES: *c.* 1150–1200: nave arcades,
part of S nave aisle and core of W front; C13i: W
façade of aisles; C15: adaptation of triforium; 1891:
restoration and remodelling of aisles.

REFERENCES: Notes in *Buckinghamshire Architect
Archaeol Soc Recs* X, 272. S. Gardner: 'Dunstable
Priory Church', *Clapton Architect Club Proc* (1891),
41. W. G. Smith in *Proc Soc Antiq ser 2* XXIII
(1910), 151–7. Screens: Vallance (1947), 101. History: VCH *Beds* III, 364–8.

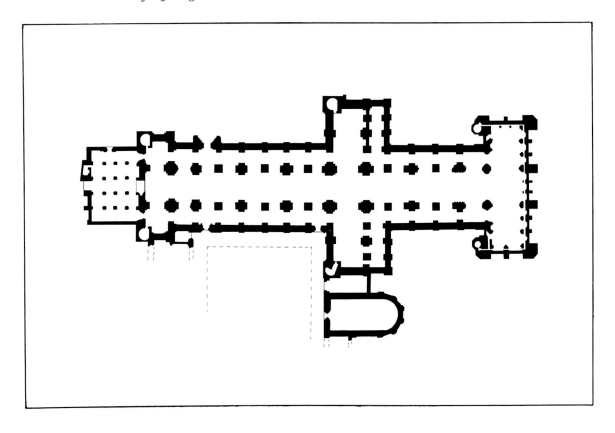

DURHAM
St Mary and St Cuthbert
See: 997
997: secular canons. Refd 1093: Benedictine Monks. D. 1540.

MAIN BUILDING DATES: 1093–1100: choir and presbytery; *c.* 1100–37: nave and lower stages of W towers; C12ii: chapter-house; *c.* 1170– : Galilee; C13i: upper stages of W towers; C13ii–iii: eastern transept; C15iii–iv: central tower heightened.

REFERENCES: R. W. Billings: *Durham Cathedral* (1843). Browne Willis: *Mitred Abbeys* (1718), 253–65. W. A. Pantin: *Durham Cathedral* (1948). R. B. Dobson: *Durham Priory* (1973). R. A. Cordingly: 'Cathedral Innovations: James Wyatt Architect at Durham Cathedral 1795–7', *Trans Ancient Mon Soc new ser* 3 (1955), 31–55. W. Greenwell: 'Drawings of parts of the cathedral at Durham, made at the end of the eighteenth century', *Durham Northumberland Architect Archaeol Soc* 5 (1904), 29–36. J. Bilson: 'On the Recent Discoveries at the East End of the Cathedral Church at Durham', *Archaeol J* 53 (1896), 1–18. J. Bilson: 'Durham Cathedral and the Chronology of its Vaults', *Archaeol J* 79 (1922), 101. E. W. Hudson: 'The beginnings of Gothic architecture and Norman vaulting: the Durham example further considered and compared', *J Roy Inst Brit Architects ser 3* IX, 509–17. G. M. Hills: 'The cathedral and monastery of St Cuthbert at Durham', *J Brit Archaeol Ass* XXII (1866), 197–237. R. A. Cordingly: 'Norman Decoration in Durham Cathedral', *Archaeol Aeliana ser 4* 10 (1933). Rev. C. W. Greenwell: 'The history of Durham Cathedral', *Berwickshire Nat Club* IX, 57–73. See also Greenwell in *Durham Northumberland Architect Archaeol Soc* II, 163–234. Rev. H. Fowler: 'Excavations on the site of the chapter-house of Durham . . .' *Durham Northumberland etc.* II, 235–70. Reopening of St Cuthbert's tomb: E. J. Taylor in *Proc Soc Antiq Newcastle* 9 (1904), 18–20. History: VCH *Durham* II, 86–103; architecture: III, 93–137.

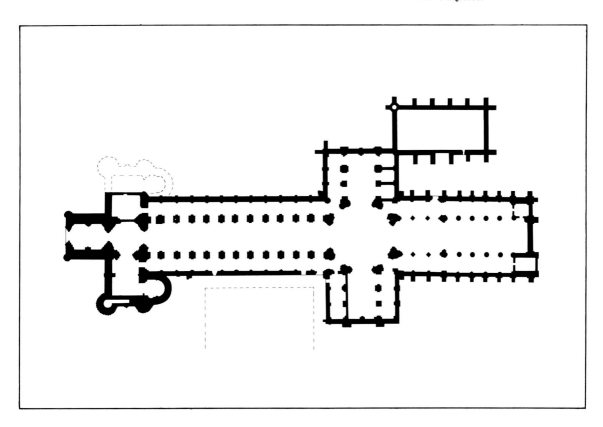

ELY

Holy Trinity (formerly St Peter and St
Etheldreda)
See: 1109
Fd *c*. 673: nuns ?double monastery. C9: ?secular
canons. Refd 970: Benedictine Monks. D. 1540.

MAIN BUILDING DATES: C11iv–C12ii transept and
nave; C12iv: western transept; C13ii: presbytery;
1321–C14ii: Lady Chapel, choir, octagon and lantern, Prior Crauden's Chapel; C15iv: Bishop
Alcock's Chapel; C16i–ii: Bishop West's Chapel.
1845– : restoration.

REFERENCES: Browne Willis: *Mitred Abbeys* (1718),
265–81. J. Bentham: *The History and Antiquities of the
Cathedral Church of Ely* 2 vols (1771); 2nd ed. vol. I:
1812; supplement by W. Stephenson: 1817. J. Ben-
tham: 'Extract of a letter . . . to the Dean of Exeter
concerning certain discoveries in Ely minster',
Archaeologia II (1773), 364–6. C. W. Stubbs: *Histor-
ical Memorials of Ely Cathedral* (1897). D. J. Stewart:
The Architectural History of Ely Cathedral (1868).
T. D. Atkinson: *Architectural History of the Benedictine
Monastery of St Etheldreda at Ely* (1933). W. Wilkins:
'An account of the Prior's Chapel at Ely',
Archaeologia XIV (1803), 105. R. Gough: 'A mosaic
pavement in the prior's chapel at . . .', *Archaeologia*
X (1792), 151–5. Pulpitum: see W. St John Hope
in *Archaeologia* 68 (1917), 43–110. M. R. James:
'The sculptures in the Lady Chapel at Ely',
Archaeol J 49 (1892), 345–62. G. Zarnecki: *Early
Sculpture of Ely* (1958). Wall paintings: *Archaeol J* 34
(1877), 276; Tristram II, 541– ; Tristram III, 168.
F. R. Chapman: *Sacrist Rolls of Ely, 1291–1360*
(1907). C. J. P. Cave: 'The Roof Bosses in . . .' *Proc
Cambridge Antiq Soc* 32 (1932). Screens: Vallance
(1947), 42. Chantry chapels: Cook (1947), 85–6.
VCH *Cambs*, IV, 50–77. Masons' drawings:
Pritchard (1967), 37–42.

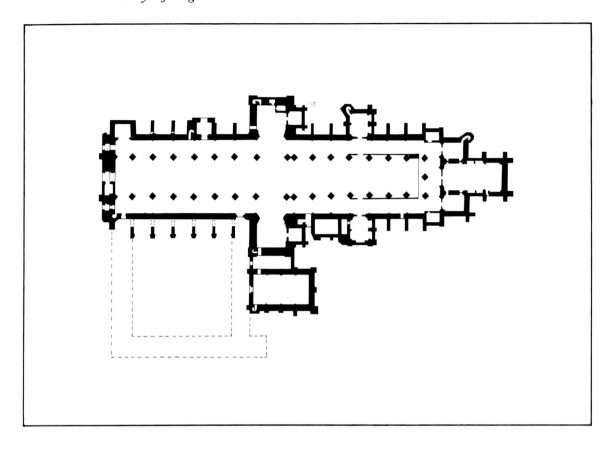

EXETER
BVM and St Peter
See: 1050 (transferred from Crediton)
Fd ?before *c*. 690. 932: 'Benedictine' Monks. Refd
1019. 1050: secular canons.

MAIN BUILDING DATES: C12i–ii: transept, transeptal towers; C13ii: chapter-house; C13iv–C14ii:
presbytery, choir, crossing, nave; C14ii–iii: west
front, vault of nave; 1870–7: restoration (Scott).

REFERENCES: H. E. Bishop & E. K. Prideaux: *The
building of the cathedral church of St Peter in Exeter*
(1922). P. Freeman: *The architectural history of Exeter
Cathedral* (revised by E. V. Freeman 1888). W. R.
Lethaby: 'How Exeter Cathedral was built',
Architect Review (1903). G. Oliver: *Lives of the bishops
of Exeter and a history of the cathedral* (1861). V. Hope
& L. J. Lloyd: *Exeter Cathedral: a short history and
description* (1977). C. Fox: 'The siting of the Monastery of St Mary and St Paul in Exeter', in *Dark Age
Britain*, ed. D. B. Harden (1956), 202. Misericords:
K. M. Clarke in *Devon Assoc* 39 (1907), 231–41; 40
(1908), 193–200. Glass in W window: C. A. Bell in
Proc Soc Antiq ser 2 19 (1903), 204–6. Notes on
military figures: T. V. Brushfield in *Proc Soc Antiq
ser 2* 19 (1903), 216–18. Carvings of medieval musical instruments: E. K. Prideaux in *Archaeol J* 72
(1915), 1–36. Reconstruction of C14 altar-screen:
P. Morris in *Antiq J* 23 (1943), 122–47; 24 (1944),
10–21. Woodwork: see *Exeter Dioc Architect Soc* IV,
323–31; V, 173–81. Stained glass: J. L. Fulford in
Exeter Dioc Architect Soc II, 181–8. Norman work: J.
Helling in *Exeter Dioc Architect Soc* V 120–5. Chantry chapels: Cook (1947), 102. Pulpitum: Vallance
(1947), 65.

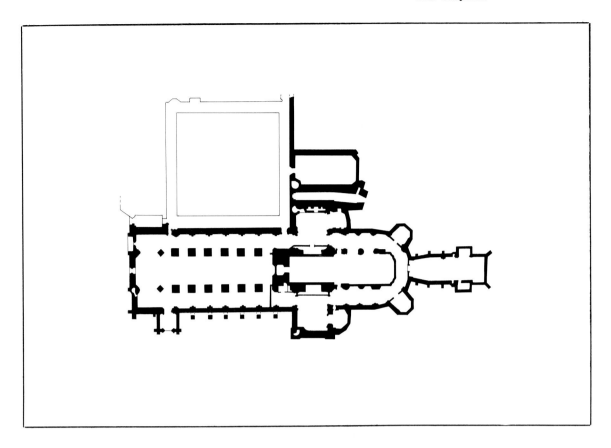

GLOUCESTER
St Peter

See: 1541 (united with Bristol 1836; separated 1897)
Fd *c*. 681: double monastery; 823: secular canons.
Refd 1022: Benedictine Monks. D. 1539.

MAIN BUILDING DATES: 1089–1100: crypt and eastern arm; C12i–iii: nave; C13ii: nave vault; 1318–29: S aisle of nave; 1331–7: remodelling of S transept arm; 1337–57: alterations to choir; 1347–50: glazing of E window; C14iii: remodelling of N transept arm; 1351–C14iv: cloister; C15i–ii: W front and S porch; *c*. 1450–60: central tower; 1457–83: Lady Chapel.

REFERENCES: W. St John Hope: 'Notes on the Benedictine Abbey of St Peter at Gloucester', *Archaeol J* 54 (1897), 77–119; see also *Gloucester Cath Soc* III, 90–134. Norman work: see *Records of Gloucester Cath* I, 106–8. Early English Lady Chapel: W. Bazeley in *Shropshire Archaeol Nat Hist Soc ser 2* 4 (1892), 183–98. Builders and architecture: T. G. Parry in *Records of Gloucester Cath* I, 38–58; see also Freeman in *Records of Gloucester Cath* I, 18–37; II, 79–155. East window: C. Winston in *Archaeol J* 20 (1863), 239–53; T. D. Grimké-Drayton in *Trans Bristol Gloucestershire Archaeol Soc* 38 (1915), 69–97; G. McN. Rushforth, *Trans Bristol Gloucestershire etc* 44 (1922), 293–304. J. Bony: 'Gloucester et l'origine des voûtes d'hémicycle gothiques', *Bull Monumental* 98 (1939), 329. Effigies: W. Bazeley in *Trans Bristol Gloucestershire etc* 28 (1904), 289–326. Misericords: *Trans Bristol Gloucestershire etc* 28 (1905), 61–85. Screens: Vallance (1947), 106. Chantry chapels of Abbots Parker, Seabroke and Browne: Cook (1947), 142. History: VCH *Glos* II, 53–61.

GREAT MALVERN

St Mary and St Michael

Fd *c.* 1075: Benedictine Monks. D. 1540.

MAIN BUILDING DATES: (*c.* 1100– : transept); *c.* 1120– : nave arcades, S wall of nave; C12iii–iv: Lady Chapel crypt; *c.* 1420–55: presbytery, N transept arm, N and S arches of crossing, N nave aisle, nave clerestory; *c.* 1450–60: central tower; C16: blocking of demolished S transept arm; *c.* 1815: repairs; 1841: alterations; 1860–1: restoration (Scott); 1894: NW porch rebuilt; 1895: extensive repairs to tower.

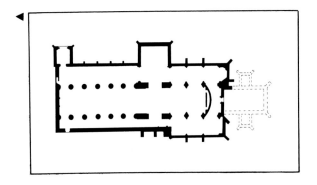

REFERENCES: W. Thomas: *Antiquitates Prioratus Majoris Malverne* (1725). M. Southall: *A Description of Malvern* (1822). A. C. Deane: *Short Account of Great Malvern Priory Church* (1914). B. Smith: *A History of Malvern* (1964). Glass: H. Fowler in *Assoc Architect Soc Rep and Pap* XVII, 115–20; R. W. Paul in *Archaeologia* 57 (1901), 353–8; G. McN. Rushforth: *Medieval Christian Imagery as Illustrated in the painted windows of* . . . (1936); J. A. Knowles: 'John Thornton of Coventry and the East Window of Great Malvern Priory', *Antiq J* 39 (1959), 274–82; L. A. Hamand: *Angel Musicians and their Instruments* (1963). Tiles: Eames (1968), 23. See also *The Builder* (Jan. 1897). History: VCH *Worcs* II, 136–43; architecture: IV, 127–31.

HEREFORD

St Mary and St Ethelbert

See: 676

Secular canons.

MAIN BUILDING DATES: C12i–ii: eastern arm, transept and nave; C12iv–C13i: retrochoir and Lady Chapel; C13iii: N transept arm; C13iv: remodelling of aisles; C14i– : central tower; C16i: extension to N porch; 1786–96: alteration of nave and W front; 1902–8: W front (J. O. Scott).

REFERENCES: RCHM *Herefordshire*, I. G. M. Hills: 'The Architectural History of Hereford Cathedral', *J Brit Archaeol Ass* 27 (1871), 46–84; 496–513. W. W. Capes (ed.): *The Charters and Records of Hereford Cathedral* (1908). G. Scott: 'Hereford Cathedral', *Archaeol J* 34 (1877), 323–48. G. Marshall: *Hereford Cathedral* (1951). A. J. Bannister: *The Cathedral Church of Hereford, its history and constitution* (1924). N. Drinkwater: 'Hereford Cathedral: the Chapter House', *Archaeol J* 112 (1956), 61–75. R. K. Morris: 'The remodelling of the Hereford aisles', *J Brit Archaeol Ass* 37 (1974), 21–39. R. K. Morris: 'The Local Influence of Hereford Cathedral in the Decorated Period', *Trans Woolhope Natur Fld Club* 41 (1973), 48–67. G. Marshall: 'The Shrine of St Thomas Cantilupe in Hereford Cathedral', *Trans Woolhope Natur Fld Club* (1930–2). Screens: Vallance (1947), 70. Chantry chapels: Cook (1947), 107. Tombs and monumental sculpture: C. Boutell in *J Brit Archaeol Ass* 27 (1871), 191–202.

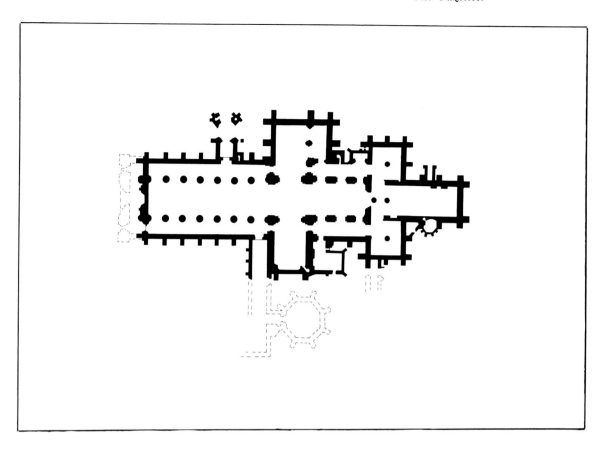

HEXHAM
St Andrew
See: 678–*c.* 821
Refd 1113: Augustinian Canons. D. 1537.
MAIN BUILDING DATES: *c.* 674: crypt; C13i–ii: eastern arm, transept, E end of nave; 1858–60: E end of church; 1869–70: restoration; 1889–1908: restoration and rebuilding of nave.

REFERENCES: J. Raine: *The Priory of Hexham*, 2 vols (1864–5) (*Surtees Soc* 44.46). C. C. Hodges: *Ecclesia Hagustaldensis: the Abbey of St Andrew, Hexham* (1888). C. C. Hodges: *Guide to the Priory Church of* . . . (1913). C. C. Hodges and J. Gibson: *Hexham and its Abbey* (1919). E. S. Savage and C. C. Hodges: *A Record of all Works connected with Hexham Abbey* (1907). J. Micklethwaite: 'On the crypts at Hexham and Ripon', *Archaeol J* 39 (1882). J. Hewitt: *A Handbook of Hexham and its Antiquities*

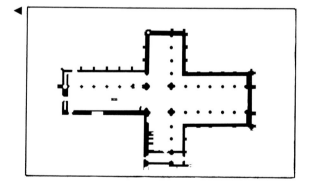

(1879). D. P. Kirby (ed.): *Saint Wilfrid at Hexham* (1974). H. M. and J. Taylor: 'The seventh-century church at Hexham: a new appreciation', *Archaeol Aeliana* 39 (1961), 103–34. See also Hexham entry in *Anglo-Saxon Architecture* (1965). *A History of Northumberland* III.1, 105–200. R. N. Bailey (1976).

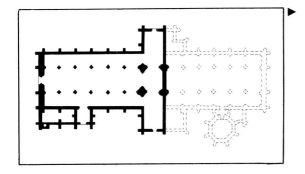

HOWDEN
St Peter
Fd 1267: secular canons. D. 1550.

MAIN BUILDING DATES: *c.* 1260– : transept; *c.* 1280–1310: nave, S porch, W front; C14i–ii: eastern arm, extension of transept; 1388–1405: lower stage of central tower; C15: upper stage of central tower.

REFERENCES: VCH *Yorks* III, 361–2. S. Glynne in *Yorkshire Archaeol J* 12 (1893). J. L. Petit in *Archaeol J* 25 (1868), 179–91. J. Bilson: 'Howden Church, Some Notes on its Architectural History', *Yorkshire Archaeol J* 22 (1903). See also *Archaeol J* 91 (1934), 398. Brasses: F. R. Fairbank in *Yorkshire Archaeol Topograph J* 11 (1891), 169–73. Pulpitum: Vallance (1947), 149. Skirlaw chantry chapel: Cook (1947), 66.

LANERCOST
St Mary Magdalene
Fd *c.* 1166: Augustinian Canons. D. 1537.
MAIN BUILDING DATES: C12iii–iv: transept, S wall of nave and part of N wall of nave; C13: eastern arm, S nave clerestory, N aisle of nave.

REFERENCES: *Archaeol J* 115 (1958), 220–5. E. R. Tate in *The Builder* (Oct. 1898). See also G. Baldwin Brown and M. Whitehead: 'The monuments in the choir and transepts of Lanercost Abbey', *Trans Cumberland Westmorland Architect Archaeol Soc* XII, 312–43. J. R. H. Moorman: *Guide to Lanercost Priory* (1945).

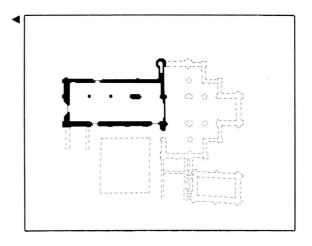

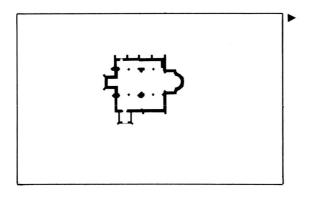

LASTINGHAM
St Mary
Fd *c.* 654. Refd 1078: Benedictine Monks; removed to York *c.* 1086.
MAIN BUILDING DATES: *c.* 1078–86: crypt, apse, presbytery, crossing; C13: presbytery arcade, N aisle; C14: S aisle; C15i–ii: W tower; 1879: vault of chancel, S porch and restoration (Pearson).

REFERENCES: VCH *Yorks North Riding* I, 524–9. J. C. Wall: *The Monastic Church of Lastingham* (1894). S. Glynne in *Yorkshire Archaeol J* 13 (1895).

LEOMINSTER
SS Peter and Paul

Fd *c*. 660. ?Refd C9: secular canons . . . nuns –1046. Refd 1123: Benedictine Monks. D. 1539.

MAIN BUILDING DATES: C12ii–iii: N nave arcade and aisle, lower stage W tower, W door; C13iii: S nave; C14i–ii: S nave aisle, S porch; C15: upper stages of W tower; *c*. 1539: blocking of W side of crossing; 1699–1705: rebuilding of S nave aisle arcade; 1866: restoration (Scott); 1886: restoration of S aisle; 1891: restoration of W tower; 1923: refacing of external stonework of S aisle.

REFERENCES: RCHM *Herefordshire* III, 111–14. E. Freeman: 'Excavations at Leominster Priory Church', *Archaeol J* 10 (1853), 109–15. E. Freeman: 'Leominster Priory Church', *Archaeol Cambrensis* 4 (1853), 9–33, 180–8. E. Roberts' 'On Leominster Priory Church', *J Brit Archaeol Ass* XXVII (1871), 438–45. J. T. Smith: 'The Norman Structure of Leominster Priory Church', *Trans Ancient Mon Soc* 11 (1963), 97. G. McN. Rushforth: 'The wheel of the ten ages of life on the walls of Leominster church', *Proc Soc Antiq* XXVI (1913–14), 47. Restoration of tower: see F. R. Kempson in *Woolhope Club Trans* (1890–2), 291.

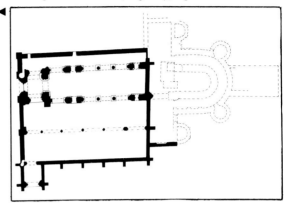

LICHFIELD
St Mary and St Chad

See: 669. Archbishopric 785–803. Removed to Chester St John 1075; to Coventry 1095. Coventry and Lichfield 1148. Lichfield 1826.

Secular canons.

MAIN BUILDING DATES: C12iv–C13i: parts of choir and crossing; C13ii: transept and chapter-house; C13iii–iv: nave; C14i: central tower; C14ii: Lady Chapel; C14ii–iii: presbytery; 1661–9: repairs and rebuilding; 1788– : restoration and remodelling of west front; 1842: repairs to nave and north arm of transept; 1856– : restoration (Scott).

REFERENCES: VCH *Staffs* III, 140–99. T. Harwood: *History and Antiquities of the City and Church of Lichfield* (1806). Browne Willis: *Survey* etc. (1727). R. Willis: 'Foundations of Early Buildings in Lichfield Cathedral', *Archaeol J* 18 (1861), 1–24. J. T. Irvine: 'The West Front of Lichfield Cathedral', *J Brit Archaeol Ass* 38 (1882), 349. H. E. Savage: 'The Architectural Story of Lichfield Cathedral', *Trans North Staffs Fld Club* 48, 115. J. Gould: 'Letocetum, Christianity and Lichfield', *Trans South Staffordshire Archaeol Hist Soc* 13 (1973), 30–1. Mortuary chapels: *J Derby Archaeol Soc* I, 116–26. Sacrist's roll: *J Derby Archaeol Soc* IV, 107–38.

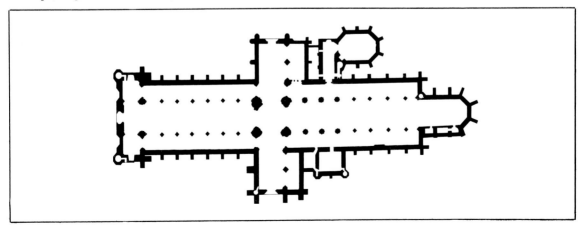

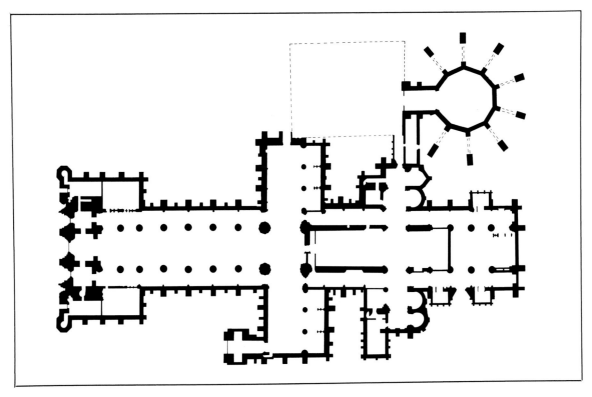

LINCOLN
St Mary

See: 678. Refd *c*. 954 (with Dorchester). Refd 1072. Secular canons.

MAIN BUILDING DATES: –1092: core of west front; C12ii: lower stages of W towers and W doorways; 1192–*c*. 1207: eastern transepts and choir; *c*. 1207–20: main transept; *c*. 1218: repairs to west front; *c*. 1220–5: chapter-house (first phase); *c*. 1227–140: nave; 1238–*c*. 1244: central tower; 1256–80: Angel Choir; *c*. 1253– : completion of chapter-house; 1307– : upper stage of central tower; *c*. 1335: 'Bishop's Eye' window; *c*. 1375– : upper stages of W towers.

REFERENCES: E. Venables: 'The architectural history of Lincoln Cathedral', *Archaeol J* 40 (1883), 159–92, 377–418; see also Venables on St Hugh's Choir, *Archaeol J* 32 (1875), 229–38; and on foundations uncovered at E end of church, *Archaeol J* 44 (1887), 194–202. J. Essex: 'Some observations on Lincoln Cathedral', *Archaeologia* IV (1777), 149. E. Sharpe: 'On Lincoln Cathedral', *Assoc Architect Socs Rep and Pap* IX, 179–90. Dimock: 'Record history of Lincoln Cathedral', *Assoc Architect Socs Rep and Pap* IX, 190–201. J. Smith: 'Architectural drawings of Lincoln Cathedral in Norman times', *Assoc Architect Socs Rep and Pap* XXVIII (1908). F. Bond & W. Watkins: 'Notes on the Architectural History of Lincoln Minster from 1192–1255', *Roy Inst Brit Architects J* 26/11/10; 10/12/10; 27/5/11. J. Bilson: 'Lincoln Cathedral: The New Reading', *Roy Inst Brit Architects J* 6/5/11; 17/6/11. J. Bilson: 'The Plan of the First Cathedral Church at Lincoln', *Archaeologia* 62.ii (1911), 543–64. P. Frankl: 'The crazy vaults of Lincoln Cathedral', *Art Bulletin* 35 (1953). P. Frankl: 'Lincoln Cathedral', *Art Bulletin* 44 (1962). J. W. F. Hill: *Medieval Lincoln* (1948). D. Owen: *Church and Society in Medieval Lincolnshire* (1971), 37–46. F. Saxl: 'Lincoln Cathedral: the eleventh-century design for the West Front', *Archaeol J* 103 (1946), 105. J. Romilly Allen: 'Early Norman Sculpture at Lincoln and Southwell', *J Brit Archaeol Ass* 48 (1892), 292–9. G. Zarnecki: *Romanesque Sculpture at Lincoln Cathedral* (1963). M. R. James: 'Sculptures at Lincoln Cathedral', *Cambridgeshire Archaeol J* 10 (1901), 148–52. Lethaby: '. . . The Judgement Porch and the Angel Choir', *Archaeologia* 60 (1908), 379–90.

LITTLE MALVERN
St Giles
Fd *c*. 1171: Benedictine Monks. D. 1537.
MAIN BUILDING DATES: C14: crossing, eastern arm, first stage of tower; *c*. 1480– : arcades to (ruined) side chapels, upper stage of tower.

REFERENCES: VCH *Worcs* III, 451–3. J. Willis-Bund: 'Little Malvern', *Proc Soc Antiq* XXIII (1909–11), 26. Screen: Vallance 1947, 112. East window: E. Oldfield in *Archaeol J* 22 (1865), 302–25.

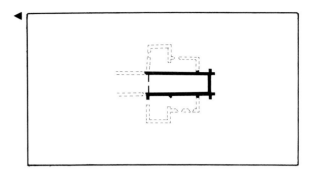

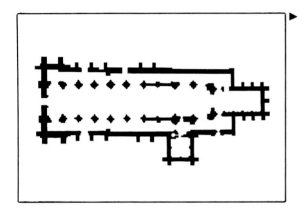

LLANDAFF
SS Peter and Teilo
See: C6
Refd 1107: secular canons.
MAIN BUILDING DATES: *c*. 1120– : (Norman church); C12iv–C13ii: church; *c*. 1250: chapter-house; C12iii–iv: Lady Chapel; C14: alterations to presbytery; *c*. 1490; NW tower; 1734–52: 'Italian temple' church; 1835–57: restoration; 1858–69: restoration of nave, SW tower; 1945– : repairs.

REFERENCES: Bibliography given in *Archaeol Cambrensis* (1925), 392–404. F. J. North: *The Stones of Llandaff* (1977).

London
St Paul's
(*see over*)

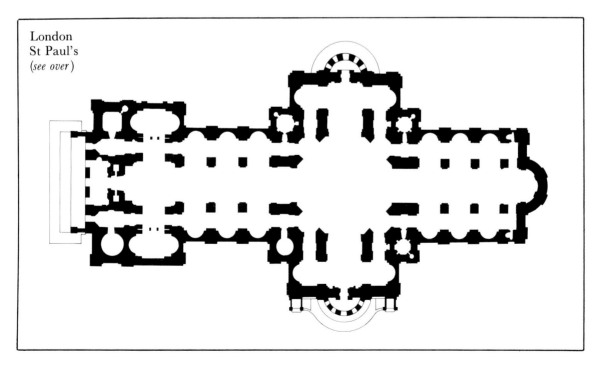

LONDON
St Paul's
See: 604
Secular canons.
MAIN BUILDING DATES: 1675–1710 (Wren).

REFERENCES: RCHM *City of London*, 44–53. W. S. Simpson: *Gleanings from Old St Paul's* (1839). H. Milman: *Annals of St Paul's Cathedral* (1869). W. Benham: *Old St Paul's Cathedral* (1902). W. R. Matthews & W. M. Atkins: *A History of St Paul's Cathedral and the men associated with it* (1957); contains full bibliographical notes: 361–9. See also C. N. L. Brooke and G. Keir: *London 800–1216: the shaping of a city* (1975).

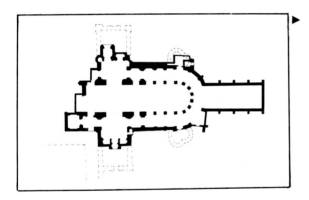

LONDON, SMITHFIELD
St Bartholomew
Fd 1123: Augustinian Canons. D. 1539.
MAIN BUILDING DATES: *c.* 1123– : presbytery and ambulatory; *c.* 1150: crossing, western bay of presbytery arcade, parts of N and S transept arms, eastern bay of nave; *c.* 1335: Lady Chapel and crypt; C14iv: part of presbytery N aisle wall, presbytery clerestory; 1628: W tower; 1863–6: restoration of presbytery and ambulatory; 1886– : N and S arms of transept, W porch; 1896: restoration of Lady Chapel.

REFERENCES: RCHM *London* IV, 123. B. Savory: 'The ancient priory church of St Bartholomew the West, Smithfield', *Hampstead Antiq Hist Soc* (1901), 47–9. E. A. Webb: 'Notes on the Augustinian priory of . . .' *Archaeologia* 59 (1905), 375–90. T. H. Lewis: 'The church of . . .' *London Middlesex Archaeol Soc* III, 79–86. VCH *London* I, 480–4.

MALMESBURY
SS Peter and Paul
–965: secular canons. Refd 965: Benedictine Monks. D. 1539.
MAIN BUILDING DATES: *c.* 1160: crossing, nave arcades and aisle walls (S arcade and aisle complete; N arcade and aisle six bays surviving), S porch, S portion of W front; C14i–ii: nave clerestory, fenestration, cladding of S porch; C15: pulpitum, doorway to cloister; C16: blocking of W side crossing and reduction of W end.

REFERENCES: H. Brakspear: 'Malmesbury Abbey', *Archaeologia* 64 (1912–13), 399–436. (See also *Archaeologia* 81 (1931), 1.) C. H. Talbot: 'On the architecture of Malmesbury Abbey', *Wiltshire Archaeol Nat Hist Mag* XXI, 26–34. J. E. Jackson: 'Malmesbury Abbey in its best days', *Wilts Archaeol Mag* XXI, 35–60. M. R. James: 'On the sculptures of the south portal of the abbey church of Malmesbury', *Cambridge Antiq Soc* X, 136–47. K. J. Galbraith: 'The iconography of the biblical scenes at Malmesbury Abbey', *J Brit Archaeol Ass* 28 (1965), 39–56. W. Bazely: 'The architecture of Malmesbury Abbey Church', *Trans Bristol Gloucestershire Archaeol Soc* 16 (1892), 6–15. E. Freeman: 'The architecture of Malmesbury church', *Wiltshire Archaeol Mag* VIII, 82–101. VCH *Wilts* III, 210–31.

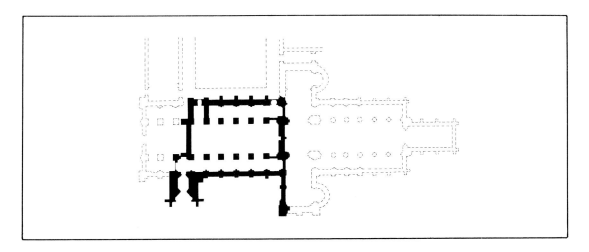

MELBOURNE
SS Michael and Mary

MAIN BUILDING DATES: *c.* 1130–60: chancel, tran-, sept, nave, W towers and narthex; C14: E end of chancel; C15: nave aisle walls; C16i–ii: reduction of transeptal chapels; C17i: central tower; 1859–62: restoration (Scott).

REFERENCES: W. Wilkins and T. Bensley: 'A description of the Church of Melbourne', *Archaeologia* XIII (1800). J. C. Cox: *Notes on the Churches of Derbyshire* III (1877). A. W. Clapham: in *Archaeol J* 90 (1933), 393–5. Wall paintings: Tristram III, 222. See also: *J Brit Archaeol Ass* XVI (1860), 286; W. D. Fane in *J Derbyshire Archaeol Soc* XVII, 82–94.

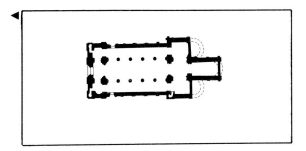

MILTON ABBAS
SS Mary and Michael
Refd 964: Benedictine Monks. D.1539.

MAIN BUILDING DATES: 1309– : choir and transept, tower; 1789: restoration (Wyatt); 1865: W porch and restoration (Scott).

REFERENCES: R. Paul in *The Builder* 5 January 1901. VCH *Dorset* II, 58–62.

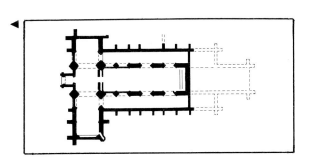

NEW SHOREHAM
St Mary de Haura

MAIN BUILDING DATES: 1103–30: transept, eastern bay of nave; *c*. 1185–1200: choir and choir aisles; C13i: choir triforium and clerestory; *c*. 1715: blocking of eastern end of nave; 1876–9: refenestration of aisles.

REFERENCES: E. Sharpe: *The Architectural History of St Mary's Church, New Shoreham* (1861). *Archaeol J* 116 (1959), 251, 253.

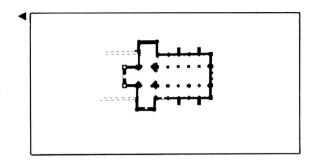

NORWICH
Holy Trinity

See: at *Dommoc* (631) and Elmham (673); transferred to Thetford 1070; Norwich 1094. Refd 1096: Benedictine Monks. D. 1539.

MAIN BUILDING DATES: C11iv–C12i: eastern arm and transept; C12i–ii: central tower and nave; C14i: refenestration of N nave aisle; C14iii: clerestory of presbytery; C15ii: W front; C15iii: nave vault; C15iv: presbytery vault; 1830– : restoration; 1930: eastern chapel.

REFERENCES: J. Britton: *Antiquarian and Architectural Memoranda Relating to* ... (1817). D. J. Stewart: 'Notes on Norwich Cathedral', *Archaeol J* 32 (1875), 16–47, 155–87. W. St John Hope and W. T. Bensley: 'Recent Discoveries in Norwich Cathedral', *Norfolk Archaeol* XIV (1901), 105–27. J. Gunn: 'The trinitarian arrangement of part of Norwich cathedral built by Bishop Herbert . . .' *J. Brit Archaeol Ass* XXXVI (1880), 409–12. B. Dodwell: 'The Foundation of Norwich Cathedral', *Trans Roy Hist Soc ser 5* 7 (1957), 1–18. E. C. Fernie (1976), 77–86. E. C. Fernie (1977), 383–5. Misericords: *Norfolk and Norwich Archaeol Soc* II, 234–52. Summary history, plan and biography: *Archaeol J* 106 (1949), 85–7. VCH *Norfolk* II, 315–28. Roof bosses: *Archaeologia* 83 (1933), 45–65. Wall paintings: *Norfolk Archaeol* 6 (1864), 272–6; VCH *Norfolk* II, 530–5; Tristram I, 138, Pls 84–5; II, 583, Pls 200–4; III, 230, Pls 11a, 12a, 12b, 29a. Screen and pulpitum: Vallance (1947), 46. Chantry chapels: Cook (1947), 88. Eastern chapels: D. H. S. Cranage in *Antiq J* 12 (1932), 117–26.

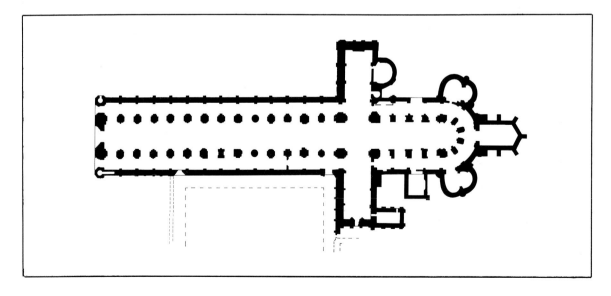

NUN MONKTON
St Mary
Fd *c*. 1145: Benedictine Nuns. D. 1536.
MAIN BUILDING DATES: C12iv: lower level of nave walls and W front; C13i: nave gallery and upper stage of W front, W tower; 1873: E end of chancel (J. W. Walton; glass by W. Morris).

REFERENCES: M. Spence: 'Nun Monkton Church', *East Riding Antiq Soc* 13.i (1906), xxvii. W. Richardson: *Monastic Ruins of Yorkshire* II, 87. VCH *Yorks* III, 122–3.

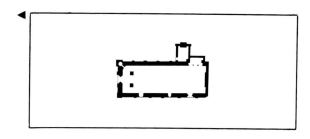

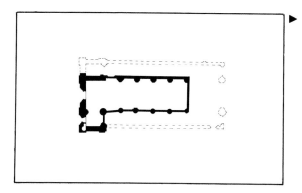

OLD MALTON
St Mary
Fd 1150: Gilbertine Canons. D. 1539.
MAIN BUILDING DATES: C12iv–C13i: S nave arcade and three eastern bays of N nave arcade, SW tower, W front; C15: five western bays of N nave arcade (W bay now solid); 1636– : blocking of nave arcades and east wall.

REFERENCES: VCH *Yorks* III, 253–4. VCH *Yorks N Riding* I. E. C. Walcott: 'Notes on Some Northern Minsters', *The Antiquary* I (1850), 113–17. Restoration: *The Antiquary* VI (1882), 34. Excavation: *Antiq J* 23 (1943), 53–4.

OXFORD
St Frideswide, now Christ Church
See: 1546 (removed from Oseney)
Fd *c*. 727: nuns. Church rebuilt 1004: secular canons. Refd 1122: Augustinian Canons. Priory suppressed 1524.
MAIN BUILDING DATES: *c*. 1150– : church; *c*. 1200–25: upper stage of central tower and spire; –*c*. 1250: Lady Chapel; C14ii: Latin Chapel; C15iv: presbytery clerestory and vault; 1524–9: demolition of W part of nave; 1629–38: alterations; 1856: restoration; 1870– : restoration, incl. rebuilding of south presbytery aisle (Scott).

REFERENCES: Browne Willis: *Mitred Abbeys*. (1718), 281–5. S. A. Warner: *Oxford Cathedral* (1924). RCHM *Oxford*. J. P. Harrison: 'On a pre-Norman clerestory window . . .' *Archaeol J* 49 (1892), 155–60; see also *J Brit Archaeol Ass* XLVII (1891), 141–3; *Archaeol Oxoniensis* I, 23–31. Chantry chapel: Cook (1947), 149. VCH *Oxford* II, 97–101.

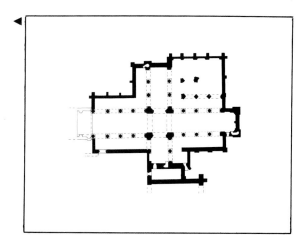

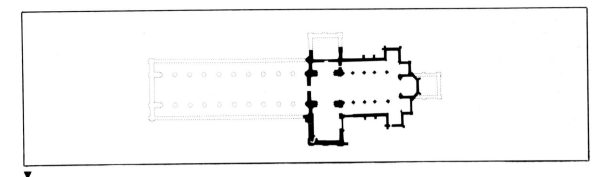

PERSHORE

St Mary the Virgin and SS Peter and Paul (later SS Mary and Eadburga)

Fd *c*. 689: secular canons. Refd 972: Benedictine Monks. D. 1539.

MAIN BUILDING DATES: –*c*. 1100: S arm of transept, parts of N arm of transept, east end of nave; C13i–ii: Lady Chapel, choir; 1290s: choir vault; C14i–ii: central tower; *c*. 1686– : blocking of reduced N transept arm; 1847: eastern apse; 1852–5: restoration (Scott); 1871: pinnacles on tower.

REFERENCES: VCH *Worcs* IV, 159–63. R. Styles: *The History and Antiquities of the Abbey of Pershore* (1838). M. E. C. Walcott: 'The Benedictine Abbey of St Mary Pershore', *J Brit Archaeol Ass* XXXII (1876), 330–43. W. J. Hopkins: 'Abbey Church of Holy Cross, Pershore', *Assoc Architect Socs Rep and Pap* IV (1857–8), 355–63. J. Maclean: 'Pershore Abbey Church', *Trans Bristol Gloucestershire Archaeol Soc* X, 230–7. C. R. Peers in *Archaeol J* 63 (1906), F. Andrews in *Birmingham Midland Inst Trans* LIII, 196. J. Bony: 'Tewkesbury et Pershore', *Bulletin Monumental* 96 (1937), 288. R. Stalley and M. Thurlsby: 'A Note on the Architecture of Pershore Abbey', *J Brit Archaeol Ass* 37 (1974), 113–18.

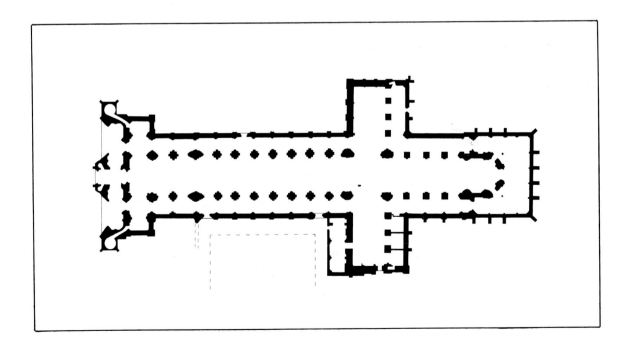

PETERBOROUGH

St Peter

See: 1540

Fd *c*. 655–870. Refd *c*. 966: Benedictine Monks. D. 1539.

MAIN BUILDING DATES: C12i–iii: eastern arm, transept, nave; C12iv: west transept; *c*. 1195–1230: west front; C14ii: central tower; C15iv–C16i: eastern extension ('New building'); 1883–6: rebuilding of central tower.

REFERENCES: Anglo-Saxon church: J. T. Irvine in *Assoc Architect Socs Rep and Pap* 17 (1883–4), 277–83; *J Brit Archaeol Ass* 50 (1894), 45–54; H. M. and J. Taylor (1965); VCH *Northants* II 83–95. S. Gunton: *The history of the church of Peterborough* (1686). W. Fickling: 'The builders of Peterborough Cathedral', *Assoc Architect Socs Rep and Pap* XXX, 141–6. Poole: 'On the abbey church of . . .' *Assoc Architect etc.* III, 187–285. West front: G. F. Webb in *Archaeol J* 106 (supplement) (1952), 113. T. Craddock: *Peterborough Cathedral* (1864). Painted ceiling: C. J. P. Cave and T. Borenius in *Archaeologia* 87 (1931), 297–300; F. Nordstrom: 'Peterborough, Lincoln and the Science of Robert Grosseteste', *Art Bulletin* 37 (1955), 241–72. Roof bosses: *Archaeologia* 88 (1932), 271–80. W. D. Sweeting: *The Cathedral Church of Peterborough* (1898). Screens: Vallance (1947), 117.

RIPON

SS Peter and Wilfrid

See: 1876

Fd –660. Refd 661: monks. Refd ?C10: secular canons.

MAIN BUILDING DATES: C7iii: crypt; C12iii–iv: parts of choir and nave, transept, chapter house; C13ii–iii: west front; C13iv: eastern end of presbytery; C15iii: central tower; C15iv: two western bays on south side of choir; C16i: nave arcades and aisles; 1861–70: restoration and alterations to W front (Scott).

REFERENCES: Crypt: J. T. Micklethwaite in *Archaeol J* 39 (1882), 347–54; C. R. Peers in *Antiq J* II (1931), 113–22; R. J. Walbran in *Proc Architect Ass: Winchester 1845* (1846), 339–54; H. M. and J. Taylor in *Anglo-Saxon Architecture* (1965), 561; W. T. Jones in *Yorks Archaeol J* 31 (1934), 74–6; R. A. Hall: 'Rescue Excavations in the Crypt of Ripon Cathedral', *Yorks Archaeol J* 49 (1977), 59–63. G. G. Scott: 'Ripon Minster', *Archaeol J* 31 (1874), 309–18. T. S. Gowland: 'Ripon Minster and its Precincts', *Yorks Archaeol J* 35 (1943), 270–87 (comp. 1860). J. R. Walbran: 'On St Wilfrid and the Saxon Church of Ripon', *Assoc Architect Socs Rep and Pap* V, 63–96. M. F. Hearne: 'On the Original Nave of Ripon Cathedral', *J Brit Archaeol Ass* 35 (1972), 39–45. See also Hearne's 'Postscript' in JBAA CXXIX (1976), 93–4. Pulpitum: Vallance (1947), 168. Woodcarvers: J. S. Purvis in *Archaeologia* 85 (1935), 107–28; *Yorkshire Archaeol J* 29 (1929). Roof bosses: C. J. P. Cave: *Archaeologia* 38 (1940), 271–9. VCH *Yorks* III, 367–72.

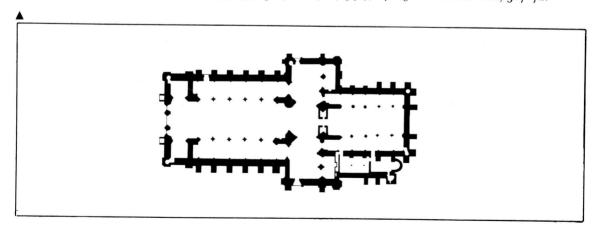

ROCHESTER

St Andrew

See: 604

−1080: secular canons. Refd 1080: Benedictine Monks. D. 1540.

MAIN BUILDING DATES: *c*. 1077–80: north tower; *c*. 1080– : crypt; C12i–ii: modifications to choir, nave, and original west front; 1138– : repairs after fire; *c*. 1190– : start of original central tower; 1195–1227: undercroft, E transept, presbytery; *c*. 1220–7: choir and pulpitum; *c*. 1240: N transept arm; *c*. 1280– : S transept arm and eastern bays of nave; *c*. 1320: modifications to transept and choir aisles; 1343: completion of original central tower; *c*. 1470: west window; *c*. 1500: Lady Chapel; 1591: serious fire in eastern arm, repairs; 1664: repairs to S aisle of nave; 1670: partial rebuilding of N aisle of nave; 1826– : restoration (Cottingham); 1872: restoration (Scott); 1904: central tower rebuilt.

REFERENCES: J. Denne: *The History and Antiquities of Rochester and its Environs* (ed. T. Fisher, 1817).

Anglo-Saxon church: G. M. Livett in *Archaeol Cantiana* 18 (1889), 261–78. W. St John Hope: *Architectural History of St Andrew's, Rochester* (1900). See also *Archaeol Cantiana* 23 (1898), 194–328. W. St John Hope: 'Gundulf's Tower at Rochester, and the first Norman cathedral there', *Archaeologia* 49 (1884) 323–34. F. H. Fairweather: 'Gundulf's Cathedral . . . some critical remarks upon the hitherto accepted plan', *Archaeol J* 86 (1929), 187–212. F. Bond: 'Rochester . . .' *J Roy Inst Brit Architects ser 3* VIII, 105–6. A. Ashpitel: 'On Rochester . . .' *J Brit Archaeol Ass* IX, 271–85. See also *Archaeol J* 32 (1875), 205–28. A. M. Oakley: 'The Cathedral Priory of . . .', *Archaeol Cant* 91 (1975), 47–60. Anglo-Saxon graves: *Medieval Archaeol* (1961), 309. Pre-Conquest sculptural fragment: *Archaeol Cantiana* 88 (1973), 201–3. Pulpitum: Vallance (1947), 47. C. A. R. Radford '. . . a new fragment of pre-Conquest wall' *Annual Report of the Friends of Rochester Cathedral* (1969), 13–16. VCH *Kent* II, 121–6.

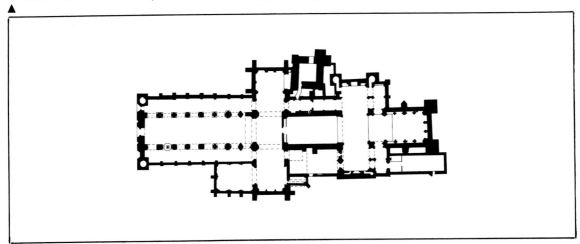

ROMSEY

SS Mary and Elfleda

Fd *c*. 907. Refd 967: Benedictine Nuns. D. 1539.

MAIN BUILDING DATES: *c*. 1120–50: eastern arm, transept; *c*. 1150–90: four eastern bays of nave; C13i–ii: three western bays of nave, nave clerestory and W front.

REFERENCES: VCH *Hants* IV, 460. A. M. Davis: 'Some Norman details in Romsey Abbey', *Hampshire Fld Club* (1891), 8–14. E. P. Loftus Brock in

The Builder (Oct. 1895). Pre-Conquest church: H. M. and J. Taylor (1965), 520–2. Excavations: W. J. C. Morens: 'Recent discoveries in . . .' *Proc Soc Antiq ser* 18 (1901), 246–9. C. R. Peers in *Archaeologia* 57 (1901), 317–20. Excavation of Lady Chapel: note in *Medieval Archaeol* (1973), 189. Discussion of significance of design: M. Hearne in *Gesta* 14 (1975), 27. See also *Archaeol J* 58 (1901), 99. H. G. D. Liveing (1906). A. R. Green; 'The Romsey Painted Wooden Reredos' *Archaeol J* 90 (1933), 306–14.

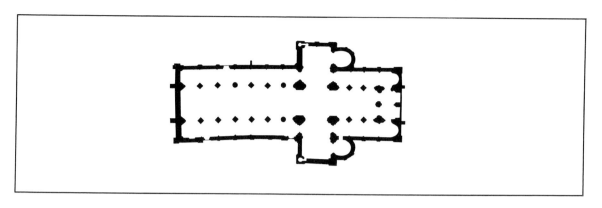

ST ALBANS
St Alban
See: 1877
Shrine in existence by 429. Fd/Refd *c*. 793. Refd *c*.
976: Benedictine Monks. D. 1539.
MAIN BUILDING DATES: C11iv–C12i: western part
of presbytery, transept, tower and portion of nave
arcades; C12iv–C13i: west front and three western
bays of nave; C13ii–iv: presbytery; C14i: Lady
Chapel; C14ii: five bays of S nave arcade; C15iv:
reredos; 1856–77: restoration (Scott); 1879–85:
restoration and alterations (Grimthorpe).

REFERENCES: C. R. Peers in VCH *Herts* II. RCHM
Herts (1910). J. C. Buckler: *A history of the architecture
of the abbey church of . . .* (1847). J. Neale: 'Notes

on . . .' *Assoc Architect Socs Rep and Pap* XIII, 255–
64; 'Four periods of Gothic Architecture in . . .'
Assoc Architect etc XIV, 115–27. J. T. Micklethwaite: 'The shrine of . . .' *Archaeol J* 29 (1872),
201–10. Restorations: G. E. Street in *Proc Soc Antiq
ser 2* VII (1876–8), 461–9; E. Grimthorpe: *St Albans
Cathedral and its Restoration* (1893). Plan and discoveries: *Archaeologia* 56, 21–6. Wall paintings: W.
Page in *Archaeologia* 58 (1908), 275–92; RCHM
Herts (1910), 19, 182–6; Tristram III, 132; Eileen
Roberts: *A Guide to the Abbey Murals* (1971). J. Carter: *Observations of the Abbey Church of St Alban*
(1813). Restorations: *Antiquary* I (1880), 88, 186,
280; IV, 30; VI, 33. Chantry chapels: Cook (1947),
138. Screen: Vallance (1947), 90. Graffiti: Pritchard (1967) 105–10. R. Runcie (1977).

▲

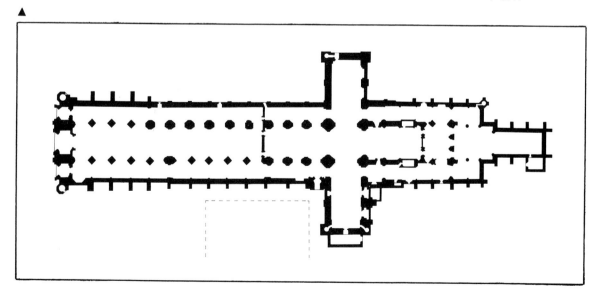

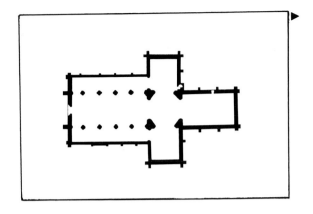

ST ASAPH

St Asaph

See: *c*. 553

Refd 1143: secular canons.

MAIN BUILDING DATES: C13ii: choir; *c*. 1286–1300: nave walls; –1381: crossing, nave arcades, S arm of transept, upper stage of N transept, central part of west front, tower; C15iv: restoration; C18iv: rebuilding of choir; 1810: restoration; 1867– : restoration (Scott).

REFERENCES: Architectural history: E. W. Lovegrove in *Archaeol Cambrensis* (1921), 215–36; 328–34. See also E. Freeman in *Archaeol Cambrensis* (1854), 279–89.

ST DAVID'S

SS Andrew and David

See: *c*. 580

Refd 1116: secular canons.

MAIN BUILDING DATES: (*c*. 1116–31: first Norman church); *c*. 1180– : west front, nave, choir aisles; *c*. 1215– : presbytery; 1220: collapse of central tower, repairs and continuation of presbytery; *c*. 1275– : eastern extension; 1293–1328: Lady Chapel; 1328–47: upper portions of nave aisles, chapterhouse, second stage of tower, screen; C15iv–C16i:

nave roof; 1509–23: upper stage of tower, roofing of eastern chapel; 1862– : restoration (Scott).

REFERENCES: W. B. Jones and E. A. Freeman: *The History and Antiquities of St David's* (1856). E. W. Lovegrove: 'St David's Cathedral', *Archaeol Cambrensis* (1922), 360–82. Woodwork: *Archaeol Cambrensis* (1957), 9, 12, 23, 26–40. Misericords: *Archaeol Cambrensis* (1900), 43–54. Pulpitum: Vallance (1947), 62. Chantry chapels: Cook (1947), 124.

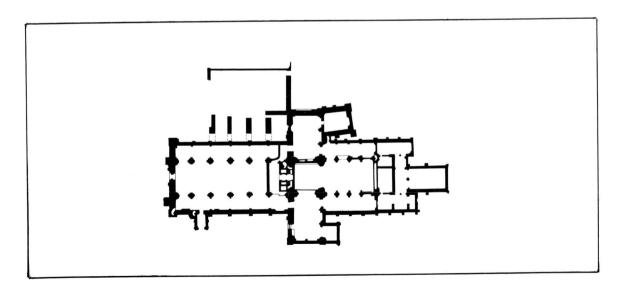

ST GERMANS

See: *c.* 936–1042.
Secular canons. Refd –1184: Augustinian canons.
D. 1539.

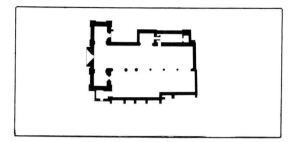

MAIN BUILDING DATES: *c.* 1180: two W bays of S nave arcade, W towers, W door; C13: NW tower octagon; C14ii: chapel in S nave aisle; C15: upper stage of SW tower; C15ii: S nave aisle, S porch; C16: S nave arcade, blocking of E end of nave.

REFERENCES: C. A. R. Radford in *J Roy Inst Cornwall n ser* 7 pt 3 (1975–6), 190–6. See also *Archaeol J* 130 (1973), 289–91; J. Furneaux in *Exeter Diocesan Architect Hist Trans* III.

SALISBURY

St Mary

See: 1075 (Old Sarum, removed from Sherborne); transferred to Salisbury 1227. Secular canons.
MAIN BUILDING DATES: 1220–58: church; –1266: west front; *c.* 1265–75: chapter-house; C14i–ii: upper stage of tower and spire; ?c. 1450: strainer arches in N and S arches of crossing; 1787– : alterations and demolition of campanile; 1862– : restoration (Scott).

REFERENCES: W. Dodsworth: *An historical account of the episcopal see and Cathedral Church of Sarum* (1814). Davis: 'Salisbury Cathedral', *J Brit Archaeol Ass* XV (1859), 46–62. Central tower: W. A. Forsyth in *J Roy Inst Brit Architect* 53 (1946), 85–7. Sites of medieval altars: C. Wordsworth in *Dorset Nat Hist Antiq Fld Club* XIX, 1–24. Roof painting: *Wiltshire Archaeol* XVII, 129–35. Chantry chapels: Cook (1947), 118. Screen: Vallance (1947), 81. Norman cathedral: W. St John Hope in *Proc Soc Antiq* XXVI (1913–14), 100–19; W. St John Hope: 'The Sarum Consuetudinary and its relation to the Cathedral Church of Old Sarum' *Archaeologia* 68 (1916–17), 111–26. VCH *Wilts* VI, 60–2. Close: VCH *Wilts* VI, 73–9. H. Braun: Building of Salisbury Cathedral re-examined *WAM* LVII, 371–5. J. M. J. Fletcher: Old Belfry in the Close: *WAM* XLVII, 608–16. F. Price: *Series of Observations upon that Admirable Structure the Cathedral Church of Salisbury* (1753).

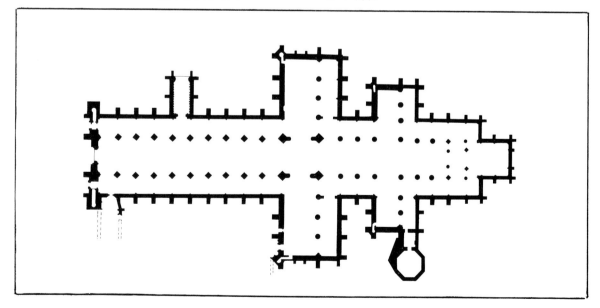

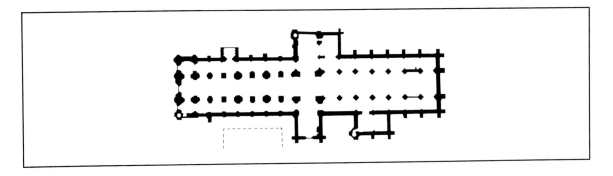

SELBY

Fd *c*. 1070: Benedictine Monks. D. 1539. P. 1618.
MAIN BUILDING DATES: *c*. 1100–10: N arm of transept; 1110–20: nave arcades; 1115–1230: galleries and clerestory of nave; *c*. 1290–1335: eastern arm and sacristy; 1871–3: restorations (Scott); 1889–90: restorations; 1908: central tower; 1912: S arm of transept; 1935: upper stages of W towers.

REFERENCES: J. B. Mitchell-Withers: *Ass Architect Socs Rep and Pap* XIII, 144–50. W. W. Morrell: *The History and Antiquities of Selby* (1867). J. P. Prichett: *J Brit Archaeol Ass* XLVIII (1892), 93–9, 285–91. S. Glynne: *Yorks Archaeol J* 12 (1893). C. C. Hodges: 'The Architectural History of . . .' *Yorks Archaeol J* 12 (1893), 344–94. C. H. Compton: *J Brit Archaeol Ass* 13 (1907), 241–8. J. T. Fowler (ed.): *Coucher Book of Selby* II (*Yorks Archaeol Soc Record Ser* Vols X and XIII (1891–3)). R. B. Dobson: *Selby Abbey and Town* (1969). W. St John Hope: 'On the Great Almery for Relics in the Abbey of Selby' *Archaeologia* 60 (1907). East window: J. Fowler in *Yorks Archaeol J* 5 (1879), 331–49. VCH *Yorks* III, 95–100.

SHERBORNE

St Mary the Virgin
See: 705–1075
Fd 705: secular canons. Refd 998. Refd 1122: Benedictine Monks. D. 1539.
MAIN BUILDING DATES: Pre-Conquest: portions of W front and crossing; C12i–ii: transept, nave aisle walls, S porch, parts of N choir aisle; C13: Bishop Roger's Chapel, Lady Chapel; C14: S transeptal chapels; *c*. 1430–40: choir and aisles; *c*. 1475–90: nave, central tower; 1856: rebuilding of choir vault; 1921: E end of Lady Chapel.

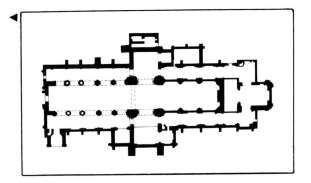

REFERENCES: R. Willis: 'Sherborne Minster', *Archaeol J* 22 (1865), 179–99. R. H. Carpenter: 'On the Benedictine Abbey of . . . with notes on the restoration of its church', *Trans Roy Inst Brit Architects* (1876–7), 137–51. W. B. Wildman: *A Short History of Sherborne* (1911). RCHM *Dorset* I (1952) and *Addendum* (1974). J. H. P. Gibb: 'The Anglo-Saxon Cathedral at Sherborne', *Archaeol J* 132 (1975), 71–110. W. Leedy: 'Wells Cathedral and Sherborne Abbey: a workshop connection in the late fifteenth century', *Gesta* 16 (1977), 39–44. Screen etc.: Vallance (1947), 121. History: VCH *Dorset* II, 62–70.

SHREWSBURY

SS Peter and Paul (nave dedicated to Holy Cross)
Fd *c*. 1080: Benedictine Monks. D. 1540.

MAIN BUILDING DATES: C12i–ii: western piers of
crossing, parts of N and S transept arms; C12iii:
three eastern bays of nave, nave aisles, W front;
C13i–ii: lower stage of N porch; *c*. 1360–70: W
tower and W end of nave arcade; C15: upper storey
of N porch; 1886– : chancel and east side of
crossing, clerestory (Pearson).

REFERENCES: H. Owen and J. B. Blakeway: *History
of Shrewsbury* (1825). *Archaeol J* 85 (1928), 215.
Archaeol J 113 (1956), 219–21. D. H. S. Cranage: *An
architectural account of the churches of Shropshire* II,
867–92. W. A. Leighton: 'Shrewsbury Abbey',
Shropshire Archaeol Soc Trans ser 2 IX, 246–50. Alterations: *The Antiquary* VII (1883), 85. Screen doors:
Vallance (1947), 170.

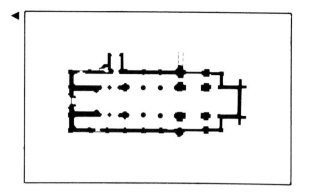

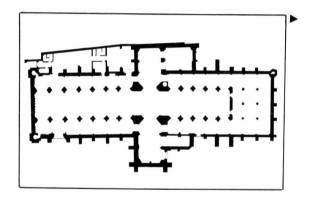

SOUTHWARK

St Mary
See: 1905
Pre-Conquest minster. Refd 1106: Augustinian
Canons. D. 1539.

MAIN BUILDING DATES: C13i–ii: eastern arm and
retrochoir; C13iv: transept; C14iv: lower part of
tower; C16i: upper stage of tower; 1822– : restoration; 1889–97: nave (Blomfield).

REFERENCES: W. Thompson: *The history and antiquities of the collegiate church of St Saviour (St Marie
Overie) Southwark* (2nd ed. 1906). F. T. Dollman:
'Priory Church of . . .' *Trans Roy Inst Brit Architect
new ser* VII (1891), 389–97. VCH *London* I, 480–4.
T. P. Stevens: *The Story of Southwark Cathedral*
(1922).

Southwell
St Mary
(see over)

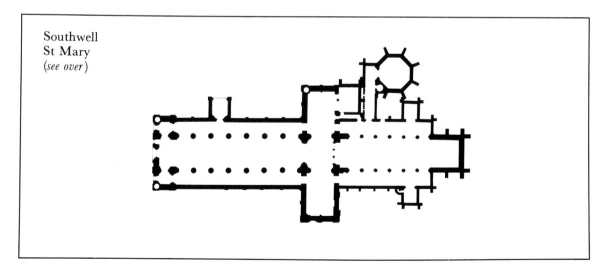

SOUTHWELL
St Mary
See: 1884
Secular canons.

MAIN BUILDING DATES: C12i–ii: transept, nave, western towers; C13ii: eastern arm; C13iv: chapter-house; *c*. 1330: pulpitum; 1851– : restoration (Christian).

REFERENCES: W. D. Rastell: *History and antiquities of the town and church of Southwell* (1787). N. Summers: *A Prospect of Southwell* (1974). A. Hamilton Thompson: 'The cathedral church of . . .' *Trans Thoroton Soc* 15 (1912), 1–50. G. T. Harvey: 'Foundations of the Norman choir of . . .' *Assoc Architect Soc Rep and Pap* XX, 55–6. Architectural history: Dimock in *Assoc Architect etc* X, 39–56. Discovery of (? Roman) pavement: *Trans Thoroton Soc* (1901), 58–9; Roman villa: *Trans Thoroton Soc* 70 (1966), 13–37. A. F. Leach: *Visitations and Memorials of* . . . (Camden Soc 48) (1891). Documentary history: *Assoc Architect etc* XIV, 26–40. Pulpitum: Vallance (1947), 170. N. Pevsner: *The Leaves of Southwell* (1945). W. J. Conybeare: 'The Carved Capitals of . . .', *J Brit Archaeol Ass* 39 (1933), 176–85. VCH *Notts* II, 152–61.

TEWKESBURY
Blessed Virgin Mary
Refd as cell of Cranborne *c*. 980. Trans. from Cranborne to Tewkesbury 1102: Benedictine Monks. D. 1540.

MAIN BUILDING DATES: 1087– *c*. 1150: arcades of eastern arm, N choir aisle wall, transept, nave, central tower; *c*. 1230: St Nicholas' chapel; *c* 1330: nave vault; C14ii: ambulatory and presbytery vault; 1877–92: restoration (Scott).

REFERENCES: T. Blashill: 'The architectural history of . . .' *Assoc Architect Socs Rep and Pap* XIV, 97–104. T. Blashill: 'Tewkesbury Abbey Church', *J Brit Archaeol Ass* XXXII (1876), 44–53. J. L. Petit: 'Tewkesbury Abbey Church', *Trans Bristol Gloucestershire Archaeol Soc* V, 70–85. See also A. Hartshorne in *Archaeol J* 47 (1890), 290–301. J. Bony: 'Tewkesbury et Pershore', *Bulletin Monumental* 96 (1937), 288. A. W. Clapham in *Archaeol J* 106 (Supplement), 1952. Tiles: A. S. Porter in *Archaeol J* 48 (1891), 83–4. Heraldry: F. Were in *Bristol Gloucestershire etc*. 26 (1903), 162–72. Glass in choir clerestory: J. McN. Rushforth in *Bristol Gloucestershire etc*. 46 (1924), 289–324. Tombs: S. Lysons in *Archaeologia* XIV (1803), 143. Roof bosses: C. J. P. Cave in *Archaeologia* 79 (1929), 73–84. Chantry chapels: Cook (1947), 142. History: VCH *Glos* II, 61–6; architecture: VIII, 156–63.

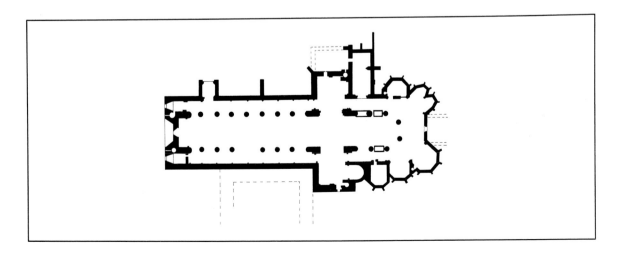

WALTHAM
Holy Cross
Fd ?1016–35. Refd *c.* 1060: secular canons. Refd
1117: Augustinian Canons. D. 1540.
MAIN BUILDING DATES: C11iii–*c.* 1160: W wall of S
transept arm, W crossing, nave arcades and nave
aisle walls; *c.* 1315–20: W bay of nave remodelled,
W front; *c.* 1320–30: S chapel and undercroft;
1556–8: W tower; C16 and modern: blocking of W
side of crossing; *c.* 1850: restoration; 1905: upper
stage of W tower.

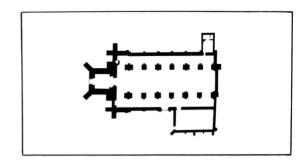

REFERENCES: VCH *Essex* V, 171–4. RCHM *Essex*
II, 237. E. Freeman: 'The architectural and early
history of Waltham Abbey Church', *Essex Archaeol
Soc* II, 1–40. Full bibliography in VCH *Essex
Bibliography*, 294–5. Screens: Vallance (1947), 122.
Excavations on site of SE transept of Henry II's
church: *Medieval Archaeol* 21 (1977), 207.

WELLS
St Andrew
See: 909 (transferred to Bath 1090; Bath and Wells
1218)
Fd *c.* 704: secular canons.
MAIN BUILDING DATES: C12iv: choir; C12iv–C13ii:
transept, nave, N porch; C13ii–iii: W front;
C13iii–iv: chapter-house; C14i: Lady Chapel, central tower; C14ii: retrochoir and remodelling of
choir, strainer arches in crossing; C14iii–iv: SW
tower; C15ii: NW tower; 1842– : repairs and
alterations.

REFERENCES: W. St John Hope: 'The site of the
Saxon Cathedral . . .' *Archaeol J* 67 (1910), 223–34.
J. A. Robinson: 'Documentary evidence relating to
the building of . . . *c.* 1186–1247' and J. Bilson:
'Notes on the history of . . .', *Archaeol J* 85 (1928),
1–22; 23–68. West front: W. St John Hope and
W. R. Lethaby in *Archaeologia* 59 (1904), 143–206.
L. S. Colchester and J. H. Harvey: 'Wells
Cathedral', *Archaeol J* 131 (1974), 200–14. C. M.
Church: *Chapters in the early history of Bath and Wells*
(1894; 1903). E. A. Freeman: *History of the Cathedral
Church of Wells, as illustrating the history of the cathedral
churches of the old foundation* (1870). E. Buckle: 'On
the Lady Chapel by the cloister at . . .' *Somerset
Archaeol Nat Hist Soc Proc* XL, 32–63. Notes on
arabic numerals on sculpture of west front: W. R.
Lethaby in *Proc Soc Antiq ser 2* XXI (1906), 199–
203. West front sculpture: E. S. Prior in *J Roy Inst
Brit Architect* XI (1904), 325–41. T. J. Pettigrew:
'On the cathedral of Wells', *J Brit Archaeol Ass* XII
(1856), 344–69. Architectural history: J. Irvine in
Somerset Archaeol etc. XIX, 1–47; C. M. Church in
Somerset Archaeol etc. XXXIV, 1–11; Ferrey in
Somerset Archaeol etc. XIX, 73–93. Glass: C. M.
Church in *Somerset Archaeol etc.* VI, 125–30;
Archaeologia 81 (1931), 85–118. Lady Chapel: J. A.
Robinson in *Archaeol J* 88 (1931). Chantry chapels:
Cook (1947), 121. Pulpitum: Vallance (1947), 82.
VCH *Somerset* II, 162–9.

Wells
St Andrew
(*see previous page*)

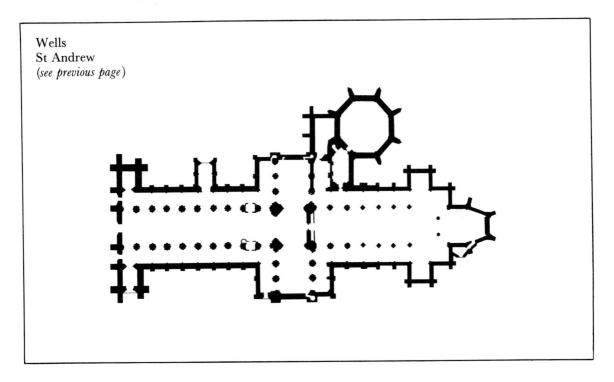

WESTMINSTER
St Peter
See: 1540–50
Fd/?Refd *c*. 960: Benedictine Monks. D. 1540.
Rest. 1556. D. 1559.
MAIN BUILDING DATES: (–1065: Edward the Confessor's church; 1220– : Lady Chapel); 1246–59: presbytery, ambulatory, transept and chapter-house; –1272: five eastern bays of nave; *c*. 1376–1471: western bays of nave; 1471–98: W window and nave roof; 1498–1502: completion of nave vault; 1503– *c*. 1512: Henry VII's Chapel; 1698–1745: western towers; 1808–22: restoration of Henry VII's Chapel; 1849–1906: restorations and rebuilding.

REFERENCES: R. Widmore: *History of . . . Westminster Abbey* (1751). W. R. Lethaby: *Westminster Abbey and the King's Craftsmen* (1906). F. Bond: *Westminster Abbey* (1909). W. R. Lethaby: *Westminster Abbey Re-examined* (1925). G. G. Scott: *Gleanings from Westminster Abbey* (2nd ed., 1863). R. A. Brown, H. M. Colvin and A. J. Taylor: *The History of the King's Works* (1963). VCH *London* I, 433–57. C. A. R. Radford: 'Westminster Abbey before King Edward the Confessor', *Westminster Abbey Occasional Papers* 15 (1965), 1–7. J. Armitage Robinson: 'The Church of Edward the Confessor at Westminster', *Archaeologia* 62 (1910), 81–100. L. E. Tanner and A. W. Clapham: 'Recent Discoveries in the Nave of Westminster Abbey', *Archaeologia* 83

(1933), 227–36. E. C. Fernie: 'Enclosed Apses and Edward's Church at Westminster', *Archaeologia* 105 (1973), 235–60. F. Barlow: *Edward the Confessor* (1970), esp. 229–33. F. Stenton (ed.) *et al.: The Bayeux Tapestry* (1957). R. P. Howgrave-Graham: '. . . the Sequence and Dates of the Transepts and Nave', *J Brit Archaeol Assoc ser 3* 11 (1948), 60–78. S. E. Rigold: *The Chapter House and the Pyx Chamber of Westminster Abbey* (1976). R. Branner: 'Westminster Abbey and the French Court Style', *J Soc Architect Hist* (1964). R. B. Rackham: 'The Nave of Westminster Abbey', *Proc Brit Acad* 4 (1909–10); 'Building at Westminster Abbey, 1298–1348', *Archaeol J* 67 (1910). R. W. MacDowall, J. T. Smith & C. F. Stell: 'The Timber Roofs of the Collegiate Church of St Peter at Westminster', *Archaeologia* 100 (1966). J. Heyman: 'An apsidal timber roof at Westminster', *Gesta* 15 (1976), 53–60. W. C. Leedy: 'The design of the vaulting of Henry VII's Chapel, Westminster: a reappraisal', *Architectural History* 18 (1975), 5–11. J. G. O'Neilly and L. E. Tanner: 'The Shrine of St Edward the Confessor', *Archaeologia* 100 (1966), 129–54. H. J. Plenderleith and H. Maryon: 'The Royal Bronze Effigies in . . .' *Antiq J* (1959), 87–90. W. H. St John Hope: 'The Funeral, Monument, and Chantry Chapel of King Henry the Fifth', *Archaeologia* 65 (1914). P. Clayton: 'The Inlaid Tiles of Westminster Abbey', *Archaeol J* 69 (1912), 36–73. See also Eames 1968. H. F. Westlake: *Westminster Abbey: the church, convent, cathedral and college of St Peter* 2 vols (1923). RCHM *London* I (1924). H. Poole: '. . . some account of the four northern chapels of the apse . . .' *London Middlesex Archaeol Soc Trans* VI, 488–519. J. T. Micklethwaite: 'Notes on the imagery of Henry VII's Chapel, Westminster', *Archaeologia* 47 (1883), 361–80; 'Further notes on Abbey buildings at Westminster', *Archaeol J* 51 (1894), 1–27; 'On the present state of the Royal tombs in Westminster Abbey', *Proc Soc Antiq ser 2* 15 (1900), 412. J. H. Harvey: 'The Masons of Westminster Abbey', *Archaeol J* 108 (1957), 82–101. Chantry chapels: Cook (1947), 128. Screens: Vallance (1947), 125.

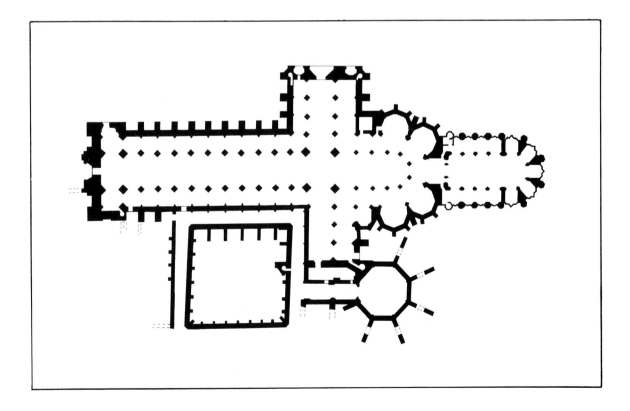

WIMBORNE
St Cuthberga
Fd –705: nuns. Refd –1066: secular canons. D. 1547.
MAIN BUILDING DATES: ? –1066: portions of transept; C12ii–iii: crossing, transept; 1160– : nave arcades, upper stages of central tower, W bay of presbytery; C13i–ii: Lady Chapel, presbytery and aisles; C14: remodelling of eastern arm, crypt, two W bays of nave, S vestry, N porch; 1448–64: W tower, upper stages of N porch and S vestry; 1855–7: restoration, rebuilding of N and S chapels, nave clerestory (T. H. Wyatt); 1891: restoration.

REFERENCES: RCHM *Dorset* V, 78–83. VCH *Dorset* II, 107–13.

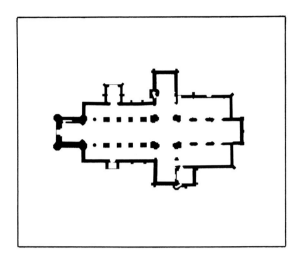

WINCHESTER
Holy Trinity and SS Peter and Paul
See: 662–3.
Fd *c*. 642. Secular canons –964. Refd 964: Benedictine Monks. D. 1539.
MAIN BUILDING DATES: C11iv: crypt and transept; 1108– : central tower; 1202– : retrochoir and Lady Chapel; C14i–iii: presbytery; C14iii: west front; C14iv–C15ii: remodelling of nave; C15iv: reredos and extension to Lady Chapel; C16i–ii: alterations to presbytery; 1905–12: restoration (T. G. Jackson).

REFERENCES: *Old Minster*: R. N. Quirk: 'Winchester cathedral in the tenth century', *Archaeol J* 114 (1957), 28–68. Interim reports on excavations in *Antiq J* 44 (1964), 188–219; 45 (1965), 230–64; 48 (1968), 250–84; 49 (1969), 295–329; 50 (1970), 277–326. See also Birthe Kjølbye-Biddle: 'A cathedral cemetery: problems in excavation and interpretation', *World Archaeol* 7.I (1975), 87–108; Martin Biddle: 'Felix Urbs Winthonia: Winchester in the Age of Monastic Reform', in *Tenth-Century Studies*, ed. D. Parsons (1975), 123–40. Cathedral priory: R Willis: 'The architectural history of Winchester cathedral', *Proc Roy Archaeol Inst at Winches-* ter (1845–6; repr. 1972). C. R. Peers and H. Brakspear in VCH *Hants* V (1912), 50–9. T. G. Jackson: '. . . an account of the building and of the repairs now in progress', *Trans St Paul's Ecclesiolog Soc* VI, 215–36. J. H. Harvey: 'Had Winchester Cathedral a central spire?', *Winchester Cath Record* 27 (1958), 9–13. T. D. Atkinson: 'Medieval Figure Sculpture in Winchester Cathedral', *Archaeologia* 75 (1935). Bosses: see *Archaeologia* 76 (1936), 161–78. Inigo Jones screen: J. M. G. Blakiston in *Winchester Cath Record* 46 (1977), 13–17. N. Pevsner: 'A Note on the East End of Winchester Cathedral', *Archaeol J* 116 (1959), 133–5. Medieval tiles: G. E. C. Knapp in *Winchester Cath Record* 25 (1956). Chantry chapels: Cook (1947), 82. Screens: Vallance (1947), 53. Cathedral Close: T. D. Atkinson in *Proc Hampshire Fld Club Archaeol Soc* 15.I (1941), 9–26. Wall paintings: Tristram I, 152; II, 168–71, Pls. 28–54; M. R. James and E. W. Tristram: 'The Wall Paintings in . . . the Lady Chapel of . . .' *Walpole Soc* 17 (1928–9), 13–39. R. W. and E. Baker: 'An account of the conservation of the painted vault in the chapel of the Guardian Angels, Winchester Cathedral', *The Conservator* I (1977), 17–21. J. H. Harvey: 'The Later Architects of Winchester Cathedral', *Winchester Cath Record* 15 (1946).

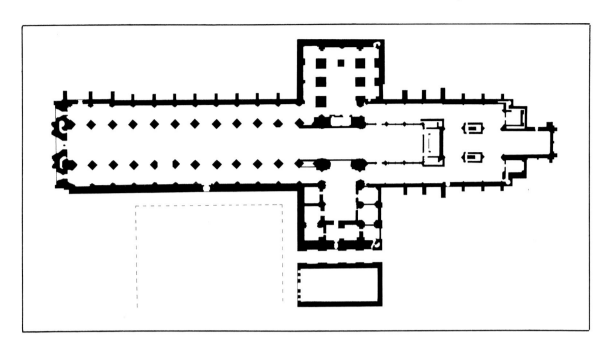

WINCHESTER

St Cross
Fd *c.* 1136. Hospital.
MAIN BUILDING DATES: 1136– : sacristy; 1160–1200: chancel, transept, E bay of nave, E bay of S nave wall, two eastern bays of N nave wall; C13i: two western bays of nave and aisle walls, W front, N porch; 1334–5: nave clerestory and W window; 1864–5: restoration (Butterfield).

REFERENCES: VCH *Hants* V, 59. *Archaeol J* 123 (1967), 216.

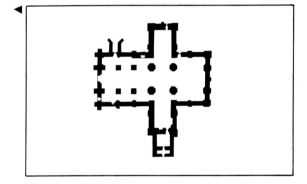

WORCESTER

St Mary
See: 680
Fd 680: secular canons (St Peter's). Separate church est. 743 (St Mary's). Refd 969: 'Benedictine' monks. D. 1540.
MAIN BUILDING DATES: 1084–9: crypt; *c.* 1120–5: chapter-house; *c.* 1175– : two western bays of nave; 1224–C13iii: eastern transept and choir; C14i–iii: nave; 1357–74: central tower; 1375/6– : alterations to N and S arms of transept; C14iv: nave vault, N porch, modifications to chapter-house; 1756–62: repairs; 1858–74: restoration, west front (Perkins, Scott).

REFERENCES: W. Thomas: *A survey of the cathedral church of Worcester* (1736). Browne Willis: *Mitred Abbeys* (1718), 302–12. R. Willis: 'The architectural history of Worcester cathedral and monastery', *Archaeol J* 20 (1863), 83–132 (cathedral), 254–72, 301–18 (monastic buildings). C. C. Dyer: 'The Saxon Cathedrals of Worcester', *Trans Worcestershire Archaeol Soc* (1968), 34. J. Noake: *The monastery and cathedral of Worcester* (1866). History: VCH *Worcestershire* II, 94–112; architecture IV,

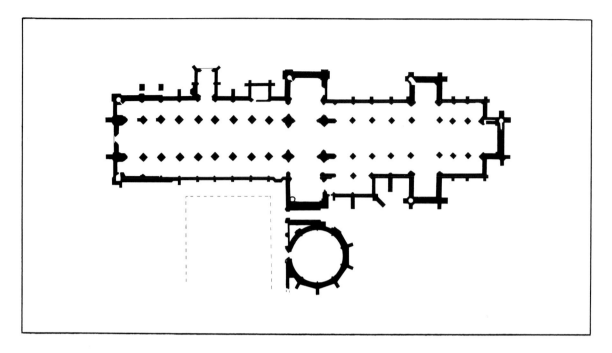

394–408. St John's Chapel: see *Assoc Architect Rep and Pap* XXX (1910), 605–18. M. D. Cox: 'The Twelfth-Century Design Sources of the Worcester Cathedral Misericords', *Archaeologia* 97 (1959), 165–78. *Medieval Art and Architecture at . . .* Brit Archaeol Ass Conference Trans for 1975 (1978);

classified bibliography: 186–9. J. K. Floyer: 'The medieval library of the Benedictine Priory of . . .' *Archaeologia* 58 (1903), 561–70. I. Atkins: 'The Church of Worcester from the Eighth to the Twelfth Century', *Antiq J* 17 (1937), 371–91; 20 (1940), 1–38.

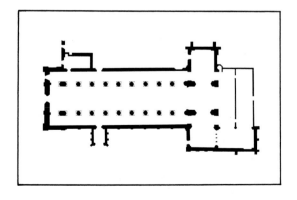

◀ WORKSOP
SS Mary and Cuthbert
Fd after 1119: Augustinian Canons. D. 1539.
MAIN BUILDING DATES: *c*. 1140: eastern bay of nave; *c*. 1170– : nave arcades; *c*. 1240: Lady Chapel; 1558–68: repairs; 1845–9: restorations (Nicholson); 1883– : repairs to S tower; 1922: renovation of Lady Chapel; 1929: renovation of S transept; 1958: restoration (King); 1970–4: east end.

REFERENCES: A. Trollope: in *Assoc Architect Socs Rep and Pap* V, 208–28. VCH *Notts* II, 125–9.

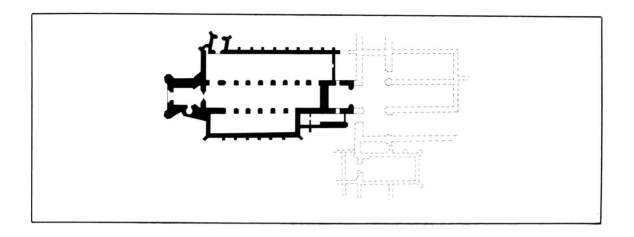

WYMONDHAM

St Mary the Virgin
Fd 1107: Benedictine Monks. D. 1538.
MAIN BUILDING DATES: *c*. 1107–30: nave arcades; *c*. 1400: octagon tower; 1445– : nave clerestory, N nave aisle; 1473– : W tower.

REFERENCES: J. L. Petit: 'Wymondham Church', *Archaeol Inst of Great Brit and Ireland Proc* (1847). H.

Harrod: 'Some particulars relating to the history of the abbey church of . . .' *Archaeologia* XLIII (1871), 264–72. Excavations: S. Woodward in *Archaeologia* XXVI (1836), 287–99; A. Parker: *Restoration of . . .* (1902); *Archaeol J* 80 (1923), 327–8; F. H. Fairweather in *Ingleby's Supp. to Blomefield's Norfolk*, 328. VCH *Norfolk* II, 336–43.

YORK

St Peter
See: 627
Secular canons.
MAIN BUILDING DATES: (*c*. 1080–1100: Norman church; fragments in crypt, transept and Undercroft); *c*. 1154–70: central crypt; *c* 1225–55: S and N arms of transept; *c*. 1260–90: chapter-house; 1291–*c*. 1345: nave and W front; 1361–1402: eastern arm; 1408–23: central tower (completed in 1470s): 1432–56: SW tower; 1470–4: NW tower; 1829– : repairs and reroofing after fire in eastern arm; 1840– : repairs and reroofing after fire in nave; 1875– : restoration of S arm of transept; 1887–1910: restoration; 1967–72: restoration and Undercroft.

REFERENCES: J. Browne: *The History of the Metropolitan Church of St Peter York* (1847). J. Browne: *The Fabric Rolls of York Minster* (1863). J. Raine: *The Fabric Rolls of York Minster, Surtees Soc* 35 (1859). G. Benson: *Handbook to the cathedral church of . . .* (1893). VCH *Yorks* III, 375–82; *City of York*,

337–57. F. Harrison: *York Minster* (1927). G. E. Aylmer and R. Cant (eds): *A History of York Minster* (1977). Anglo-Saxon church(es) and cemetery: K. Harrison: 'The Saxon Cathedral at York', *Yorkshire Archaeol J* 39 (1956–8), 436–44; H. M. and J. Taylor: *Anglo-Saxon Architecture* II (1965), 700–9; B. Hope-Taylor: *Under York Minster* (1971); A. D. Phillips: 'Excavations at York Minster 1967–73', *Friends of . . . Annual Report* 46 (1975), 19–27. R. Willis: 'The architectural history of York cathedral', *Proc Roy Archaeol Inst* (1848) (repr. 1972). See also chapters by E. A. Gee and J. H. Harvey in Aylmer and Cant (1977). D. F. Robertson: 'On the newly discovered crypt at . . .' *Trans Roy Inst Brit Architects* I (1836), 105–8. C. R. Peers: 'Recent discoveries in the minster of Ripon and York', *Antiq J* 11 (1931), 113–22. J. S. Miller: 'The Norman Staircase Turrets', *Friends of . . . Annual Reports* 38 (1967), 15–19. J. Quentin Hughes: 'The Timber Roofs of York Minster', *Yorkshire Archaeol J* 38 (1955), 474–95. Chapter-house: N. Coldstream in *J Brit Archaeol Ass* 35 (1972); C. J. Bassham and

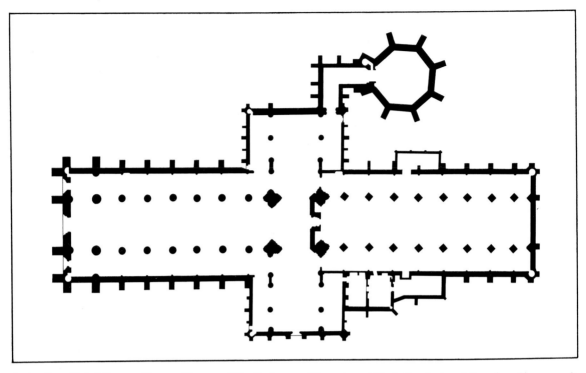

E. A. Gee: *York Minster: Chapter-House and Vestibule* (1974). Tracing house: J. H. Harvey in *Friends of . . . Annual Report* 40 (1968–9), 9–13. Glass: F. Harrison: 'The west choir clerestory windows . . .' *Yorkshire Archaeol J* 26 (1922), 353–74; W. R. Lethaby: 'Archbishop Roger's Cathedral at York and its stained glass', *Archaeol J* 72 (1915), 37. J. A. Knowles: 'Technical notes on the St William Window in . . .', *Yorkshire Archaeol J* 37 (1949), 148–61; 'Notes on some windows in the choir and Lady Chapel . . .' *Yorkshire Archaeol J* 39 (1958), 91–118. Sculpture: A. W. Clapham: 'The York Virgin and its Date', *Archaeol J* 105 (1948), 6–13. A. Maclagen: 'A Romanesque Relief in . . .' *Proc Brit Acad* 10 (1921–3), 481. J. Bilson: 'Notes on a sculptured representation of a Hell Cauldron . . .' *Yorkshire Archaeol J* 19 (1907), 435–45. C. Wilson: *The Shrines of St William of York* (1977). De Gray and De Ludham tombs: H. Ramm *et al* in *Archaeologia* 103 (1971), 101–47.

YORK

Holy Trinity (Micklegate)
Fd –1069: secular canons. Refd 1089: Benedictine Monks. D. 1538.

MAIN BUILDING DATES: *c.* 1090–1110: W crossing piers, fragment on N side of W front; *c.* 1180: nave arcade, N respond of W doorway; C16: NW tower and blocking of N nave arcade; C19 and modern: extensive alteration and restoration of E and W ends, S aisle and N porch.

REFERENCES: Description: RCHM *York* III (1972). See also J. Solloway, *The Alien Benedictines of York* (1910). K. Harrison: 'The Pre-Conquest Churches

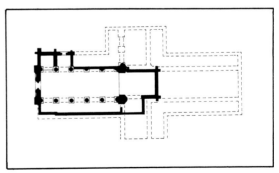

of York', *Yorks Archaeol J* 40 pt 2 (1960), 232–3. VCH *Yorks* III, 389–90.

Glossary

Abacus Horizontal slab of stone above a capital

Abutment Structure designed to resist or accept lateral thrust

Ambo Form of pulpit in early church

Ambulatory Route for procession incorporated in the architectural layout of the east end of a church

Apse Semi-circular (sometimes semi-polygonal) projection from or termination to a plan

Ashlar Block of dressed stone worked to a clean finish at the face

Bar tracery Strips of masonry subdividing a window

Bay Compartment of a building (e.g. as between pairs of columns, buttresses, tie-beams, etc.)

Boss Embellished block of stone or wood at junction of vaulting ribs

Buttress Masonry projection which receives the lateral thrust delivered by another part of the building, usually a vault

Calme (pronounced 'came') H-section strip of lead used to secure window glass

Campanile Free-standing bell-tower

Canon Secular cleric belonging to a cathedral or collegiate church

Capital Topmost part of a pier or column

Centring Temporary wooden framework used to assist in the construction of an arch or vault

Chancellor Member of cathedral chapter with responsibility for education

Chantry Office endowed for the purpose of saying mass for the soul of the founder

Chapter-house Room or building used for formal meetings of monastic body or chapter of canons

Chevet The ensemble of a presbytery, ambulatory and radiating chapels at the east end of a great church

Choir The central part of a cruciform church, used for most of the offices

Clerestory Uppermost tier of windows positioned to admit light to the central aisle of a church

Cloister Quadrilateral enclosure with a covered walk on each side. The heart of a monastic layout

Corbel Stone projecting beyond the plane of a wall for purpose of supporting some other feature

Crypt Chamber below part of the main body of a church

Cupola Miniature dome

Dead load The weight of a structure, acting downwards

Dean The president of a secular chapter

Double monastery Monastic house accommodating monks and nuns (segregated), normally under the authority of an abbess

Eccentric load Load which is not in alignment with the axis of the structure upon or through which it acts

Falsework Temporary wooden framework used to support part of a masonry building during construction

Fan vault A vault in which all the ribs are of equal spacing and curvature

Feretory Bay (usually east of high altar) assigned for the keeping of important relics or shrine

'Gesta' Record of official activities

Label stop Small boss or terminal at the end of a moulding over a door or window

Lantern Tower with walls which rise above surrounding roofs and are pierced by windows which admit light to the area below

Lierne vault A vault including vault ribs which do not connect either with the springing of the principal structure ribs or with the ridge ribs (see Pl. 107)

Live load Pressure exerted by a transient force of variable intensity (e.g. wind)

Metropolitan Archbishop exercising jurisdiction over a province

Minster Literally, an English form of Latin *monasterium*: a monastery; in practice often a church serving a large territory staffed by a body of secular canons

Nave Western limb of a great church: the place of the people

Obedientiary roll Record of accounts kept by monastic official responsible for a specific aspect of domestic management (e.g. cellarer, guest-master)

Oratory Small chapel or prayer house

Orthographic projection Representation of an elevation or plan in which all parts of the structure are seen as though the line of vision is perpendicular to them

Pendant vault A vault including elongated bosses which hang below the surface of the main shell (see Pl. 155)

'Porticus' Adjunct to the main body of a church (pre-Conquest)

Prebend Portion of the endowment of a secular cathedral used for the support of a member of the chapter

Precentor Member of cathedral chapter with responsibility for supervision of music and musical training

Presbytery That part of the eastern arm of a cruciform church which contains the principal altar

Pulpitum Screen, usually solid, at the west end of the choir

Putlog hole Temporary recess left in masonry to secure the end of a horizontal scaffold pole

Reredos Screen providing a back-drop to an altar

Rib An arch forming part of the structural skeleton of a vault

Rood screen Screen marking the boundary between the area of the people (nave) and the area to the east designated for the use of monks or canons. The rood screen normally stood near the east end of the nave (see Pl. 64)

Rule Written instructions governing monastic life

Sacrist(an) Monastic or clerical official in charge of contents of a great church, often responsible for the administrative oversight of building

Sacristy Annex to a church used for keeping sacred vessels and vestments

Scriptorium Monastic writing house

Secretarium Annex adjacent to the eastern arm (see Sacristy)

See The place where a bishop's chair (*cathedra*) is located

Spandrel Triangular area above the haunch of an arch

Statics Forces acting in equilibrium; acting as a weight without motion

Stilting Condition in which the curve of a vault, arch or apse begins at a point above or beyond the impost or origin

String course Horizontal strip of masonry projecting beyond the place of a wall, sometimes moulded

Strip footing Continuous substructure carrying a wall or arcade

Succentor Deputy to precentor

Tierceron vault A vault including secondary vault ribs which spring from the same point as the principal structural ribs (see Pl. 142)

Transept Limb of a cruciform church set at right-angles to the main axis of the building, consisting of two arms and a central crossing. The word is often used to denote one or other of the arms (e.g. 'north transept')

Tribune Second storey arcade which corresponds with the spacing of the ground storey arcade (see Pl. 115)

Triforium Second storey gallery which occupies space above side aisles

Vault Masonry covering of space based on the principle of an arch

Vault cell Panel of masonry bounded by vaulting ribs

Volute Embellished projection at the angle of a capital

Bibliography

ACKERMAN, J. S. 1949. 'Ars Scientia Nihil Est': Gothic Theory of Architecture at the Cathedral of Milan. *Art Bulletin* 31, 84–111.

ANDERSON, R. B. 1875. Notice of Working Drawings Scratched on the walls of the crypt at Roslin Chapel. *Proc Soc Antiq Scotland* 10, 63–4.

ANDREWS, F. B. 1925. *The Medieval Builder and His Methods*. Oxford.

ARNOLD, T (ed.) 1882. *Symeonis Monachi Opera Omnia*. 2 vols. Rolls series.

BAILEY, R. N. 1976. The Anglo-Saxon Church at Hexham. *Archaeol Aeliana* 5th ser. 4, 47–67.

BARLEY, M. W. and HANSON, R. P. C. (eds) 1968. *Christianity in Britain, 300–700*. Leicester.

BARLOW, F. 1963. *The English Church 1000–1066*. London.

BATSFORD, H. and FRY, C. 1940. *The Greater English Church of the Middle Ages*. London.

BERGEN, H. (ed.) 1906. *Lydgate's Troy Book*. Early English Text Society (Extra Ser) 97, i.

BIDDLE, M. 1962–71. Excavations at Winchester. Interim reports annually in *Antiq J* 44–50; 52; 55. For further details see:

BIDDLE, M. 1975. *Felix Urbs Winthonia*: Winchester in the Age of Monastic Reform. In Parsons 1975, 123–40.

BIDDLE, M. 1976. The Archaeology of the Church: a widening horizon. In *The Archaeological Study of Churches*, eds P. V. Addyman and R. K. Morris, CBA Research Report 13, 65–71.

BIDWELL, P. T. 1978. The Cathedral Close, Exeter. *Bulletin* of the CBA Churches Committee 8, 8–11.

BILSON, J. 1911. The Plan of the First Cathedral Church at Lincoln. *Archaeologia* 62. ii, 543–64.

BILSON, J. 1922. Durham Cathedral and the Chronology of its Vaults. *Archaeol J* 79, 101–60.

BIRCH, W. (ed.) 1892. *Liber Vitae: Register and Martyrology of New Minster and Hyde Abbey, Winchester*.

BLAGG, T. F. C. 1976. Tools and Techniques of the Roman Stonemason in Britain. *Britannia* 7, 152–72.

BLAKE, E. O. (ed.) 1962. *Liber Eliensis*. Camden Soc. (Ser. 3), 92.

BLUNT, C. E. and BRAND, J. D. 1970. Mint Output of Henry III. *Brit Numis J* 39, 61–5.

BOND, F. 1905. *Gothic Architecture in England*. London.

BOND, F. 1912. *The Cathedrals of England and Wales*. London.

BOND, F. and WATKINS, J. 1910–11. Notes on the Architectural History of Lincoln Cathedral from 1192 to 1255. *J Roy Inst Brit Architects* 26/11/10; 10/12/10; 27/5/11.

BOYCE, E. J. 1888. *A Memorial of the Cambridge Camden Society, Instituted May, 1839 and the Ecclesiological (late Cambridge Camden), May 1846*. London.

BRAKSPEAR, H. 1922. Bardney Abbey. *Archaeol J* 79, 1–92.

BRANNER, R. 1958. Drawings from a Thirteenth-Century Architect's Shop: the Reims Palimpsest. *J Soc Architect Hist* 17, 9–22.

BRANNER, R. 1963. Villard de Honnecourt, Reims, and the Origin of Gothic Architectural Drawing. *Gazette des Beaux-Arts*, 129–46.

BRIDBURY, A.R. 1973. The Black Death. *Econ Hist Rev* (2nd ser.) 26, 577–92.

BRIDBURY, A. R. 1975. *Economic Growth: England in the Later Middle Ages*. Hassocks, near Brighton.

BRIDBURY, A.R. 1977. Before the Black Death. *Econ Hist Rev* (2nd ser.) 30, 393–410.

BRIGGS, M. S. 1927. *The Architect in History*. Oxford.

283

BRIGGS, M. S. 1952. *Goths and Vandals: A Study of the Destruction, Neglect, and Preservation of Historical Buildings in England*. London.

BROOKE, C. 1977. St Albans: The Great Abbey. In Runcie 1977, 43–70.

BROWN, P. D. C. 1972. The Church at Richborough. *Britannia* 2, 225–31.

BROWN, R. A., COLVIN, H. M., and TAYLOR, A. J. 1963. *The History of the King's Works*. Vol. I: *The Middle Ages*. London.

BUCHER, F. 1968. Design in Gothic Architecture – a Preliminary Assessment. *J Soc Architect Hist* 27, 49–71.

BURNE, R. V. H. 1962. *The Monks of Chester*. London.

BUTLER, L. A. S., RAHTZ, P. A., and TAYLOR, H. M. 1975. Deerhurst 1971–4; The Society's Research Project on the English Church. *Antiq J* 55, 346–65.

CAIGER-SMITH, A. 1963. *English Medieval Mural Paintings*. Oxford.

CAMERON, K. 1968. Eccles in English Place-Names. In Barley and Hanson 1968, 87–92.

CAMPBELL, A. (ed. and trans.) 1967. *Æthelwulf, De Abbatibus*. Oxford.

CAMPBELL, J. 1971. The First Century of Christianity in England. *Ampleforth J* 76, 16–29.

CAPES, W. W. (ed.) 1908. *The Charters and Records of Hereford Cathedral*.

CHAPMAN, F. R. 1907. *Sacrist Rolls of Ely*. 2 vols.

CLAPHAM, A. 1930. *English Romanesque Architecture Before the Conquest*. Oxford.

CLAPHAM, A. 1934. *English Romanesque Architecture After the Conquest*. Oxford.

CLARKE, B. F. L. 1938. *Church Builders of the Nineteenth Century: A Study of the Gothic Revival in England*. London.

COCKE, T. H. 1975. James Essex, Cathedral Restorer. *Architect Hist* 18, 12–22.

COLCHESTER, L. S. and HARVEY, J. H. 1974. Wells Cathedral. *Archaeol J* 131, 200–14.

COLDSTREAM, N. 1976. English Decorated Shrine Bases. *J Brit Archaeol Ass* 129, 15–34.

COLGRAVE, B. and MYNORS, R. A. B. (eds) 1969. *Bede's Ecclesiastical History of the English People*. Oxford.

COLVIN, H. M. (ed.) 1969. *Daniel King – The Cathedral and Conventvall Churches of England and Wales*. Farnborough.

COLVIN, H. M. (ed. and trans.) 1971. *Building Accounts of Henry III*. Oxford.

CONANT, K. J. 1944. Observations on the Vaulting Problems of the Period 1088–1211. *Gazette des Beaux-Arts* 26, 127–34.

CONANT, K. J. 1963. Medieval Acadamy Excavations at Cluny, ix: Systematic Dimensions in the Buildings. *Speculum* 38, 1–45.

COOK, G. H. 1947. *Medieval Chantries and Chantry Chapels*. London.

COX, J. C. 1897. The Treatment of our Cathedral Churches in the Victorian Age. *Archaeol J* 54, 239–74.

CRAMP, R. 1976. Window Glass from the monastic site of Jarrow. *J Glass Stud* 17, 88–96.

CRANAGE, D. H. S. 1932. Eastern Chapels in the Cathedral Church of Norwich. *Antiq J* 12, 117–126.

CROMBIE, A. C. 1953. *Robert Grosseteste and the Origins of Experimental Science*. Oxford.

DARBY, H. C. 1977. *Domesday England*. Cambridge.

DARLINGTON, R. R. 1936. Ecclesiastical Reform in the Late Old English Period. *Eng Hist Rev* 51, 385–428.

DAVIS, R. H. C. 1954. A Catalogue of Masons' Marks as an Aid to Architectural History. *J Brit Archaeol Ass* (3rd ser.) 17, 43–76.

DEANSELY, M. 1976. *A History of the Medieval Church 590–1500*. London.

DICKENS, C. 1866. Article on Jonathan Martin in *All the Year Round*, 1 December 1866. Repr. in *York History* 2 (n.d.), 75–81.

DICKINSON, J. C. 1968. The Buildings of the English Austin Canons after the Dissolution of the Monasteries. *J Brit Archaeol Ass* (3rd ser.) 31, 60–75.

DIMOCK, J. F. 1860. *Metrical Life of St Hugh*. Lincoln.

DOBSON, R. B. 1973. *Durham Priory, 1400–1450*. Cambridge.

DOBSON, R. B. 1976. The Historical Documentation of Monastic Sites (to 1500). In *Working Party on the Archaeology of Monasteries – a Compilation of Papers*. Council for British Archaeology, 9–13.

DOBSON, R. B. 1977. Urban Decline in Late Medieval England. *Trans Roy Hist Soc* (5th ser.) 27, 1–22.

DODWELL, B. 1957. The Foundation of Norwich Cathedral. *Trans Roy Hist Soc* (5th ser.) 7, 1–18.

DODWELL, C. R. (ed. and trans.) 1961. *Theophilus: De Diversis Artibus*. London.

DOUGLAS, D. 1957. The Norman Episcopate Before the Norman Conquest. *Cambridge Hist J* 13.ii, 101–15.

EAMES, E. S. 1968. *Medieval Tiles: a handbook*. London.

EASTLAKE, C. L. 1872. *A History of the Gothic Revival*. London.

EDWARDS, K. 1967. *The English Secular Cathedrals in the Middle Ages*. Manchester.

EISENHOFER, L. and LECHNER, J. 1961. *The Liturgy of the Roman Rite*. Trans. A. J. and E. F. Peeler; ed. H. E. Winstone. Edinburgh, London.

FAIRWEATHER, F. H. 1929. Gundulf's Cathedral at Rochester: some critical remarks upon the hitherto accepted plan. *Archaeol J* 86, 187–212.

FERNIE, E. 1976. The Ground Plan of Norwich Cathedral and the Square Root of 2. *J Brit Archaeol Ass* 129, 77–86.

FERNIE, E. 1977. The Romanesque Piers of Norwich Cathedral. *Norfolk Archaeol* 36, 383–5.

FITCHEN, J. 1961. *The Construction of Gothic Cathedrals: a study of Medieval Vault Erection*. Oxford.

FORSYTH, W. A. 1946. The Structure of Salisbury Cathedral Tower and Spire. *J Roy Inst Brit Architects* 53, 85–7.

FOWLER, J. T. (ed.) 1902. *Rites of Durham*. Surtees Soc. 107.

FRANKL, P. 1960. *The Gothic: Literary Sources and Interpretations through Eight Centuries*. Princeton N. J.

FRASER, C. M. 1969. The pattern of trade in the north-east of England, 1265–1350. *Northern History* 4, 44–57.

FRERE, S. 1976. The Silchester Church: the excavation by Sir Ian Richmond in 1961. *Archaeologia* 105, 277–302.

GARMONSWAY, G. N. (ed. and trans.) 1972. *The Anglo-Saxon Chronicle*. London.

GELLING, M. 1977. Latin loan-words in Old English place-names. *Anglo-Saxon England* 6, 1–13.

GELLING, M. 1978. *Signposts to the Past. Place-names and the history of England*. London.

GEM, R. D. H. 1970. The Anglo-Saxon Cathedral Church at Canterbury: a further contribution. *Archaeol J* 127, 196–201.

GEM, R. D. H. 1975. A Recession in English Architecture During the Early Eleventh Century, and its Effect on the Development of the Romanesque Style. *J Brit Archaeol Ass* 128, 28–49.

GERMANN, G. 1972. *Gothic Revival in Europe and Britain: Sources, Influences and Ideas*. London.

GIBB, J. H. P. 1975. The Anglo-Saxon Cathedral at Sherborne. *Archaeol J* 132, 71–110.

GIBSON, S. and WARD-PERKINS, B. 1977. The Incised Architectural Drawings of Trogir Cathedral. *Antiq J* 57, 289–311.

GILBERT, E. C. 1970. The Date of the late Saxon Cathedral at Canterbury. *Archaeol J* 127, 202–210.

GILYARD-BEER, R. 1958. *Abbeys: An Introduction to the Religious Houses of England and Wales*. London.

GOULD, J. 1976. *Lichfield: Archaeology and Development*. Birmingham.

GRAHAM, R. 1945. An Appeal about 1175 for the Building Fund of St Paul's Cathedral Church. *J Brit Archaeol Ass* (3rd ser.) 10, 73–6.

GREENE, J. P. 1977. A Medieval Bell Pit at Norton Priory, Cheshire. *Bulletin* of the CBA Churches Committee 6, 12–14.

GRIERSON, P. 1952–4. The Canterbury (St Martin's) hoard of Frankish and Anglo-Saxon coin-ornaments. *Brit Numis J* 27, 39–51.

HAHNLOSER, H. R. 1972. *Villard de Honnecourt*. Vienna.

HALCROW, E. M. 1954–5. The Decline of Demesne Farming on the Estates of Durham Cathedral Priory. *Econ Hist Rev* (2nd ser.) 7, 345–56.

HANDBOOK 1848. *A Hand-Book of English Ecclesiology*. London.

HARDEN, D. B. 1961. Domestic Window Glass, Roman, Saxon and Medieval. In Jope 1961, 39–63.

HARRISON, K. 1956–8. The Saxon Cathedral at York. *Yorkshire Archaeol J* 39, 436–44.

HARRISON, K. 1960. The Pre-Conquest Churches of York. *Yorkshire Archaeol J* 40, 232–41.

HARVEY, J. H. 1947. *Gothic England: A Survey of National Culture 1300–1550*. London.

HARVEY, J. H. 1954. *English Mediaeval Architects: A Biographical Dictionary down to 1550*. London.

HARVEY, J. H. 1961. The Origins of the Perpendicular Style. In Jope 1961, 134–65.

HARVEY, J. H. 1968. The Origins of Gothic Architecture: Some Further Thoughts. *Antiq J* 48.i, 87–99.

HARVEY, J. H. 1969. The Tracing Floor in York Minster. *The Friends of York Minster 40th Annual Report* (for 1968), 9–13.

HARVEY, J. H. (ed. and trans.) 1969. *William Worcestre: Itineraries*. Oxford.

HARVEY, J. H. 1972. *The Mediaeval Architect*. London.

HARVEY, J. H. 1974. *Cathedrals of England and Wales*. London.

HARVEY, J. H. 1975. *Mediaeval Craftsmen*. London.

HASKINS, C. H. 1924. *Studies in the History of Medieval Science*. Harvard.

HASKINS, C. H. 1971. *The Renaissance of the Twelfth Century.* (Original edition 1928.) Harvard.

HATCHER, J. 1977. *Plague, Population and the English Economy 1348–1530.* London, Basingstoke.

HAZLITT, W. 1864. *Early Popular Poetry.*

HE: see Colgrave and Mynors 1969.

HEIGHWAY, C. 1978. Excavations at Gloucester. Fourth Interim Report: St Oswald's Priory, Gloucester. 1975–6. *Antiq J* 58, 103–32.

HERTZ, C. 1963. *Recherches sur les Rapports entre Architecture et Liturgie à l'Epoque Carolingienne.* Paris.

HEWETT, C. A. 1974. *English Cathedral Carpentry.* London.

HEWETT, C. A. 1977. Understanding standing buildings. *World Archaeol* 9, 174–84.

HEWETT, C. A. and TATTON-BROWN, T. 1976. New Structural Evidence regarding Bell Harry Tower and the South-East Spire at Canterbury. *Archaeol Cantiana* 92, 129–36.

HEYMAN, J. 1966. The Stone Skeleton. *Internat J Solids Structures* 2, 249–57.

HEYMAN, J. 1967. Spires and Fan Vaults. *Internat J Solids Structures* 3, 243–57.

HEYMAN, J. 1967–8. Beauvais Cathedral. *Trans Newcomen Soc* 40, 15–32.

HEYMAN, J. 1968. On the Rubber Vaults of the Middle Ages, and other matters. *Gazette des Beaux-Arts*, 177–88.

HEYMAN, J. 1976. An Apsidal Timber Roof at Westminster. *Gesta* 15, 53–60.

HOLLIS, D. (ed.) 1949. *Calendar of the Bristol Apprentice Book 1532–1565.* Part I: *1532–1542.* Bristol Record Soc. 14.

HOPE-TAYLOR, B. 1971. *Under York Minster: Archaeological Discoveries 1966–71.* York.

HORN, W. and BORN, E. 1966. The 'Dimensional Inconsistencies' of the Plan of St Gall and the Problem of the Scale of the Plan. *Art Bulletin* 48, 285–308.

HOWARD, F. E. 1911. Fan Vaults. *Archaeol J* 68, 1–42.

JAMES, J. 1973. Medieval Geometry. *Architect Ass Quarterly* 5.ii, 4–11.

JENKINS, F. 1961. *Architect and Patron.* Oxford.

JOPE, E. M. (ed.) 1961. *Studies in Building History.* London.

JOPE, E. M. 1964. The Saxon Building-Stone Industry in Southern and Midland England. *Medieval Archaeol* 8, 91–118.

KEEN, L. 1969. A Series of Seventeenth- and Eighteenth-Century Lead-Glazed Relief Tiles from North Devon. *J Brit Archaeol Ass* (3rd ser.) 32, 144–70.

KERSHAW, I. 1973. *Bolton Priory: the Economy of a Northern Monastery.* Oxford.

KITCHIN, G. W. (ed.) 1892. *Compotus Rolls of the Obedientiaries of St Swithun's Priory, Winchester.* Hampshire Record Soc. London, Winchester.

KJØLBYE-BIDDLE, B. 1975. A cathedral cemetery: problems in excavation and interpretation. *World Archaeol* 7, 87–108.

KNOOP, D. and JONES, G. P. 1932. Masons and Apprenticeship in Medieval England. *Econ Hist Rev* 3, 346–66.

KNOOP, D. and JONES, G. P. 1933. *The Medieval Mason: an Economic History of English Stone Building in the Later Middle Ages.* Manchester.

KNOOP, D. and JONES, G. P. 1938. The English Medieval Quarry. *Econ Hist Rev* 9, 17–37.

KNOOP, D., JONES, G. P. and HAMER, D. 1938. *The Two Earliest Masonic MSS.*

KNOWLES, D. 1948, 1955, 1959. *The Religious Orders in England.* 3 vols. Cambridge.

KNOWLES, D. (trans.) 1951. *The Monastic Constitutions of Lanfranc.* Edinburgh, London.

KNOWLES, D. and HADCOCK, R. N. 1971. *Medieval Religious Houses: England and Wales.* London.

KNOWLES, J. A. 1959. John Thornton of Coventry and the East Window of Great Malvern Priory. *Antiq J* 39, 274–82.

KOSTOF, S. (ed.) 1977. *The Architect: Chapters in the History of the Profession.* New York.

KREUSCH, F. 1963. *Beobachtungen an der Westanlage der Klosterkirche zu Corvey.* Beihefte der Bonner Jahrbücher. 9. Cologne, 49–73.

KUBLER, G. 1944. A Late Gothic Computation of Rib Vault Thrusts. *Gazette des Beaux-Arts* 26, 135–48.

LAPIDGE, M. 1975. Some remnants of Bede's lost *Liber Epigrammatum. Eng Hist Rev* 90, 798–820.

LENERZ-DE WILDE, M. 1977. *Zirkelornamentik in der Kunst der Latènezeit.* Munich.

LETHABY, W. R. 1906. *Westminster Abbey and the Kings' Craftsmen.* London.

LETHABY, W. R. 1925. *Westminster Abbey Re-examined.* London.

LEVISON, W. 1941. St Alban and St Albans. *Antiquity* 15, 337–59.

LIVEING, H. G. D. 1906. *Records of Romsey Abbey: an account of the Benedictine House of Nuns, with notes on the Parish Church and Town.* Winchester.

LUARD, H. R. (ed.) 1861. *Epistolae Roberti Grosseteste episcopi Lincolniensis*. Rolls Series 57.

MACAULAY, J. 1975. *The Gothic Revival 1745–1845*. Glasgow, London.

MADDICOTT, J. R. 1975. The English Peasantry and the Demands of the Crown, 1293–1341. *Past and Present*, supp. 1.

MATE, M. 1973. The Indebtedness of Canterbury Cathedral Priory 1215–95. *Econ Hist Rev* (2nd ser.) 26, 183–97.

MAYHEW, N. J. 1974. Numismatic Evidence of Falling Prices in the Fourteenth Century. *Econ Hist Rev* (2nd ser.) 27, 1–15.

MAYHEW, N. J. (ed.) 1977. *Edwardian Monetary Affairs (1279–1344)*. Brit Archaeol Rep 36. Oxford.

McKINNON, J. W. 1974. The Tenth-Century Organ at Winchester. *Organ Yearbook* 5, 4–19.

MELLERS, W. 1968. *Caliban Reborn*. London.

METCALF, D. M. 1977. A Survey of Numismatic Research into the pennies of The First Three Edwards. In Mayhew 1977, 1–31.

MILLER, E. 1952. *The Abbey and Bishopric of Ely*. Cambridge.

MILLER, E. 1971. England in the Twelfth and Thirteenth Centuries: An Economic Contrast? *Econ Hist Rev* (2nd ser.) 24, 1–14.

MOODY, E. A. and CLAGETT, M. 1952. *The Medieval Science of Weights: Treatises Ascribed to Euclid, Archimedes, Thabit ibn Qurra, Jordanus de Nemore and Blasius of Parma*. Madison.

MORGAN, B. G. 1961. *Canonic Design in English Medieval Architecture*. Liverpool.

MORGAN, M. H. (trans.) 1960. *Vitruvius: the Ten Books on Architecture*. New York.

MORRIS, J. R. 1968. The Literary Evidence. In Barley and Hanson 1968, 55–73.

MORRIS, R. (ed.) 1872. *An Old English Miscellany*. Early English Text Soc. 49. London.

MORTET, V. (ed.) 1911. *Recueil de Textes relatifs à l'Histoire de l'Architecture . . . XIe–XIIe siècles*. Paris.

MORTET, V. and DESCHAMPS, P. (eds.) 1929. *Recueil de Textes relatifs à l'Histoire de l'Architecture . . . XIIe–XIIIe siècles*. Paris.

MUSSET, L. 1966. Les conditions financières d'une réussite architecturale: les grandes églises romanes de Normandie. In *Mélanges offerts à René Crozet*, 307–13. Poitiers.

MYERS, A. R. (ed.) 1969. *English Historical Documents 1327–1485*. London.

NEALE, J. M. 1910. *Letters of John Mason Neale, D.D., Selected and Edited by His Daughter*. London.

NICHOLSON, C. B. 1937. *England's Greater Churches*. London.

NORDSTROM, F. 1955. Peterborough, Lincoln, and the Science of Robert Grosseteste: a Study in Thirteenth-Century Architecture and Iconography. *Art Bulletin* 37, 241–72.

OWEN, D. M. 1971. *Church and Society in Medieval Lincolnshire*. Lincolnshire Local Hist Soc. Lincoln.

PAGE, F. M. 1934. *The Estates of Crowland Abbey*. Cambridge.

PANOFSKY, E. (ed.) 1946. *Abbot Suger on the Abbey Church of St Denis*. Princeton N.J.

PANOFSKY, E. 1973. *Gothic Architecture and Scholasticism*. New York.

PARSONS, D. 1969. The Pre-Conquest Cathedral at Canterbury. *Archaeol Cantiana* 84, 175–84.

PARSONS, D. (ed.) 1975. *Tenth-Century Studies: Essays in Commemoration of the Millennium of the Council of Winchester and Regularis Concordia*. London, Chichester.

PARSONS, D. 1977. The Pre-Romanesque Church of St-Riquier: the Documentary Evidence. *J Brit Archaeol Ass* 130, 21–51.

PEERS, C. R. 1930. Mattersey Priory, Nottinghamshire. *Archaeol J* 87, 16–20.

PEVSNER, N. 1972. *Some Architectural Writers of the Nineteenth Century*. Oxford.

PHELPS BROWN, E. H. and HOPKINS, S. V. 1955. Seven Centuries of Building Wages. *Economica* 22, 195–206.

PHILLIPS, A. D. 1975. Excavations at York Minster 1967–73. *The Friends of York Minster 46th Annual Report*, 19–27.

PHILLIPS, A. D. 1976. Excavation techniques in Church Archaeology. In *The Archaeological Study of Churches*, eds. P. V. Addyman and R. K. Morris, CBA Research Report 13, 54–9.

PLATT, C. 1976. *The English Medieval Town*. London.

POSTAN, M. M. 1950. Some Economic Evidence of Declining Population in the Later Middle Ages. *Econ Hist Rev* (2nd ser.) 2, 221–46.

POSTAN, M. M. 1972. *The Medieval Economy and Society. An Economic History of Britain 1100–1500*. London.

PRESTWICH, M. 1977. Currency and the Economy of early Fourteenth-Century England. In Mayhew 1977, 45–58.

PRIOR, E. S. 1905. *The Cathedral Builders in England*. London.

PRITCHARD, V. 1967. *English Medieval Graffiti*. Cambridge.

QUENTIN HUGHES, J. 1955. The Timber Roofs of York Minster. *Yorkshire Archaeol J* 38, 474–95.

QUIRK, R. N. 1957. Winchester cathedral in the tenth century. *Archaeol J* 114, 28–68.

RACKHAM, O. 1972. Grundle House: on the quantities of timber in certain East Anglian buildings in relation to local supplies. *Vernacular Architecture* 3, 3–8.

RACKHAM, O. 1976. *Trees and Woodland in the British Landscape*. London.

RADFORD, C. A. R. 1968. The Archaeological Background on the Continent. In Barley and Hanson 1968, 19–36.

RADFORD, C. A. R. 1971. Christian Origins in Britain. *Medieval Archaeol* 15, 1–12.

RAFTIS, J. A. 1957. *The Estates of Ramsey Abbey: A Study in Economic Growth and Organization*. Toronto.

RAHTZ, P. A. 1976. *Excavations at St Mary's Church, Deerhurst 1971–3*. CBA Research Report 15. London.

RAINE, J. (ed.) 1835. Reginald of Durham, *Libellus de Admirandis Beati Cuthberti Virtutibus*. Surtees Soc. 1.

RAINE, J. (ed.) 1859. *The Fabric Rolls of York Minster*. Surtees Soc. 35.

RAINE, J. (ed.) 1879–94. *The Historians of the Church of York and its Archbishops*. 3 vol. Rolls Series 71.

RCHM Royal Commission on Historical Monuments: inventories by county.

REMNANT, G. C. 1969. *A Catalogue of Misericords in Great Britain*. Oxford.

RICKMAN, T. 1835. *An Attempt to Discriminate the Styles of Architecture in England from the Conquest to the Reformation*. (4th ed.) London.

RIGOLD, S. E. 1963. The Anglian Cathedral of North Elmham, Norfolk. *Medieval Archaeol* 6–7, 67–108.

RIGOLD, S. E. 1977. *Litus Romanum* – the Shore forts as mission stations. In *The Saxon Shore*, ed. D. E. Johnston, CBA Research Report 18, 70–5.

ROBERTS, E. 1971. *A Guide to the Medieval Murals in St Albans Abbey*.

RODWELL, W. J. 1976. The Archaeological Investigation of Hadstock Church, Essex. *Antiq J* 56, 55–71.

RUNCIE, R. (ed.) 1977. *Cathedral and City: St Albans Ancient and Modern*. London.

RUSHFORTH, G. McN. 1936. *Medieval Christian Imagery as illustrated by the painted windows of Great Malvern Priory Church Worcestershire*. Oxford.

RUSKIN, J. 1956. *The Seven Lamps of Architecture*. (Original edition 1849.) London.

SALZMAN, L. S. 1967. *Building in England down to 1540 – A Documentary History*. (Second edition.) Oxford.

SAUNDERS, H. W. 1930. *An Introduction to the Rolls of Norwich Cathedral Priory*.

SAVAGE, H. (ed.) 1924. *The Great Register of Lichfield Cathedral known as the Magnum Registrum Album*. William Salt Archaeol. Soc. (1926).

SAWYER, P. H. 1965. The Wealth of England in the Eleventh Century. *Trans Roy Hist Soc* (5th ser.) 15, 145–64.

SAWYER, P. H. 1975. Charters of the Reform Movement – the Worcester Archive. In Parsons 1975, 84–93.

SAWYER, P. H. 1978a. Some sources for the history of Viking Northumbria. In *Viking Age York and the North*, ed. R. A. Hall, CBA Research Report 27, 3–7.

SAWYER, P. H. 1978b. *From Roman Britain to Norman England*. London.

SCHOLES, P. A. 1956. *The Oxford Companion to Music*. Oxford.

SCOTT, G. G. 1879. *Personal and Professional Recollections*, ed. G. Gilbert Scott. London.

SHELBY, L. R. 1972. The Geometrical Knowledge of Medieval Master Masons. *Speculum* 47, 395–421.

SIMSON, O. VON, 1956. *The Gothic Cathedral: Origins of Gothic Architecture and the Medieval Concept of Order*. New York.

SKINNER, F. G. 1967. *Weights and Measures: their ancient origins and their development in Great Britain up to AD 1855*. London.

SMITH, L. T. (ed.) 1907. *The Itinerary of John Leland in or about the Years 1534–43*. London.

SMITH, R. A. L. 1943. *Canterbury Cathedral Priory: A Study in Monastic Administration*. Cambridge.

SNEYD, C. A. (trans.) 1847. *A Relation, or Rather a True Account, of the Island of England; with Sundry Particulars of the Customs of these People, and of the Royal Revenues under King Henry VII*. Camden Soc. 37.

ST JOHN HOPE, W. 1884. Gundulf's Tower at Rochester, and the first Norman cathedral there. *Archaeologia* 49, 323–34.

ST JOHN HOPE, W. 1917. Quire Screens in English Churches. *Archaeologia* 68, 43–110.

STENTON, F. M. 1971. *Anglo-Saxon England*. Oxford.

SUMNER, W. L. 1952. *The Organ: Its Evolution, Principles of Construction and Use*. London.

TATTON-BROWN, T. 1978. Canterbury Cathedral. *Bulletin* of the CBA Churches Committee 9, 6–7.

TAYLOR, A. J. 1961. Castle-building in Wales in the later thirteenth century: the prelude to construction. In Jope 1961, 104–33.

TAYLOR, H. M. and TAYLOR, J. 1965. *Anglo-Saxon Architecture* I and II. Cambridge.

TAYLOR, H. M. 1969a. Corridor crypts on the Continent and in England. *North Staffs J Field Stud* 9, 17–52.

TAYLOR, H. M. 1969b. The Anglo-Saxon Cathedral Church at Canterbury. *Archaeol J* 126, 101–30.

TAYLOR, H. M. 1975. Tenth-century church building in England and on the Continent. In Parsons 1975, 141–68.

TAYLOR, H. M. 1976. The Foundations of Architectural History. In *The Archaeological Study of Churches*, eds P. V. Addyman and R. K. Morris, CBA Research Report 13, 3–9.

TAYLOR, H. M. 1977. *Deerhurst Studies I*.

TAYLOR, H. M. 1978. *Anglo-Saxon Architecture* III. Cambridge.

THOMAS, C. 1971. *The Early Christian Archaeology of North Britain*. London.

THOMPSON, A. H. 1925. *The Cathedral Churches of England*. London.

THOMPSON, D. V. 1936. *The Materials of Medieval Painting*. London.

TOYNBEE, J. M. C. and PERKINS, J. W. 1956. *The Shrine of St Peter*. London.

TRISTRAM, E. W. 1944. *English Medieval Wall Paintings: the Twelfth Century*. Oxford.

TRISTRAM, E. W. 1950. *English Medieval Wall Paintings: the Thirteenth Century*. London.

TRISTRAM, E. W. 1955. *English Wall Painting of the Fourteenth Century*. London.

TURNER, H. L. 1971. *Town Defences in England and Wales; an Architectural and Documentary Study: AD 900–1500*. London.

URRY, W. 1965. Cardinal Morton and the Angel Steeple. *Friends of Canterbury Cathedral 38th Annual Report*, 29, 18–24.

VALLANCE, A. 1947. *Greater English Church Screens*. London.

VENABLES, E. 1887. Some Account of the Recent Discovery of the Foundations of the Eastern Termination of Lincoln Minister, as erected by St Hugh. *Archaeol J* 44, 194–202.

VERDIER, P. 1954. Transepts de nef. *Arte del primo millenio*. Pavia, 354–61.

WELLDON FINN, R. 1971. *The Norman Conquest and its effects on the economy*. London.

WEST, S. E. with PLOUVIEZ, J. 1976. The Roman Site at Icklingham. *East Anglian Archaeol* 3, 63–125.

WHITE, J. F. 1962. *The Cambridge Movement: the Ecclesiologists and the Gothic Revival*. Cambridge.

WHITEHILL, W. M. 1941. *Spanish Romanesque Architecture of the Eleventh Century*. Oxford.

WHITELOCK, D. 1972. The pre-Viking age church in East Anglia. *Anglo-Saxon England* I, 1–22.

WILLIAMS, G. 1962. *The Welsh Church from the Conquest to the Reformation*. Cardiff.

WILLIAMS, J. 1977. St Peter, Northampton. *Bulletin* of the CBA Churches Committee 7, 9–10.

WILLIS, R. 1842. On the Construction of Vaults of the Middle Ages. *Trans Roy Inst Brit Architects* I.ii, 1–69.

WILLIS, R. 1845. *The Architectural History of Canterbury Cathedral*. London.

WILLIS, R. 1846. The architectural history of Winchester cathedral. *Proc Roy Archaeol Inst at Winchester*.

WILSON, C. 1977. *The Shrines of St William of York*. York.

WILTON-ELY, J. 1967. The Architectural Model. *Architect Review* 142, 26–32.

WOLFE, M. I. and MARK, R. 1976. The Collapse of the Vaults of Beauvais Cathedral in 1284. *Speculum* 51, 462–76.

WREN, C. 1750. *Parentalia*.

WRIGHT, T. (ed.) 1843. *Letters Relating to the Suppression of the Monasteries*. Camden Soc. 26.

ZARNECKI, G. 1951. *English Romanesque Sculpture 1066–1140*. London.

ZARNECKI, G. 1970. *Romanesque sculpture at Lincoln Cathedral*. (2nd. ed.) Lincoln.

ZARNECKI, G. 1972. *The Monastic Achievement*. London.

Index

Skirlaw, Robert, bishop of Durham 86
Snow, C. P. 55
Society for the Protection of Ancient Buildings 49
Somerset House 34
Southwark cathedral 200, 271
    reredos 150
    tower 227
    diocese 26
    Roman remains 117
Southwell Minster 1, 16, 82, 200, 272; *115*
    bells 78
    chapter-house 63; *22, 134, 135*
    prebends 16
    pulpitum 144
    Roman remains 117
    diocese 26
Southwell, Richard 165
Spence, Sir Basil 82
Speyer, 190
stability 125
Standish, bishop of St Asaph 227
Stapledon, Walter de, bishop of Exeter 86
Statute of Mortmain 157
Staunton Harold 31
Stephen, King of England 24, 194
Stow, Lincolnshire 13
Strata Marcella 2
Strik, Hendrik 4, 39
Suger, abbot of St Denis 98–9, 105
suppression of chantries 157–8
Swansea, diocese 26
Swithun, St 139
Synod of Mainz 136
Tallie 2
Tasker, David 4
Tatton-Brown, Tim 4, 39
Taverner, John 171
Taylor, Dr A. J. 214
Taylor, Dr H. M. 4, 133, 141, 163
    on principles of architectural history 38
Teinfrith 67
Tewkesbury abbey, Gloucestershire 3, 26, 188–9, 272; *4, 110, 111, 140, 141*
    abbot of Cheltenham's tomb 50
    apses 153
    campanile 78
    collapse at 113
    furnishings and fittings 35
    Lady Chapel 153
    organ 35
    wall painting 168
    west towers (projected) 194
Theodore, archbishop of Canterbury 12
Theophilus 167
theoretica 105
Thetford, see at 16
Thomas, abbot of Crowland 224
Thomas of Bayeux, archbishop of York 19, 86, 97, 100, 142
Thomas II, archbishop of York 162
Thomas Cantilupe, St 162
Thompson, J. H. 51
Thorney abbey, Cambridgeshire 140
thrusts 119, 124, 127
Tillich, Paul 176

timber 96–7, 119
    alder 96
    ash 96
    beech 96
    conifers 96
    elm 96
    lengths of 97
    oak 96
    piles 96
    poplar 96
    reinforcement 118–19
    roofs 121
    woodland management 96
Tintern abbey, Monmouthshire 2
tools
    adze 65, 69
    axe 65
    blokker 67
    bolster 66
    carpenter's tools 69–70
    chisels 65–6
    compasses 65, 69, 106, 110
    dividers 111
    dolobrium 67
    drag 66
    gaveloks 67
    grozing iron 72
    kevelles 67
    metroddes 69
    pulyngaxes 67
    rule 69
    ruler 111
    saw 70
    skantyllyon 69
    square 65, 69, 106, 110, 111
    stanexes 65
    wedges 67
Torrigiano, Pietro 77
Tours, John of, bishop of Bath 19
towers 113, 121, 227
tracing houses 61
transport, water 92–3
Tredington 139
Trent, Council of 131
Trogior cathedral, Yugoslavia 112
Truro, diocese 26
tufa 94–5
Turner, Mrs Alison 4
Tye, Christopher 172
Ubanford *see* Norham
Utrecht Psalter 169
Vale Royal abbey 25, 58, 213
Valor Ecclesiasticus 178
vaults 101, 121–2, 124, 129, 181, 191–2
Verulamium 9
Victorine canons 24
Viollet-le-duc 38
Vitrivius 106, 109, 169
Wakefield 26
Walcher, bishop of Durham 185
Walcher, prior of Great Malvern 100
Wales
    diocesan reorganization 26
    dioceses 18
    monastic houses in 186
Wallace, Thomas 87
Walsingham abbey 165
Walsingham, Alan of 60, 97
Walter, bishop of Hereford 16
Waltham abbey, Essex 111, 273
    Henry II's church 25
    pre-Conquest canons 16
    projected see at 26
Warton, Michael 35
Wastell, John 227

Water Newton, Roman silver Christian treasure 5
wealth of Church 230
Wells cathedral 19, 132, 171, 186, 198, 200, 273; *70*
    external painting 168
    Lady Chapel 153
    tracing house 61
    west front 175; *102*
    see 15
Wermington, William of 105
Westminster abbey 2, 61, 95, 143, 181, 187, 206, 274; *33, 65, 128, 129*
    bar tracery 208
    campanile 78
    composition of workforce 214
    Edward the Confessor's church 67
    Henry VII's Chapel 37; *154, 155*
    Lady Chapel 177
    metal reinforcement 76–7
    nave 29; *40, 105*
    rebuilding by Henry III 83
    Roman remains 117
    tomb of Henry VII 50, 77, 156
    tomb of Edward the Confessor 165
    tracing house 61
    wall painting 168
    church of St Margaret 154
    diocese 26
west-works 137–9
Whitby
    'bishopric' at 18
    synod of 12
Wihtburh, St 161
Wilfrid, St 13, 27, 161
William the Conqueror, King of England
    II (Rufus) 185, 194
    IV 26
William of Malmesbury 120
William of Sens 59, 67, 124
Willis, Robert 39, 43
Wilson, Christopher 4
Wimborne minster, Dorset 186, 200, 276
    Elricke Tomb 50
    gift of bell 86
    Roman remains 117
Winchcombe abbey, Gloucestershire 25, 178
Winchester 19, 164, 181, 184, 185, 200, 206, 224
    cathedral 1, 43, 276; *11*
    archaeological excavations 13, 53, 70; *18*
    burial 155
    choir 144
    confraternity of donors 89
    continuity of worship 114
    cranes 79
    Inigo Jones screen 35
    Norman cathedral 39–40, 87, 188
    Old Minster 91, 114, 141; *figure 3*
    reredos 150
    Saxon organ 169, 171
    wall painting 168
    west-work 139
    Pilgrims' Hall 97
    St Cross 95, 277
    see 14

wind loads 119, 121
Windsor 67
Wing 93
Witney, Thomas 172
Wotton, Henry 33
Worcester 19, 26, 43, 59, 132, 164, 188, 198, 200, 206, 277–8; *87, 117*
    campanile 78
    charnel house 160
    confraternity of donors 89
    pre-Conquest cathedral 13, 70
    Roman remains 117
    shrines 89
    tomb of King John 50
    see 12, 14
Worcestre, William 175
Worksop priory, Nottinghamshire 278
    projected see at 26
Wren, Christopher 35, 26, 99
Wulfred, archbishop of Canterbury 141
Wulfstan, bishop of Worcester 186
Wyatt, James 36–7
Wygmor, John, abbot of Gloucester 221
Wymondham abbey, Norfolk 279; *147*
    nave roof 68; *28, 29*
    parochial nave 154, 227; *108*
Wynford, William 40
Xanten 9
Yarmouth 227
York 6, 10, 15, 16, 18, 19, 39, 43, 58–9, 61, 65, 82, 86, 95, 106, 132, 143, 144, 155, 181, 184, 185, 188, 201
    Alma Sophia 133, 136, 141
    cathedral 30, 279; *131, 132*
    central tower 227
    chapter-house 68, 97; *72–4*
    collapse at 113
    excavations 44, 53; *13, 49*
    fires at 44
    Lady Chapel 153
    nave 153
    Norman church 190–2; *12, 94; figure 9*
    painted plaster 169
    repaving 35
    shrines of St William 162–3, 164
    spans 97
    Strafford-Wentworth vault 158
    substructure 114, 117–19
    timber purchases 96
    timber reinforcement 67; *50*
    timber vaults 68
    tracing house 61; *20, 21*
    western towers 40; *151*
    domuncula cloccarum 78
    Freemen 217
    Holy Trinity Micklegate 117, 280
    pre-Conquest cemetery 160; *89*
    pre-Conquest church 11, 13, 27, 70
    Roman fortress 117; *41*
    St Mary's abbey 187–8
    St Michael-le-Belfry 155
    school 13
    see 14, 18